W9-ABI-841

EFFECTIVE WRITING

For Engineers · Managers · Scientists

EFFECTIVE WRITING
For Engineers , Managers , Scientists

H. J. TICHY

Associate Professor of English
Hunter College

John Wiley & Sons, Inc.   New York · London · Sydney

PE1408
.T5

SECOND PRINTING, FEBRUARY, 1967

Copyright © 1966 by John Wiley & Sons, Inc.

All rights reserved. This book or any part
thereof must not be reproduced in any form
without the written permission of the publisher.

Library of Congress Catalog Card Number: 66–21062
Printed in the United States of America

NOV 1 4 1967

Preface

The preface and dedication of a book are usually separate parts, but in this book they are one. It is fitting that I dedicate this book to my students with gratitude for all that they have taught me about management, science, and technology and about the writing and editing problems of the professional man in industry and government.

For fifteen years these students and others who consulted me about writing problems have been asking me to write a book that will help them maintain their improvement. And even more urgently they have been requesting such a book for "an assistant who's coming next week, just too late for your course," "an engineer at Baton Rouge who asked me how I improved my writing," or "my brother in Pomona, a professor who ought to write better if he's going to publish so many articles on chemistry."

Here it is, the book for those who want to write better, including the assistant who is coming next week, the engineer at Baton Rouge, and the professor of chemistry in Pomona. These professional men in industry and government and private practice face problems that would be difficult for even an experienced professional writer. In one morning an executive may draft an article for a scientific or technological journal and a report on the same subject for administrators who have had no technical training, compose a recruitment appeal for his professional society and a letter expressing the sympathy of his company to the family of a deceased colleague, edit minutes that convey the differing views of the members of a committee and explain his editing to the confused writer of the minutes, prepare foolproof safety directions for new workers who will perform a complicated and dangerous laboratory experiment, and write complete instructions for his secretary and the members of his division to follow while he attends a professional meeting in Europe. Much of his writing presents judgments that require fine, subtle expression: an estimate of the value of a distinguished colleague, an analysis of a budget that may determine the success or failure of a project, a discussion of the side effects of a drug for thousands of doctors who are prescribing the drug, or an evaluation of a program of experimental work that may lead to a breakthrough.

Knowing the importance of his words, the professional man is eager to write better. But he does not have time to waste on model reports, letters, memorandums, and other business forms; on lists of *do's* and *don't's* insulting to his intelligence; or on a detailed review of English grammar. He wants a book on writing, preferably his kind of writing, that will help him achieve the maximum improvement for his time and energy; he needs understanding of his problems and instruction suited to his intelligence. True, he has some of the problems of other writers, and a little help in getting started and some advice about planning may make his writing easier and more rewarding. But the main errors and weaknesses in his writing are those common in his reading. Once these have been explained and illustrated, he has the instruction in fundamentals that he needs, and he is prepared for more advanced work; he can grasp the philosophy of style and apply the techniques with imagination and originality. Thus he discovers with delighted awe that mastering the expression of ideas offers the challenge and excitement that he has found in administration or science or technology. And he becomes a good writer.

Obviously I have had no reason to regret that fifteen years ago F. J. Van Antwerpen of the American Institute of Chemical Engineers convinced me that I should attempt to help engineers to write better or that Joseph Coogan and Robert Dean of Smith Kline and French Laboratories and W. J. Sparks and Joseph Stewart of Esso Chemicals Research Division persuaded me to consult with professional men in industry and to give courses in effective writing. From those who have administered my courses I have learned about the needs and problems of professional men in all divisions of small and large companies. John B. Riley, Jack Rockett, and Earl Willauer of Esso Research and Engineering Company; William Steytler and Stokes Carrigan of Smith Kline and French Laboratories; and Louis Moll and Chester Poetsch of Vick Divisions Research and Development have permitted me freedom to experiment and have cooperated in every way to improve the writing and editing in their companies.

For patient reading of rough drafts and for advice throughout the preparation of this book, I am indebted to an excellent editor and supervisor of editors—Sylvia Fourdrinier.

H. J. Tichy

Hunter College of the
City University of New York
January 1966

Contents

Chapter I

Who Done It?

> Nearly all men die of their
> remedies, and not of their maladies.
>
> *Molière*

When the Lord High Executioner of the town of Titipu announces, "If I should ever be called upon to act professionally, I am happy to think that there will be no difficulty in finding plenty of people whose loss will be a distinct gain to society at large," he voices a sentiment of our times. With hatchet instead of snickersnee, we search for someone to blame for the faults of our society. Hollywood, we cry, is responsible for our low culture; tobacco companies are to blame for our smoking; Madison Avenue fosters materialism; publishers of pornography inspire sexual immorality; TV is the cause of juvenile violence; and our apathy is due to the bomb.

Of course, spoilsports may maintain that we are witch hunting. But the witches are more like the bad fairies who visit the cradle and are thereafter held responsible for all the weaknesses of the grown man. The hunting, however, is true hunting, especially when the villain is hard to find. Then with all the avidity and perseverance and little of the skill of Dupin, Sherlock Holmes, Philo Vance, Father Brown, Miss Marple, and Lord Peter Wimsey, we try to detect the guilty.

High on our little list of those who must be found is the villain responsible for the death of good writing. Who, we demand, is to blame for the miserable writing in government documents, in business reports, in directions of all kinds, in articles in learned journals, and in papers read at conventions? Like readers of detective stories, we are confronted by a number of suspicious-looking characters and a number of suspiciously innocent-looking characters. Which of them killed good writing?

Because we know that a reader of mystery stories cannot depend on the seemingly guilty to be innocent, we must view with suspicion the

1

likely murderer of good writing, the villain accused most frequently by the other suspects—Education. Like most scoundrels, Education has a poor reputation but is attractive and desirable. Anyone who doubts the desirability should interview the parents of high school students who have been refused admission to college. Yet obviously Education is no good. Eighth-grade children cannot read, write, or count. High school students waste their time on extracurricular activities or, according to their parents, lose their health cramming for college-entrance examinations. Why, even Ph.D.'s cannot write English. It must be the English teacher who kills good writing.

In the tradition of all likely murderers, the English teacher quickly produces an unshakable alibi: he was not there when many of the poorest writers of today were being educated. He cites the large number of middle-aged and elderly scientists and technologists who cannot write, and he proves that they received their degrees without taking even one college English course. If this does not convince us that he is blameless, the English professor will insist that students who have the benefit of college English courses write better than their fathers who did not. When employers of recent graduates deny that the graduates can write, the professor insists that they wrote well when they left his course and demands of the employers, "What have you done to them?"

Business and Industry cringe at this attack, probably out of the habit of being scapegoats for the sins of society. Indeed, the names Business and Industry are aliases: every reader knows that the villains are more properly called Big Business and Monopoly. Experts rush to testify against these scoundrels. They submit as evidence Exhibit One—poor business reports that Business and Industry force beginners to imitate; Exhibit Two—antiquated business jargon; Exhibit Three—lists of ignorant and incompetent supervisors of business writing. And disgruntled, unsuccessful employees testify to such frightening instances of the discouragement of imagination and originality by Big Business and Monopoly that our story threatens to become a horror tale of prolonged sadism.

But Business and Industry restore us to sanity with their defense. They exhibit poor letters written by college graduates applying for their first jobs. Business and Industry offer in evidence their excellent training programs and tearfully describe their courses in creativity that prove how much they really love imagination and originality, at least as described and prescribed by their instructors in creativity. Then, fretted by accusations, Business and Industry return the attack of the professor of English. They have little difficulty, they say, finding competent instructors for their courses in science, mathematics, psychology, and business management. But unless training directors conduct national talent hunts or are unusually lucky, the educators hired to improve business writing are likely to be of two kinds: those who think that old-fashioned grammar is the answer to all writing problems and those newfangled instructors who encourage employees to demonstrate their imagination and informality by replacing *Dear Sir* in their letters with *Hello, how are you this morning?*

An influential part of Industry, the Technical Writing Industry, accuses another character who is often held responsible for every infamy —the Government. Technical writers, editors, and publishers attribute the poor quality of their publications not to a lack of understanding of the technical material or to a lack of writing skill but to government specifications. The Government is responsible, they testify, for the incomprehensibility of military instruction manuals. Our detective, who has secret longings to wear a trench coat and hunt international spies, preferably female, suggests that these manuals sound like the work of saboteurs.

But readers of tax forms, the *Congressional Record*, and other government writings know that the Government does not need saboteurs to kill good writing. Readers can testify that good writing in government publications has been dead a long time. *Federal prose, gobbledygook*, and other less polite epithets for government writing are proof that the remains were beginning to smell as early as 1940, when *gobbledygook* was coined. The Government is the first character in our story to offer no defense. Perhaps the crime is too old to bother about, perhaps Government slaughter is legal slaughter, or perhaps the Government has been accused of so many more serious crimes that the murder of good writing is not a charge worth noticing. It is even possible that the Government did present a defense, but a written one, and as usual nobody could understand what the Government had written. In mitigation of the charges, the Government might have offered books written by some of its competent administrators to revive good writing in their departments. The Government might even have turned the attack on three of its favorite whipping boys: TV, Hollywood, and Advertising.

On TV the slaughter of the written word has been bloody. When words inadvertently appear on a TV screen, they are read aloud, apparently for illiterate viewers, and as though that were not insult enough, the TV voice repeats or explains any difficult words. Hollywood is quick to point out that motion pictures never treat writing this way. No, indeed, motion picture audiences are expected to read. They are expected to read not English, but subtitle English, a semiforeign variety related to pidgin. Both TV and Hollywood defend themselves by offering in evidence their best dramatic presentations to prove their sponsorship of good writing. Finally, they desperately try to divert suspicion by calling attention to the faults of another popular scapegoat, Advertising. Advertising has no alibi, no plea, no defense. It so often uses words to misinform, to mislead, and to deceive that it expects accusers to overlook the great number of well-written advertisements and to think, "Aha, the murderer!"

But any detective can see that among the accusers are men who have been poisoning good writing for some time—those in colleges and universities, in business and industry, and in government who proliferate writings to gain promotions and prestige. The prevailing belief that recognition and advancement are awarded in direct proportion to the number of pages a man publishes is frequently correct. Administrators shirk the demanding labor of evaluating publications and the task of investigating other qualifications for advancement and use quantity of writing as a test because it is easy to measure objectively. Thus quantity defeats quality. If a dozen poor papers weigh more heavily on the scale for promotion, who in industry, government, and education will spend the energy and time required for one paper of excellence?

Even where academic pressures are not so extreme as to mean "publish or perish," they do mean write or want—want money, recognition, and reduced teaching programs. Faculty members write much that should not be published. They fabricate textbooks that duplicate better ones. They send articles on the round of scholarly journals until the articles are accepted, very likely by some editor who secured one promotion for establishing a poor journal and will get another for editing it. And their students ape their methods unto the third and fourth generation of those that flourish by words alone.

In industry and government the situation is worse because a man seeking to advance himself by profuse publication does not need the assistance of a misguided editor. Such a man publishes at company or government expense a flood of memorandums, reports, articles, pamphlets, booklets, and books that other employees spend company or government time reading. Thus he demonstrates his value and enlarges his department, although the only increase in work is the burden of writing, reproducing, and reading his largely worthless papers.

Certainly basing promotions on pounds of publications is responsible for much nugatory writing, but it is difficult to say that this alone is killing excellence. A much more noxious influence is poisoning, strangling, and knifing good writing. This is the murderer who destroys completely both good writers and good writing. This is indeed a villain, an attractive and appealing deceiver, a smooth promoter disguised as a friend, a panderer to credulity and indolence—this Write-Good-Quick-and-Easy

School. Members of this school advance the belief that magically rapid improvement in writing is achieved by miraculously little work. Every teacher of the school promotes one remedy for all writers and for all faults of writing, but every teacher has a different remedy—a magic average number of words for sentences, avoiding long words, beginning every paper with a statement of the problem, using only one organization, three or five or seven (choose your own magic number) commandments. These panaceas have one feature in common: they appeal to the credulous and the lazy.

The harmful effect of belief in the amulets and fetishes of the WGQE School is a weakening of the will to work to improve writing. Convinced that there must be quick-and-easy methods, a writer disillusioned with one panacea seeks another. Thus the propaganda of this school unfits him for the work of learning to write well. Although the best authors testify that writing is hard work and that the revision essential to good writing is even harder work, the dupes of the WGQE School still dream, like Walter Mitty, of magical success. They would call anyone crazy who told them that just by holding a racket properly a poor tennis player could become an excellent player, but they hack their sentences to some ritual length or squeeze their ideas into some ritual organization and expect to become good writers. Unfortunately they do not. There is no substitute for the discipline of learning and practicing the principles of good writing, and thinking that there is has killed much good writing. But writers who study and practice will discover in the happy ending that good writing is not dead but only slumbering.

Chapter II

Steps to Better Writing

The secret of success is constancy to purpose.

Disraeli

Men and women in the professions who work properly to improve their writing can improve it with ease and pleasure. When the level of instruction is appropriate to their intelligence and training, learning to write better offers them the interest, challenge, and satisfaction of any opportunity to use reason and imagination in solving problems. But poor instruction or instruction at too low a level bores, confuses, and discourages professional men and women and thus makes their writing worse. Good writers are not born; they are made and unmade.

When men and women in the professions ask me, "Can I improve my writing by myself? What book do you recommend?" I always answer frankly that a competent editor or instructor experienced in teaching professional people is the best help that they can get. And many of them have proved this by learning to write better under the guidance of good teachers.

But others have been less lucky: they could not find competent instructors, they were not free to take courses, or for some other reason they had to study by themselves. When they tried to study by themselves, they met discouragement and failure. Some erred by trying to learn all the rules in a handbook of writing and became hypochondriacal about their writing. Others attempted to learn by copying the writing of their supervisors only to find that succeeding supervisors disapproved of their imitative styles and the styles proved difficult to unlearn. And some never wrote a sentence without stopping to change it according to some dimly remembered precept of a teacher or supervisor. They became tense and confused and soon hated the thought of writing.

Many of the engineers, scientists, and business administrators with whom I consulted were using methods of writing and of improving writing that are cumbersome, wasteful, and even painful. I wanted to devise for them some methods of studying and of writing that would avoid unnecessary labor, take advantage of what is known of the psychology of writing and of writers, and enable each writer to progress at his own pace. Varied writers from all the professions experimented with me and helped me evolve methods that assist most of the writers who try them. I believe that so many are helped because they are eager and conscientious. They know that a man who improves his writing advances in his profession and advances his profession.

The order of writing and studying that I suggest replaces some common misconceptions, obstacles, and emotional problems with a knowledge of sound principles, the practice of efficient methods, and the satisfaction of accomplishment. At each step I indicate the sections of this book that will help a writer to determine how much study and practice he needs. By avoiding details of little use and concentrating on common errors and weaknesses, I try to help writers to employ their time economically. By exploring some of the causes of common errors and weaknesses, I try to help writers to work with understanding and, therefore, with more enduring success. And assuming that writers in the professions are intelligent people, I point out their opportunities to use their own judgment, I discuss the philosophy behind my recommendations, and I consider, at least occasionally, the future of language and style.

The reader of this book may exercise his judgment immediately by deciding how much of the following suggested preliminary study he needs.

PRELIMINARY STUDY

Chapter III

Starting to write proves troublesome to nearly everyone occasionally, and some professional men and women are troubled by it every time they must write. For such writers Chapter III contains an examination of some of the mental, physical, and emotional problems involved in difficult starting and suggests some ways to avoid the irritation and delay of cold starts.

For those who think that they spend too much time on their writing, Chapter III analyzes wasteful methods of writing and presents substitute methods that have enabled many writers to accomplish more in less time. Even those who do not feel dissatisfied with their methods of writing may find it profitable to skim Chapter III for suggestions that will enable them to write more efficiently and comfortably.

Chapter IV

Chapter IV is preliminary reading for those who lament, "How shall I begin? If only I could find a first sentence I could get started." It offers two dozen ways to begin and suggests combinations of those ways. Here a writer should find at least one beginning that suits his material, his readers, and himself; and he will probably find more than one. Then the question, "Shall I begin with a summary of main points, a statement of the problem, or a quotation?" will replace his old lament, "How shall I begin?" Then a slow starter will feel like the chemist who said, "I never thought that I'd be considering five ways to begin. I'm the fellow who could never think of even one way to start a memo, but analyzing many types of beginnings works like an automatic starter."

Chapter VII

Everyone who has participated in a sport and then taken lessons from a coach remembers the need to get rid of bad habits and misconceptions. To help writers reject common misconceptions about writing I have discussed in Chapter VII some of the crippling and misleading ideas that many writers have assured me they were taught: (1) writing on science, business, and technology must be heavy and dull; (2) begin and end every paragraph with a topic sentence; (3) never end a sentence with a preposition; (4) never begin a sentence with *I*, *however*, *because*, or some other word that is taboo; (5) never repeat a word; (6) a writer need not consider his reader; and (7) write the way you talk.

THE FOUR STEPS OF WRITING

The order of writing suggested in the four following steps brings improvement by itself. The study proposed for each step may be scheduled in any order that a writer chooses, but the order of writing should be the following.

Step One—Plan

Whether one is writing a short letter or a long book, planning is the first step. Chapter V discusses the principles of organizing and analyzes the advantages and disadvantages of the organizations that are used most frequently in functional prose. This chapter is suggestive rather than definitive because once writers are familiar with a variety of plans, they tend to find and to create others.

Good style demands that a writer choose the best plan for his material, his skills, and his readers. But he cannot choose well if he lacks knowledge of suitable organizations. And he does not choose at all if he seizes the first one that comes to his mind. A writer who does not usually consider a number of plans should study Chapter V.

Once he has chosen his organization, a writer may test it by outlining his paper. Chapter VI helps him find the method of outlining that suits him best. It is designed to aid those who do not understand how to outline, those who think that they should write in the order in which ideas occur to them, and those who dislike and avoid outlining. The chapter discusses the general principles of outlining and some special uses of the outline in the professions.

When I was a neophyte consultant I thought it unnecessary to tell writers to plan before writing, instead of afterwards. In fact, I used to cite Plan Ahead signs as examples of tautology. But I know better now that I have observed many a writer dictate a work, struggle to revise it, and then in desperation finally plan it and rewrite it. Organizing thoughts before writing is pleasant and profitable, but organizing after writing is wasteful, irritating, and inefficient. Planning is not the second, third, or fourth step; it must be the first.

Step Two—Write

Once a writer has outlined his work, he is ready to write. For best results he should write a rough draft. He should protect himself against interruptions—his own interruptions when he stops to rewrite or revise and outside interruptions. As Chapter III shows, writing and revising are different activities that are best performed separately. If a man writes without delaying to polish a sentence, without stopping to dawdle over the selection of a word, without pausing to answer the question of a colleague, he writes faster, enjoys writing his first drafts more, and produces better results. Much of the unpleasantness associated with writing is due to postponing writing too long and then trying to accomplish the impossible—a polished final paper in the first draft.

When a writer's first draft must be his final draft, it can contribute little to his improvement, for improvement requires careful revision. After he revises a number of papers his first drafts will be better, but still his best writing will usually be that which he has had time to revise carefully.

Step Three—Cool

After completing his rough draft a writer is likely to feel a warm glow of contentment, and he should bask in his well-deserved reward. This is not the time to be critical of his brainchild, for he is too close to creation to view the result objectively. He is too likely to confuse what is in his mind with what is on the paper. At this time a writer may not notice that words or even whole lines are missing, he may overlook glaring errors, and his most muddled passages may seem beautifully clear.

He must wait until he is cool and objective. How long that takes depends on the individual. Trained revisers, like editors, may be able to correct a draft as soon as it is typed. But most writers need more time to become objective, four to eight hours being satisfactory for many. Each writer should experiment to find the amount of time that must elapse before he can view his work as another reader views it. Sooner or later every writer experiences the icy shock reflected in a thought like "How did I ever write that?" or "Now what does this mean?" or "I'm glad I didn't send that out." At this moment of truth, the writer is ready for Step Four.

Step Four—Revise

Here is the real work of writing. Poor writers are inclined to scorn revision and to assume incorrectly that good writers do not need to revise. Poor writers believe that articles, stories, and poems should pour forth in their complete and final forms. Until writers are disabused of this error, they are at best halfhearted about revising and at worst unwilling to change a word they have written.

Stubborn refusal to change is a major block to improvement. "Won't it become awkward or too polished if I revise it so much?" asks a chemist who was advised to make subjects and predicates agree and to see that his pronouns had unmistakable antecedents. "But style doesn't sound easy and natural if a writer hacks over it that much," says an engineer when asked to supply transitions between sentences. And a geologist wails, "Why doesn't my writing just flow onto the page the way writing flows for creative writers?"

Successful authors not only revise, they revise assiduously and interminably. This is proved by their own remarks; the comments of their biographers; and the corrections on their typescripts, galleys, and page proofs. Usually the more easy and natural their work seems, the more it has been revised. Writers of less experience are reluctant to believe this, for the myth that easy writing is natural writing has captured their minds.

Yet Ernest Hemingway told George Plimpton that he rewrote every day whatever he had written before and also went over the whole when it was completed, then corrected and rewrote the typescript, and finally revised the proofs. "You're grateful for these different chances," he mentioned. Asked how much he rewrote, he said, "It depends. I rewrote the ending to *Farewell to Arms*, the last page of it, thirty-nine times before I was satisfied." [1] And Aldous Huxley answered a similar question asked by George Wicks and Ray Frazer, " . . . I write everything many times over. All my thoughts are second thoughts. And I correct each page a great deal, or rewrite it several times as I go along." [2] Frederick Lewis Allen told Robert van Gelder that he writes two or three drafts.[3] Allan Nevins complained that he "rewrites so much that his typing bills eat up large amounts of the profits of his books." He writes four or five drafts of all his work and revises "to cut down and to brighten the phrasing." [4] H. G. Wells wrote a first draft "full of gaps." When that was typed, he made changes and additions between the lines and in the margins. Then the second draft was typed and he revised that. He said that he repeated the process "four, five, six or seven times." [5] John Gunther's corrected typescripts are interlined with handwriting and even pasted in places; van Gelder, who saw them, thought that there were more words written in than there were on the original page. Gunther also revises this revised typescript and makes many changes in proof.[6]

Every good writer on business and professional subjects that I have met has spoken of the time and labor that revision takes. "I write just as soon as my experimental procedure is established," a chemist told me. "And by the time my results are complete, I have revised and rewritten sections of the paper ten and twelve times and feel that I do not have so much more to do for them." "I try to draft an answer to every important letter the day that I receive it so that I see the letter in typescript the next morning. Then I feel fresh and can catch an error or change a stupid approach," said a vice president. "We write my speeches over and over," admitted a government official, "and I read each new version aloud several times and change it as I read." "Sometimes I seem to change a word every time I see it," said a medical writer, "except the medical terminology, of course. And I sweat over how much of that to use."

---

[1] *Writers at Work: The Paris Review Interviews*, Second Series (The Viking Press, New York, 1963), p. 222.

[2] *Ibid.*, p. 197.

[3] *Writers and Writing* (Charles Scribner's Sons, New York, 1946), p. 25.

[4] *Ibid.*, p. 83.

[5] *Ibid.*, p. 130.

[6] *Ibid.*, p. 229.

Writers seem eager to know whether others revise as much as they do; every writer wonders whether he is the only one who needs to revise so much. Even Somerset Maugham described feelingly "the heavy cost of naturalness":

> I think no one in France now writes more admirably than Colette, and such is the ease of her expression that you cannot bring yourself to believe that she takes any trouble over it. I am told that there are pianists who have a natural technique so that they can play in a manner that most executants can achieve only as the result of unremitting toil, and I am willing to believe that there are writers who are equally fortunate. Among them I was much inclined to place Colette. I asked her. I was exceedingly surprised to hear that she wrote everything over and over again. She told me that she would often spend a whole morning working upon a single page. But it does not matter how one gets the effect of ease. For my part, if I get it at all, it is only by strenuous effort. Nature seldom provides me with the word, the turn of phrase, that is appropriate without being farfetched or commonplace.[7]

Writers of functional prose who feel that they should write clear, readable first drafts are usually relieved to learn that authors whom they admire are not able to do this but must revise many times. I have never met a writer of informational prose who wrote an easy and natural style in the first draft—or even a clear one. But I have met some writers who protested that they did not have time for revision and many writers who did not know how to revise.

Those who say that they do not have time for revision have usually not tried very hard to find time. They have brushed revision aside as a luxury not suitable to a writer in the professions and have failed to consider the importance of their readers' time. High-salaried readers mulling over the meaning of confused writing and finding it necessary to query what they read are much more expensive than a writer's revision time.

The problem of time is particularly difficult when a writer first tries to improve his writing. Then he has the most faults and the least time, and he lacks experience in revising. As a writer begins to see how long it takes him to revise efficiently, he also becomes aware of the good results of purposeful revision; therefore he plans his work so that he has adequate time for the steps of writing. By starting to write earlier he can provide an adequate interval before revision and can leave more time for improving his work. A welcome, and sometimes unexpected,

---

[7] "The Summing Up," *Mr. Maugham Himself* (Doubleday and Company, Garden City, N. Y., 1954), p. 558.

result is the increased thoughtfulness of his writing. He benefits from those excellent second thoughts that would otherwise plague him too late.

Purposeful revision by a writer who has cooled to an objective frame of mind is economical. The real waste of time is an interruption of one's writing of the first draft to change it or an attempt to revise a paper that one has just written. Later revision is more efficient revision.

First revision. During the first reading of his paper a writer should have two questions in mind—

1. Does this paper contain all the material that my reader needs?
2. How much material can I remove without interfering with my reader's understanding and needs?

A good writer considers these questions first while planning his paper, then again after outlining it, and finally during this revision of his first draft.

A writer, thinking of himself rather than of his reader, may have included material to impress the reader with the writer's knowledge, ability, or diligence. He may even have written an entirely unnecessary paper just to produce another publication. To discard his own writing ruthlessly is the first lesson that he must learn. A good writer fills his own wastebasket rather than his reader's.

Another writer may have included a wealth of information in his report but not the information that his reader needs. Many a specialist sends to management useless technical information but omits the information necessary for the decisions management must make. More careful consideration of the needs of his readers should help such a writer to avoid this mistake. He should ask some of the following questions: Why is X reading this paper? What training and background does he have for understanding the subject? How does he read? What kind of thinker is he? How much of my report will he read?

Second revision. During his second reading a writer should strive for clarity. The word *strive* is used advisedly, for clarity is not easy to attain. If the writer was not clear in other papers, he should search his current work for the faults that clouded his meaning in those papers. He should rephrase any ambiguous expressions even though he thinks that his reader will know what he meant to say. A reader should never be given the opportunity to think, "Well, I know what you mean to say because I know what you ought to be saying, but you haven't said it." As soon as a reader must supply what a writer intended to say, the writer has failed.

A writer should know how to choose the best word for his meaning

(Chapter XII), how to make his sentences clear (Chapters IX and XIII), and how to construct paragraphs that develop his meaning helpfully and clearly (Chapter XIV). If a writer familiar with these chapters still is not certain about the clarity of a passage, he should ask a friend who resembles his reader to study the passage and ask questions about anything that he does not understand. A careful examination of the questions can aid a writer to achieve clarity when he revises.

Third revision. In the third reading and in as many subsequent readings as are necessary, a writer should correct his writing. The errors most common in business, science, and technology are described, illustrated, and corrected in Chapters IX and X. A writer should read these chapters, mark the mistakes that he makes, and study the correction of the mistakes. Nearly every writer can benefit from meticulously examining ten pages of his writing for the errors described in Chapters IX and X. At the end of this exercise he will know his common errors, the ones to search for in the third reading.

Every writer should check ten pages of his writing annually to make sure that he has not acquired or reacquired some errors. The poor usage corrected in Chapters IX and X appears in his reading, and it is a short step from reading errors to writing them.

Chapters IX and X sometimes illustrate more than one way to correct an error, and a writer should practice the methods illustrated; otherwise he will correct his error in only one way and may thus make his writing monotonous.

Fourth revision. The fourth revision should be a strenuous attempt to reduce the number of words. After a writer has studied how to avoid the seven kinds of wordiness discussed in Chapter VIII, he will find revising for brevity profitable. Beginners have reduced long papers by one quarter of their length. Removing unnecessary words often leads to deleting whole sentences, and thus writing becomes keener and livelier.

After a writer has revised several papers for brevity, he will find fewer superfluous words in his first drafts. Achieving brevity, at first a giant step, will later be quick and easy. But because wordiness is contagious and the disease is rife, a writer must be vigilant.

Fifth revision. The fifth and final revision, an attempt to develop better style, is advanced work. A few writers will be satisfied with the clear, brief style achieved by the end of the fourth revision and will go no further. Others will not have the time to apply the principles of effective style to everything that they write but will wish to apply them to their most important writings. And many writers will be driven by pride in themselves and their work to revise thoroughly all papers that might affect their reputations.

A decision as to how much polishing of a given work is necessary or desirable is a matter of individual judgment. The decision will be a wiser one if the writer considers his reader rather than himself. Directions for laboratory work, for example, do not justify much polishing. Once they are correct, clear, and brief, a writer's work is done. But safety advice is another matter. Because of its importance to readers, a writer should revise and rewrite safety advice beyond the point of clarity, correctness, and brevity to achieve effective emphasis. Writers should not polish just the papers that interest them, for those are likely to be written better anyway. Writers should revise for easy reading any papers addressed to many readers. To save the time of many readers is a professional courtesy.

Chapter XI is a general introduction to style; it prepares writers for a study of style in the paragraph, in the sentence, and in diction.

Unless he has numbered steps or divisions, a writer should revise to achieve good style in his paragraphs. Chapter XIV gives advice on constructing paragraphs, checking transitions between paragraphs and between sentences within a paragraph, using coherence as a device of style, and achieving proper emphasis in a paragraph.

Chapter XIII helps a writer to improve his sentence style. Concentration on one length, one grammatical type, or one rhetorical type is discouraged by an introduction to other kinds and their uses. This chapter stresses effective subordination in the sentence, the correct use of parallel construction, and the application of the other principles of sentence emphasis.

For writers who never seem able to find the exact word that they need, Chapter XII examines the principles of word selection. Because the study of words is interesting and the challenge of finding effective diction attracts many intelligent people, it is not necessary to urge writers to be thorough in their improvement. But because many writers are tempted to select words by guess or by instinct, they should know that they can improve diction more efficiently if they understand the principles.

The fifth revision ends with a careful proofreading of the final copy. This should never be neglected; a writer's four careful revisions may be nullified by errors in the final copy that irritate, amuse, or otherwise distract readers. If a competent proofreader is not available, a writer should proofread the final copy himself.

SUPERVISING WRITERS

After a man has improved his writing by using the instructions in this book and sometimes even before he has completed his studying, he may be asked to supervise or edit the writing of others. Chapter XVI helps him to avoid some common errors of those who supervise writing. Necessarily brief, this chapter is not a textbook on supervising or editing, but just advice for a supervisor or editor who wants to begin in the right way.

Many writers receive the advice of supervisors or editors. Chapter XVI helps these writers to benefit from the assistance and to avoid some common errors of writers under supervision.

THE FINAL CHAPTER

Chapter XVI is the final chapter in this book, but there is no final chapter in improving writing. If a writer is alert, everything he reads can help him. The letters, memorandums, and reports that he reads for his profession not only convey information but also illustrate techniques of writing. An aware writer notices errors and weaknesses to avoid and notes telling devices and successful methods to borrow. He may plan, for example, to avoid the tangled sentence structure that made it necessary for him to reread or the kinds of letter openings that irritate him or the unnecessary material that annoys him by wasting his time. But a gracious tone in a letter, subheads that made his reading easy, an interesting beginning that persuaded him to read further—these are more than reading pleasures; they are reminders of techniques that he has studied; they are inspiration.

And the leisure reading of a writer can contribute even more to his progress. While he enjoys an essay, a story, or an article, he absorbs, without conscious effort, a knowledge of paragraph structure, an acquaintance with sentence patterns and rhythms, and a feeling for well-chosen words. And these are difficult to acquire in any other way.

Anyone can learn much from the best writers. But many professional men choose as models the poor and average writers of their professions and neglect the excellent authors who are more helpful and more interesting. Duffers can learn more from watching Arnold Palmer than from watching other duffers, and an intelligent man can learn more about writing by reading the best books and critically observing the techniques of the best authors than he can learn in any other way.

Chapter III

Getting Started

He has half the deed done, who has made a beginning.

Horace

To start writing, simple as it may seem, is difficult for many writers. They suffer anguish when they approach writing. They postpone, prevaricate, and procrastinate so frequently and persuasively that they often deceive everyone, even themselves. Other tasks that have been waiting for months suddenly seem urgent; other disagreeable duties develop immediate appeal; and other plans, hitherto nebulous, demand instant action. Anything—daydreaming, desk-cleaning, boss-baiting—serves to postpone writing. No dodger is more artful than the reluctant writer.

And the most artful dodger of all is the occasional writer faced with that first blank page. He whose main work is writing may waste a little time, it is true, but every working day he has to write. However the field representative who reports infrequently to the home office, the scientist who turns reluctantly from his experiments to report his findings, the administrator who writes only a few reports a year, and other occasional writers become masters of the long delay. They can sit and stare at the blank page until some more pressing demand releases them. I have heard at least a thousand such evaders lament their procrastination. But I still sympathize each time because I too have experienced the problem and its frustrations. After all, for ten years I found excuses for not starting this book.

Reluctance to start is not peculiar to writers in the professions although many of them think that it is. They believe that poets and writers of prose fiction have a special inspiration that enables them to fill pages painlessly. But Anatole France declared that he grew dizzy at the sight of a blank page, and he might never have produced his masterpieces without Mme de Caillavet to force him to spend several hours a day at his desk—even when he was on vacation.[1] Other authors needed the goad of poverty. Samuel Johnson said forthrightly, "No man but a blockhead ever wrote except for money." And he composed *Rasselas* to pay for his mother's funeral. S. J. Perelman stated that he writes "with the grocer sitting on my shoulder." And Lawrence Durrell expressed the experience of many writers: "You see, the beauty of it is that when you are really frantic and worried about money, you find that if it's going to be a question of writing to live, why, you just damn well buckle to and do it."[2]

A writer who does not have the equivalent of Lawrence Durrell's wolf at his door or of Anatole France's mistress in his office must force himself to write—and to write promptly. But how? The knowledge that he will write better if he allows time for revision helps, but my experience with writers in industry and government indicates that for many of them this incentive is not strong enough. Therefore my students and I sought ways of making the first writing pleasanter and easier, and we found some simple methods that work for them.

Each writer is, of course, an individual problem best helped by separate consideration. An intelligent writer can study himself and his writing to discover which recommendations will help him. One of the following suggestions usually aids even the most stubborn starter to begin more readily and therefore to write better.

Many reluctant writers hate to begin because they try to do too much in the first draft. They are determined to produce the final copy immediately, and for most writers this is a frustrating experience because it requires constant shifting from creation to revision. In the middle of the first paragraph one of these writers stops to change a sentence. Before stopping he had the next few sentences clearly in mind and the next paragraph nearly ready. After stopping he cannot remember what he intended to say next. Hoping to pick up the thread of his thought, he rereads what he has written, consults his outline, and wastes time pressing to remember. But he cannot recapture what was ready before he interrupted himself; the words elude him. Finally he gives up the attempt to recall and forces himself to write new sentences. But they do not satisfy him, and the rightness of the words that he has forgotten haunts him. Some writers confessed to me that they suffered this irritating experience two or three times for each page and accepted it as a necessary pain of writing.

[1] Nicolas Segur, *Conversations with Anatole France*, trans. J. Lewis May (John Lane, The Bodley Head, Ltd., London, 1926), p. 22.
[2] *Writers at Work: The Paris Review Interviews*, Second Series (The Viking Press, New York, 1963), pp. 249 and 267.

Trying to revise while writing is like straining to remember a name that has slipped one's mind. The more a person strains, the more the name eludes him. But if he relaxes and thinks of something else, his memory functions painlessly and produces *Bolenciecwcz* triumphantly without conscious effort or strain. If a writer does not stop to revise, his writing may flow for pages, and then the correction he wants, like the forgotten name, will obligingly pop into his conscious mind. If it does not, he need not worry. It will appear without further summons while he is driving home that night or taking his shower the next morning.

Writing and revising require different frames of mind. Revision demands cool objectivity; writing, even technical writing, is a fiery, or at least a warm, procreation. Writing should be kept at a boil. When the creator turns critic, the fire dies. Then the energy that should have been spent writing must be devoted to starting the fire again. Doing this two to four times for every page is so exasperating that it is no wonder writers hate to approach the first blank page.

For quicker and better results, writers who have started should keep going, letting the words pour forth as long as the flow lasts. The flow will stop itself soon enough. They must cease interrupting themselves when they are writing and eliminate other interruptions. A secretary's questions, the telephone, a friend passing the time of day—any one of these may make them forget the words they were just about to write. Hemingway said it simply and clearly: "The telephone and visitors are the work destroyers. . . . You can write any time people will leave you alone and not interrupt you." [3]

Writing without interruption produces miraculous results. Students tell me that when they are alone and uninterrupted they produce in thirty minutes what would otherwise take them an hour or more. And their uninterrupted writing has fewer errors and better unity and coherence. When some medical writers who were used to working in open cubicles where disturbances and distractions were frequent tried working in a quiet library, they doubled their output and felt more relaxed at the end of their working day. And I am always a little dismayed and amused at the end of a long course by the number of students who tell me, "Well, it was a very full course, and I learned a lot, but do you know what helped me most? It was that advice you gave us the first day to write without interruption." Even executives who were reluctant to arrange do-not-disturb periods because they thought that they should always be available, soon said with Heinrich Heine, "I need solitude for my work."

[3] *Writers at Work,* p. 223.

Some writers who cannot get started are unconsciously evading work. As long as they do not start working, they do not have to work. It is much easier to moan than to write. The advice that spurs these groaners best is, "Start anywhere. The section that you write first does not have to stand first in your final paper. Choose the section that interests you most or the section that you know best and write it." Once the wheels start, they keep turning, and such writers usually find that somewhere along the way they write a good beginning. They are unconscious postponers who can bemoan their inability to start—right up to their deadline. They must learn to suspect the excuse that they do not know how to begin.

Some writers cannot begin because they are not ready to write. They have not thought their subjects through, or they have not completed their research. If they outline their papers (Chapter VI), they crystallize their thinking before they write, or they discover that they must complete their research. Incidentally, some writers who are thought to be very slow are not slow at all. They have been counting as writing time the hours they spend deciding what to say. There is nothing wrong about thinking with one's pen in hand. But it is an error to confuse time spent deciding what to say with time spent saying it and then to dislike writing because it seems slow.

Other writers are problem starters because they have an artificial concept of a paper as an introduction, body, and conclusion, each part so separate from the others that often each is on a different subject. My undergraduate writers approaching their first research papers illustrate this problem in its clearest and most elementary form. A student preparing a theme on the use of light and dark in Conrad's *Victory* has completed his research, has analyzed his findings, and should be ready to write, but he is blocked. He thinks that he has to write an introduction, and to him that means a discussion of Conrad's life and works. He is not ready to write the discussion because it is not the subject of his research, but for some reason he considers it the only way to begin his paper.

In industry the introduction devoted to another subject also obstructs some writers. A worker in a personnel department could not begin his report on three machines for processing cards. He had all the information about the machines, he had organized the material, and he had decided upon his recommendations. However he was stumped by the conviction that he had to begin with a history of the use of these machines in personnel departments in the United States or at least in his company. And a market research analyst could not start writing a short memorandum on three new reasons for marketing his product in the New England area because he was planning an introduction that summarized the whole history of the product, a history unrelated to his three reasons.

The concept of the introduction is at fault here. These writers are stopped before they start because they are trying to write the beginning of another paper, often of a book. They do not have the material for it, and it is not part of their subject; therefore all the forces that are blocking them are legitimate. But some of them have to start with unnecessary introductions even though their good sense tells them that they will discard the introductions later. They protest that this is the only way that they can get into the subject. If they are inflexible personalities, then all they can do is keep these off-the-subject introductions as brief as possible and consider writing them a warming-up period. Thus they will write shorter and shorter introductions and may gradually eliminate them.

Engineers often have difficulty beginning a paper for industry for similar reasons; they find it difficult to depart from the traditional organization used in their branch of engineering and especially difficult to start in a new way. If they have been in the habit of beginning, as many journal articles do, with a complete history of the research in the subject that they have investigated, they may find it difficult to tell a client only about the progress made in the last few months. Once such engineers understand the situation and read some good reports, most of them learn to discuss recent findings without a special introduction. But some who have been taught the traditional order too well or who are inflexible by nature will continue to waste time by writing the traditional introduction and discarding it. Familiarity with only one plan makes change difficult and unpleasant for many engineers, and sometimes those just out of college are unfortunately stubborn in their insistence on a particular organization. Engineering schools could help engineers by teaching them to use several organizations for their reports instead of encouraging them to practice only one. That one, though used in some professional journals, may not be suitable for reports in industry.

Some supervisors try to help writers by suggesting that a paper begin with a summary or with a statement of a problem. Both are often good ways of beginning (Chapter IV). But no beginning is good for all papers. When suggested methods become prescriptions, trouble starts. "There isn't any problem in my paper. How can I state one?" a writer asks in a department where all papers must begin with a statement of the problem. His supervisor, knowing that each report must use this favorite beginning of an influential executive, replies without intentional humor, "Make one up." "How can I write a summary beginning for this paper?" demands an annoyed writer. "The paper is already a summary of a summary." Here, as in other phases of supervision, salutary suggestions have become destructive commands. An assigned method of beginning all reports places the writer in a straitjacket. It sometimes results in awkward introductions that seem to be the monotonous products of an assembly line. When a beginning is prescribed, writers who never had trouble starting soon develop difficulties and waste their energies fighting this cookie-cutting instruction. Unfortunately, it is frequently the best writers who are the most annoyed and hampered by such regimentation.

Another kind of regimentation that may make writing so unpleasant that a writer hates to begin is the requirement of using one physical method, such as handwriting or typing or dictating. The unwillingness of a writer or a company to experiment with methods may be harmful. It is often true that the writer who is most reluctant to change may benefit the most from trying a new method. I have noticed several times that stiff, formal executives who need an easy informal style are determined to continue handwriting their drafts. Yet dictating by telephone, though difficult for them at first, later produces excellent results, because talking into a telephone encourages informality. And sometimes companies can be as difficult as individuals about changes. For example, many writers work best by revising triple-spaced copy. Double-spaced copy looks final to them, and they make few changes on it. But one vice president discovered to his indignation that he could not get copy as ordered because it was inconvenient for his stenographic pool to have two sets of directions. A little flexibility on the part of both company and writer is often necessary for easier starting.

For some writers, the selection of a physical method is idiosyncratic. One writer uses longhand; another finds it much too slow. One likes to dictate to a person because it helps him to achieve a conversational style; another is distracted by the presence of a secretary. One writer feels a peculiar union with his typewriter; something happens as soon as he touches the keys. Another hates the clacking of keys; he enjoys the convenience of turning a dictating machine on and off as he pleases. Experimenting for a few weeks may help a writer to discover a congenial method that will take some of the unpleasantness out of writing. If he does not like one dictating machine, he should try others. Dictating machines come in all shapes and types these days, and some writers are much happier with one kind than with another. Also, some writers find that they like to dictate certain kinds of writing, such as letters, but prefer longhand for more formal writing. It is always easier for a writer to begin if the physical method is congenial.

Even successful authors are eccentric about their methods of work. Henry Miller noticed that often writers and painters seek uncomfortable positions and miserable circumstances as though discomfort helps them work.[4] Hemingway always wrote standing; others must write at the same time every day or in the same place. One executive in my course was convinced that a special kind of cigar helped him to write, and one medical writer believed that her favorite perfume was necessary. Habits and sense appeals that sound silly may prove useful. We know very little about the relation of habits and senses to the writing process. When some poor spellers write with crayons on huge sheets of paper, they spell correctly. If muscular actions aid spellers, why should not writers experiment to see what assists them? There is no doubt that habitual actions and experiences encourage some writers to achieve a working mood—sharpening pencils, raising the blinds, enjoying a particular scent, or sitting in a special position may start the words flowing.

Many of my students who had difficulty starting to write found that formulating a plan or outline of their writing was the most helpful of all devices. Some of them were used to outlining long reports but did not outline letters or short memorandums. Jotting down the few points to be covered often brought to mind a good beginning. And writers in the habit of dictating found preliminary outlines particularly useful. Their minds were relieved of worry about forgetting a point while dictating. Their struggle to remember to include everything had often interfered with their expression of preliminary thoughts. But once they had planned, they no longer sat staring at a secretary or machine and wondering how to begin. Their first point was on the plan before them, and it was usually a better beginning than they would have thought of in a rush to dictate. When they did not organize before writing, they frequently used a poor order that buried an ideal beginning in the middle of their letter or memorandum. Planning enabled them to place this idea first and to begin easily.

Some writers resist planning because they dislike the outline method that they were taught in school—the detailed plan with many subdivisions descending from Roman numerals to small letters in double parentheses. But that kind of plan is seldom necessary for a short work (Chapter VI). Simply jotting down the main ideas and then numbering them is much less painful. Yet even the simplest plan can make a work more logical and effective because it helps a writer to use the best order for his material.

Writing simple outlines revealed to my students and to me that they were familiar with few methods of organizing ideas, perhaps only one or two. Their writing suffered from being forced into one of the few plans familiar to them, and the familiar plans did not provide suitable

[4] *Writers at Work*, p. 171.

beginnings. An acquaintance with the methods of organizing discussed and illustrated in Chapter V enabled such writers to choose from many plans and therefore to make a better choice. The thinking involved in the selection of plans with suitable first topics prepared such writers to begin their papers more easily.

A knowledge of a number of beginnings appropriate in functional prose, such as those discussed and illustrated in Chapter IV, also helps writers. Once writers know the advantages and disadvantages of a number of beginnings, they are less likely to sit waiting vainly for some ideas to pop into their heads.

If the reader of this book has trouble starting to write for some reason not mentioned here, I hope that he will note the information and the methods that solved similar problems—self-analysis, experimentation with new methods of writing, organizing and outlining, knowledge of many organizations, and knowledge of many ways of beginning. If none of these work, he should write some other section of his paper first and give his mind an opportunity to develop a beginning while he is writing. Many of the best beginnings are written last.

Chapter IV

Two Dozen Ways to Begin

> . . . it is a foolish thing to make a long prologue, and to
> be short in the story itself.
>
> *II Maccabees 2:32*

First words are often last words. Readers of reports and articles may never go beyond them, for writers on professional subjects do not have captive readers. Like hurried newspaper readers who do not turn to the page where a story is continued, readers in industry and government often turn to another report or article. Americans are used to thumbing the pages of newspapers, magazines, and books to decide on the basis of first sentences what they wish to read. And many influential readers in administration must estimate from first words whether to read further or to discard; otherwise they cannot keep their heads above the flood of paper. Not surprisingly, then, they judge writers by their opening sentences. Although good writing and poor writing in the middle of a paper may escape notice, opening sentences are spotlighted.

A writer who wishes to improve the introductions of his papers should study the following kinds and choose the best one for his subject, his readers, and his ability. Imaginative, experienced writers may use all these beginnings in their papers. Less experienced writers should consider the advantages and disadvantages of each kind before experimenting.

A writer can benefit from examining critically the opening sentences in his reading to see how and when various beginnings are used. Studying the best writing in his company will acquaint him with opening sentences that are appropriate and acceptable there. But he should not confine his study to the writing of his colleagues. Books, magazines, and newspapers furnish varied examples of good openings. To show the variety offered in just one Sunday newspaper, I have illustrated from a single edition of *The New York Times*. I have also cited typical examples from other publications that a writer on professional subjects is likely to read, such as those on business, science, and technology.

Studying and imitating beginnings can be interesting and productive. Study and practice prevent the stultifying waste of time of the writer who laments, "I just don't know how to start. I've been trying for three days now, but I can't think of a good beginning." Once he becomes acquainted with ways to introduce his subject, he can spend his time choosing wisely from appropriate beginnings. One executive who writes many kinds of memorandums, reports, and letters keeps a list of beginnings handy on a card on top of his desk to consult whenever he hesitates over his introduction. Another executive who writes most of his business day has memorized the standard beginnings, but he keeps a file of new kinds and of original or unusual adaptations of familiar beginnings that he finds in his reading, and he soon uses them in his writing. Just being alert to good introductions has helped many professional men to begin papers effectively. A writer who fashions a successful opening sentence is likely to find it easy to continue. Like Gibbon writing *The Decline and Fall of the Roman Empire,* he discovers that once he has the first sentence, the rest follows.

BEGINNINGS

Summary

The popular summary beginning takes several forms: (1) a brief statement of the main ideas; (2) a digest of all sections of the paper; or (3) an abridgment of results, conclusions, or recommendations. This beginning is so useful that many professional journals preface each article with a summary. Some research institutes consider the summary important enough for a writer to spend months reducing a summary of years of research to a single page. At least one institute never sends a customer more than one page, no matter how lengthy the research; and its customers do not ask for more even though upper management bases some decisions on these few summary sentences of scientists and technologists. Therefore a writer should expend his best efforts on opening summaries. The ability to summarize the main ideas of a report is one of the most important skills a writer in industry can acquire.

A brief statement of main ideas is considered by many writers the most helpful beginning of all. I suggest it when a report is organized in the order of climax or reverse climax (Chapter V), and it is also suitable for reports organized on other plans. Although a summary of main ideas at the beginning of a paper is sometimes considered useful only to those who are not experts, it may also help specialists. Specialists say that knowing the main points helps them to read a report more intelligently and more rapidly. And this summary also saves the time of specialists who like to glance over reports to get the gist of each before starting to read the most urgent one. Nonspecialists, many of them in management, may read only the summary or only the summary and one other section. Therefore, many writers supply, in addition to the general summary of main points, informative subheads and an expository table of contents.

Unfortunately, the useful summary beginning, which is often compared to the first sentence in a news story, is frequently misunderstood. Some writers, thinking of the five W's in newspaper leads (Who? What? Where? When? Why?), try to place too much unimportant material in their first sentences. But a good story answers only the important W's in the lead sentence:

> Dr. James Bryant Conant, in a sweeping critique of teacher training in America, has called for the abolition of the existing teacher certification system.[1]

> Pope Paul VI announced today that a number of qualified laymen would be permitted to attend the second session of the Ecumenical Council and to take an active part in commission meetings.[1]

> Tales of a spider that casts a net over its prey have long been related in South Africa and Australia. The Australian netting spider (*Deinopis subrufa*), shown slightly larger than life-size in this picture sequence, practices this strange predatory method.[2]

> As a probe for examining the structure of the atomic nucleus, the neutron offers several advantages.[3]

A study of such examples should help the writer who begins, "This memo summarizes the discussion that Drs. Jones, Smith, Cadwallader, and I had at the Scientific Trivial Verbosity Plant with Drs. Brown, Greene, and Fitzgibbon on June 11, 1965." He is using valuable space—the position of major emphasis, the main clause of his opening sentence—to say that he is summarizing. Instead of telling what he is doing, he should do it. If the talks at the Scientific Trivial Verbosity Plant disclosed that scientific articles are attenuated by the persistent use of unnecessary passives, he might begin, "Scientific articles are attenuated by the persistent use of unnecessary passives," and tell his reader who and where in a footnote

[1] *The New York Times* (Sunday, September 15, 1963). Copyrighted 1963 by *The New York Times* Company. Reprinted by permission.
[2] "Predator Nets a Sugar Ant," *Natural History*, LXXIII (March, 1964), 54.
[3] Lawrence Cranberg, "Fast-Neutron Spectroscopy," *Scientific American*, CCX (March, 1964), 79.

or later in the text of the report. If the plant name is important, he might begin, "The Scientific Trivial Verbosity Plant attenuates scientific articles by the persistent use of unnecessary passives." But he should avoid the incorrect emphasis of a main clause stating that he is writing or summarizing or describing or reporting because this relegates his main thought to a subordinate construction. Moreover he insults his own writing and his readers' intelligence when he tells his readers what he is obviously doing. Such a writer should take pity on the executives who face stacks of reports beginning tritely:

> This memo summarizes
> This report is written in answer to
> This memo recommends
> This memo reports
> This memo covers
> This memo concerns
> This report gives the results of . . .

Instead of saying, "This paper describes an instrument which is useful to measure the total enthalpy content of high-energy gas streams at temperatures where dissociation effects become important," the writer should subordinate the unimportant and stress the important: "The instrument described in this paper measures the total enthalpy content of high-energy gas streams at temperatures where dissociation effects become important."

A digest of all sections of a paper, sometimes called an abstract or a descriptive abstract, is helpful to some readers, but it may become repetitive. Examples from the *Times* and professional journals show that a digest is useful for a short paper that is not highly specialized. For a long specialized report, however, it must usually be technical if it is to be brief, and it is then useful only to readers with technical knowledge. In reports on scattered subjects, it solves coherence problems.

The digest may be written from an outline, and indeed, it often borrows the wording of an outline. Thus it assists readers who wish to find certain sections and librarians who must describe reports and refer them to appropriate readers.

Although a descriptive abstract is an unusual beginning in newspapers, Robert E. Bedingfield uses one with easy informality in the *Times:*

> Percy Uris is an unusual real estate man for several reasons. In the first place, it isn't too great a flight of fancy to say that he started at the top—his father helped erect the Eiffel Tower in Paris in 1889—and kept going higher.
>
> The Uris Buildings Corporation, of which he is chairman and chief executive officer, often has several buildings going up at once, each of which contains more metal than Paris' famed landmark.

> For another distinction, Mr. Uris is not eager to build his structures by committing. . . .

Professional journals may preface short papers with abstracts, as the following examples from *Science* illustrate:

> The first cases in the United States of swine infections caused by the fungus *Microsporum nanum* are reported. The infections occurred in a herd of Yorkshire swine in Pennsylvania. The dermatophyte, which readily produced experimental infections, was identified by isolation and studies in pure cultures.[4]

> It is known that cells of *Escherichia coli* B exposed to 2537-Å ultraviolet radiation will show a higher survival (photoreactivation) if subsequently irradiated at 3650 Å, and that they will also show a higher survival (liquid holding recovery) if subsequently held in a liquid. We find that cells given an optimal recovery treatment of one type show no further recovery if also subjected to the other type of treatment. It is concluded that liquid holding treatment acts only upon photoreactivable damage.[5]

In the *A.I.Ch.E. Journal* a paper entitled "Heat Transfer in the Critical Region—Temperature and Velocity Profiles in Turbulent Flow" also begins with a descriptive abstract:

> Unusual heat transfer phenomena have been observed between solid surfaces and fluids near their thermodynamic critical point. To understand better these phenomena, temperature and velocity profiles and local heat transfer coefficients were measured for turbulent flow of carbon dioxide in a tube at 1,075 lb./sq. in. abs. . . . . The results indicate a severe flattening of the radial temperature profiles, a maximum in the velocity profile between the wall at the tube axis, and a maximum in h' when the bulk fluid temperature passes through the transposed critical temperature.
> The results can be explained qualitatively by considering the variation with temperature of thermal conductivity near the tube wall and specific heat in the turbulent core.[6]

When the writer of a long specialized paper does not have the advantage of writing mainly for technically trained readers, as journal writers do, he will probably find some other beginning easier to adapt for his readers. But long reports that are not highly specialized, short reports, and memorandums often begin effectively with a digest of all sections. Beginning with such a summary is also effective in reports treating several

[4] George Bubash, Oliver J. Ginther, and Libero Ajello, CXLIII (January 24, 1964), 366.
[5] A. Castellani, J. Jagger, and R. B. Setlow, CXLIII (March 13, 1964), 1170.
[6] Rodney D. Wood and J. M. Smith, X (March, 1964), 180.

unrelated subjects because the digest introduces each subject to the readers. Thus the writer, by establishing at the beginning the separate nature of each subject in his report, avoids the need to create artificial connections between subjects.

An abridgment of results, conclusions, or recommendations in terms intelligible to all readers is a suitable and helpful beginning for many papers, particularly those that recommend action. It may be used even though the complete technical description of results is important to the specialist. He can find that later in the paper.

John A. Osmundsen reporting on interferon in the *Times* summarizes conclusions clearly:

> A husband-and-wife team of Belgian scientists reported experimental results here today that may explain one way that certain chemicals cause cancer.
>
> The chemicals do this, the findings indicated, by suppressing the production of a substance called interferon that is normally put out by cells in response to virus infection. Interferon prevents the spread of the infection by interfering with virus reproduction.

Many memorandums and reports begin quite properly and helpfully with summaries of results, conclusions, or recommendations or even with a full statement of these:

> The Marketing Committee recommends for the reasons detailed in this report that we market by May first a 2.5-mg. Blank Drug suppository.

> Preliminary trials in private medical practice and in hospitals demonstrated the efficacy of Blank capsules as an adjunct in controlling appetite and anxiety.

In many papers the initial statements of conclusions present only the most significant features. Detailed results and conclusions are reserved for discussion after the presentation of evidence.

> Decreasing the water content of the feed results in a corresponding decrease in acid consumption for hydrofluoric acid alkylation. Lower corrosion rates and less polymer formation are additional benefits.[7]

> Babies 2- to 4-days old whose mothers received heavy medication during labor were less attentive than those babies whose mothers received light medication.[8]

[7] M. D. Box, A. E. Bynum, and R. J. Schoofs, "Molecular Sieves Dry Alky Feed Better," *Hydrocarbon Processing & Petroleum Refiner*, XLIII (January, 1964), 125.
[8] Gerald Stechler, "Newborn Attention as Affected by Medication During Labor," *Science*, CXLIV (April 17, 1964), 315.

These articles express the introductory statements of results in terms intelligible to all readers. The staff-written summaries of *International Science and Technology* are also usually expressed briefly in terms clear to nonspecialists. Evan Herbert of that journal summarizes tersely the difficult results of a paper called "Perception": "Extensions of a new color perception theory lead to a principle of relativity for perception by any of the senses." [9]

When readers are concerned about recommendations, conclusions, or results and a writer can summarize them briefly and effectively, they are the best introduction. Philip E. Jacobi begins his book *Changing Values in College* [10] with a "Summary of Findings" that presents results in the order in which they are detailed in the succeeding chapters. Thus he uses a summary of results before the first chapter to inform his readers of the contents and order of his book. If readers will benefit, a summary of results, conclusions, and recommendations is appropriate for writings of any length—from a half-page memorandum to a full-length book.

Scope

The following paragraphs concern introductory statements of scope as they appear in a paper for industry, in the *Times*, and in professional journals. The discussion concludes with the advantages of this beginning and a caution about using it.

A statement of the limitation of the subject or of the amount of detail to be presented is sometimes a necessary beginning if readers are not to be misled into wasting time. When the opening sentences establish that three computers of the X Corporation have been surveyed (a) for price, (b) for dates of availability, and (c) for adaptability to the operation of X Corporation, a reader will not waste time looking through the paper for information about the experience of other companies with these computers or for information about the computers manufactured by Y Company.

To add more zest a statement of the scope of a paper may be combined with some other method of introducing a subject. In *The New York Times Magazine* Harold Wilson combines it with an opening question that leads to a definition; thus he uses three methods:

> With public opinion polls, by-election results, and the expectations of political commentators pointing firmly toward a Labor victory at the next general election, I am frequently asked, "What is British socialism today?"

[9] November, 1963, p. 76.
[10] *Changing Values in College: An Exploratory Study of the Impact of College Teaching* (Harper and Brothers, New York, 1957).

Many journal articles begin with a statement of scope. *Chemical Engineering* introduces an article on fuel storage with the statement:

> Aiming to remedy a shortage of storage sites and other facilities for peak season supply of natural gas, this test program proves the feasibility of liquefying the gas and then putting it underground in concrete tanks.[11]

A statement of scope in a learned journal is usually longer than this, the following example from *Nuclear Science and Engineering* being typical:

> Theoretical methods for computing intracell thermal-neutron densities, disadvantage factors and thermal utilizations are presented. The topics discussed are the computation of the neutron spectra in a lattice, anisotropic scattering by water, the cylindrical cell effect, correlation of spectral moments and average one-group cross sections, one-group transport-theory methods, scattering models of water, and comparison of various theories with experiment. The lattices investigated are water moderated with slightly enriched uranium metal and oxide fuel.[12]

An introductory survey of the extent of the subject covered or of the amount of detail included or of both is most useful when readers might expect a different scope or a different amount of detail. But if the scope is simple enough for a title that is not burdensome, then it is better to describe it in the title and to introduce the paper in some other way. Unless readers are unusually dense or the scope of a paper is almost unbelievable, a writer should avoid the unnecessary repetition that occurs when scope is defined in both the title and the opening sentences.

Point of View

An excellent beginning when used discreetly, point of view may be the worst of all beginnings. An initial statement of point of view is useful in the same way that a statement of scope is; both warn the reader early. A warning should be given early when it is necessary or helpful to the reader or likely to arouse his interest. A writer must judge this cautiously, because if the initial statement of point of view antagonizes, an angry reader may stop after the first sentence or may read only to disagree.

Stating point of view early is often useful in a continuing discussion or argument, particularly when others have already established their positions and a writer is adding his views. Ethel Radler, writing to the travel editor of the *Times*, begins, "This is one more vote against the railroads."

[11] "A Concrete Solution for Fuel Storage Woes," LXXI (March 16, 1964), 96.
[12] Henry C. Honeck, "The Calculation of the Thermal Utilization and Disadvantage Factor in Uranium/Water Lattices," XVIII (January, 1964), 49.

Often all that a memorandum or letter does is cast another vote for or against, and the writer might just as well say so at the start.

A less argumentative point of view may be very close to a summary of the main thought. Robert F. Hawkins writes from Venice to the *Times:* "Few films shown at the 24th Venice Film Festival, which ended its two-weeks on Sept. 7th, will go down in film history." Such a statement of point of view occurs frequently in papers for industry. Not so frequently does one meet a statement as polemic as the opening sentence of the lead editorial in the *Wall Street Journal* of February 6, 1964: "Almost everything is wrong, we fear, with the administration's proposals on overtime pay—in principle and practice."

In journals, too, argumentative opening statements of point of view occur: "My attitude toward minimum requirements for technical writers," states Erwin R. Steinberg in the *STWP Review,* "is based on a concept which at first glance may seem to be barely relevant to our topic: engineers and scientists should write their own reports." [13]

In journals of science and technology, a point of view is often combined with a statement of scope. G. A. Tokaty writes in *Technology and Culture:*

> The aim of this paper is to depict the background of well known and not so well known Soviet achievements and failures in the field of space technology, irrespective of whether it agrees or disagrees with numerous existing books, pamphlets, articles, and rumors on the subject.[14]

Specific Details

"A hyphen omitted from an equation caused the failure of a United States rocket."

"*Ain't* ain't excluded from *Webster's Third.*"

"A new method will reduce the cost of producing fuel gasoline by two cents on the dollar."

Specific details such as these arouse interest, titillate curiosity, and please readers. Because of this inherent interest, details are good beginnings, as journalists know and demonstrate in their leads. In *The New York Times Magazine* Mary Anne Guitar starts a two-page article on childhood humor with current specific details:

> Those elephant jokes, which have become such a nationwide fad, have caused some parents to wonder if indeed children have a sense of

[13] "Developing an Undergraduate Curriculum for Training Technical Writers and Editors," VII (October, 1960), 15.
[14] "Soviet Rocket Technology," IV (Fall, 1963), 515. By permission of the University of Chicago Press.

humor. (Incidentally, they have wondered this since the days of Little Audrey.) An adult may or may not find this typical elephant exchange amusing: "Why do elephants wear sneakers?" A: "To creep up on mice." But most children are convulsed by it. Children can, it is all too apparent, appreciate the most elementary form of humor.

And Richard Witkin begins a *Times* article on commercial applications of space technology with four paragraphs of specific details and does not reach his summary until the fifth paragraph:

> Solar cells developed for the space program are providing power for a phone system in South Africa and an emergency call system on a Los Angeles Freeway.
> Filament-winding techniques for making light yet sturdy rocket cases have been adapted for auto parts, chemical vats and brassiere supports.
> Inertial navigation devices for guiding missiles to targets are expected to find commercial applications in supersonic airliners.
> Heat-resistant metals developed for rocket nozzles and winged space vehicles also should find their way into future plane engines and nuclear reactors.
> These are some of the many links found between the new missile and space technology and commercial products in a survey just completed by the Denver Research Institute of the University of Denver.

Journal writers begin with specific details less often than one would expect, considering the interest-arousing possibilities of details. Perhaps a tendency to write a traditional background beginning for journal articles is responsible. But significant details in opening sentences of articles in journals of science and technology are appropriate and effective. Vernon O. Hoehne, writing on aircraft capable of vertical and short take-offs and landings, uses details effectively:

> Statistics indicate that roughly 70 per cent of the air travelers in the United States travel distances of 1,000 miles or less, with the greatest percentage of these traveling between 200 and 300 miles.[15]

Albert B. Stewart begins an article with details of two examples:

> When a man looks at a star, he sees the star not in its true position but in an apparent position. The reason is that the motion of the earth around the sun is carrying the observer through space at a speed of about 18.5 miles per second, so that the starlight he sees undergoes an apparent displacement resulting from the combined effect of his velocity and the velocity of the light. A similar phenomenon is observed by a

[15] "A Role for V/STOL Aircraft in Air Transport," *Battelle Technical Review*, XI (July, 1962), 8.

man driving a car at a modest speed through a snow storm at night; even though the snow may be falling vertically, it appears to be moving at an angle because of the combined effect of its velocity and the car's.[16]

Writers in industry and government are too often inclined to think that no one else is interested in their subject, even when it is of overwhelming general interest. Thus, when writers who have new drugs as their subject matter ask me how to write good beginnings, I tell them that news about drugs is of such general interest today that they can begin effectively with specific information. Details about people are so fascinating that a psychiatrist need never look for better opening material. And many letters, progress reports, memorandums, articles, and advertising appeals that open with dull summaries contain specific details that would be appealing introductions. Because beginning with details is a technique overlooked by most writers for industry and government, the first to use it there will gain not only the intrinsic interest of the details at the beginning but also the appeal of a fresh approach.

Purpose

To acquaint readers quickly with the purpose of his work, a writer may begin an account of a process, a procedure, or a meeting with a statement of the purpose of the writer or of the work, as in the following *Times* story and journal articles:

> Down the ages the Dutch have fought the North Sea, creating the best of their farms in its coastal shallows, suffering tragic losses again and again when storms breached the protective dikes. The last great attack by the sea in February, 1953, drowned 1,785 persons and wreaked property damage of $400,000,000. Aware that such an assault could recur at any time, the Dutch people decided not to stop with merely plugging holes in the dikes and clearing wreckage. They began a 25-year program of dike building called the Delta Plan, now well under way, to achieve permanent security.

> In a series of experiments now being conducted, we wish to determine the projections of the cochlear nuclei upon the components of the superior olivary complex.[17]

> The primary objectives of this research were to develop and test techniques for applying the dynamic Angstrom method to the measurement of heat transfer in a three-phase system, and to make some

[16] "The Discovery of Stellar Aberration," *Scientific American*, CCX (March, 1964), 100.
[17] J. M. Harrison and R. Irving, "Nucleus of the Trapezoid Body: Dual Afferent Innervation," *Science*, CXLIII (January 31, 1964), 473.

measurements on the mass diffusion contribution to heat transfer and the parameters influencing this contribution.[18]

After a project has been completed, a statement of purpose may seem out of date to readers in government and industry and is likely to be less interesting than a statement of results or conclusions. But while the work is in progress, a statement of purpose has pertinence and interest.

Plan of Development

The following examples of beginnings from the *Times*, from papers in government and industry, and from professional journals describe the organizational plans of the articles.

Bosley Crowther writes in the *Times:*

> This is one of those Sundays when the traffic on local screens appears to be pleasantly uncongested, when the only big thing of the past week has been the almost capacity-attended showings of the first New York Film Festival (about which we'll be in a position to make some critical comments next week) and when the opportunity thus is presented to jot some brief and scattered notes on a few small things.

In a less leisurely style a writer for government or industry may say in a memorandum that he is summarizing in the order of their importance the papers read at the A.I.Ch.E. meeting in Puerto Rico and that fuller summaries will be presented in two weeks. Thus a statement of plan of development is used to show from the start that topics are scattered. It may also be used for a tight development—for five reasons in the order of their importance or for a chronological report of a month's work.

Stating the plan of development is not a common way of beginning journal articles. Journals choose, instead, to summarize each section of a paper, a practice that frequently has the serious disadvantage of including unimportant material merely because it is in a separate section. One of the advantages of summarizing the development of the thought of a paper is the omission of material of minor significance. An ASME paper on drag reduction begins with the plan of development and omits part of the background:

> This paper is a progress report on an experimental and theoretical investigation of the drag and flow characteristics of a cylinder rotating in a liquid with a lubricating gas over its surface. A theoretical solution for purely laminar flow of both components is derived from the Navier-Stokes equation. Photographs of the two-phase flow pattern and

[18] A. H. Nissan, David Hansen, and J. L. Walker, "Heat Transfer in Porous Media Containing a Volatile Liquid," *Heat Transfer—Houston*, CEP Symposium Series 41 (American Institute of Chemical Engineers, New York, 1963), p. 114.

experimental data of the drag reduction with air injection in water, alcohol, and glycerine are presented. Contrary to expectations, it was found that neither in the laminar, nor in the Taylor vortex regime did air injection produce a stable film; instead, the air formed a spiral column of bubbles over the cylinder as it rose to the top of the liquid. The need for further studies, especially on the stability criteria of the system, is indicated.[19]

Problem

How to begin with the material of most importance worries some writers, particularly those who wish to start writing before their research is completed or before all their ideas are formulated. Often they solve this by beginning with a statement of the problem of the paper. Because the first step in investigation is usually defining the problem, writers not only have the definition ready when they start to write but have it well digested. Moreover, opening with a statement of the problem is a clear, logical beginning that leads easily into the next steps of the paper. No wonder this beginning is overworked.

Walter Sullivan begins a *Times* story on a new theory for the strange features of radio emissions with a statement of the problem:

> Among the most puzzling features of the solar system are the sporadic, low frequency radio emissions from Jupiter.
>
> They were discovered in 1955 by Drs. Bernard F. Burke and Kenneth L. Franklin, then at the Carnegie Institution of Washington, during their observations of radio noise from the Milky Way. They identified a pinpoint source of very strong signals that proved to be the planet.
>
> Since then a number of strange features of these signals have been identified:
>
> (1) They can be detected only when certain points on Jupiter are aimed at the earth.
>
> (2) They are almost always polarized in the same manner, that is, the radio waves spiral clockwise away from the planet.
>
> (3) They occur in bursts of seemingly explosive intensity.
>
> (4) The band of the frequencies is narrow and sharply beamed, coming, apparently, from rather small areas.
>
> (5) The frequency emitted by certain regions changes as the areas sweep past the earth's direction with the planet's rotation. Furthermore on one side of the planet this change is an increase in frequency, whereas on the opposite side it is a drop.

[19] F. Kreith, F. J. Gude, and A. G. Gibson, "Drag Reduction with a Gas Film on a Cylinder Rotating in a Liquid," *Multi-Phase Flow Symposium* (The American Society of Mechanical Engineers, New York, 1963), p. 79.

Early Theory

One of the earliest theories was that the emissions are a result of gargantuan volcanic eruptions. Some said. . . .

M. D. Morris, writing in *Consulting Engineer,* states two problems in his opening paragraph:

Many foreign visitors claim that Venice is the most magnificent of Italy's multitourist attractions, for what they see is a city unlike any other in this world. What is not visually apparent, however, is that today Venice faces two basic problems that in turn fan out into many more detailed difficulties. Physically, the main Venetian islands are sinking into the sea at an uneven rate. Socioeconomically, residents are leaving in good numbers, taking with them both hard cash and earning capacity.[20]

William H. Pierce begins "Redundancy in Computers" with a simple statement of the problem:

One of the difficult problems facing the engineer in an imperfect world is how to get reliable performance from complex electrical systems such as computers, in which any of perhaps a million things can go wrong.[21]

A more detailed and more technical statement of a problem appears at the beginning of an article in the *A.I.Ch.E. Journal* by R. J. Wethern and Robert S. Brodkey:

The use of plasma generators for chemical synthesis makes it necessary to cool gases rapidly so as to freeze the desired products. A gas may be cooled rapidly by directing its flow through a small-diameter heat exchange system, as has been done in chemical synthesis work (9). The design of such a system requires a prediction of the rates of heat and momentum transfer at temperature differences in the range of 10,000°R. Since such data are not currently available, the present investigation is concerned with the simultaneous heat and momentum transfer which occurs when a gas in laminar flow is cooled under extreme temperature gradients in a water-cooled copper tube. It is also concerned with the corresponding analogies.[22]

In the journals a statement of the problem may introduce a simple or a complex paper and present the reader immediately with the heart of the matter. The details of a problem interesting to a reader can rivet his

[20] "Venice's Physical-Economic Problems," XXII (February, 1964), 60.
[21] *Scientific American,* CCX (February, 1964), 103.
[22] "Heat and Momentum Transfer in Laminar Flow: Helium Initially at Plasma Temperature," IX (January, 1963), 49.

attention from the start. But in government and industry, beginning with a statement of the problem may be boring if the reader, having long worried that bone, finds it all too familiar. Moreover, a statement of a problem interests a reader less after the problem has been solved. By the time that a research report is written in industry, there may no longer be a problem, and the interests of both reader and writer have shifted to the solution or to another study. A general statement of problem addressed to such readers has little force. Bored by his material, the writer rushes through a bald statement of the problem already solved and omits the very details that might make it vivid. Giving specific details is the technique that can make a statement of an unsolved problem salient.

Background

Presenting background is the traditional method of beginning a paper on science or technology. Until recently nearly all journal articles began with what is sometimes called *the history of the art.* For many articles this was the dullest and least significant introduction that could have been devised. Even now, conservative writers begin with a history of a subject as though one could not understand their research without going back to the first work in the field or as though they could not present it without a sprinkling of footnotes to start them off. Readers who have had to skim the accomplishments of *et al.* in 1910 to reach the accomplishments of the experimenters of 1966 can testify to the nuisance value of these background beginnings.

A reader usually wishes to know not what has been reported in the literature during the last one hundred and fifty years but what has not been reported. William J. Rose, Herbert L. Gilles, and Vincent W. Uhl begin directly with the inadequacy of the literature and also satisfy a reader who wants to be sure that they have covered the available studies:

> There is very limited information available for subcooled nucleate boiling of mixtures. The results of the known studies are summarized in Table 1.[23]

When missing background is the subject of the research presented in a paper, summaries of the slightly related and unrelated past work of others serve merely to obscure a current subject and to deaden interest. Only when explanations of history or background are necessary, interesting, or exciting, are they satisfactory opening material.

Barbara Plumb injects a little humor into a background beginning on a real estate page of the *Times:*

[23] "Subcooled Boiling Heat Transfer to Aqueous Binary Mixtures," *Heat Transfer—Houston,* p. 62.

Instead of counting sheep at night, many New Yorkers lull themselves to sleep by ticking off the changes they would make in their rented apartments—if only they could get permission and if only they had the wherewithal.

One owner of a new East Side apartment building not only has made himself privy to these longings but also has set about satisfying some of them. . . .

Walter R. Dornberger, writing in *Technology and Culture* on the German V-2, skims over the background material with admirable speed. "The design features and performance data of the V-2," he writes, "one of the outstanding innovations of the last war, are well known and have been described extensively in many books and articles." He footnotes eight books and articles for any reader desiring more background and then advances rapidly to his own points:

Less well known is the inside story of this weapon—how the Germans came to build it, what inspired them, how they succeeded, and especially why this weapon, in spite of all efforts, failed to become what its creators intended.[24]

In "Heat Transfer in the Critical Region—Temperature and Velocity Profiles in Turbulent Flow" in the *A.I.Ch.E. Journal*, Rodney D. Wood and J. M. Smith refer just as briskly to material more technical than Dornberger's.

Heat transfer from a solid surface to a fluid near its critical temperature and pressure has been studied for the past decade (*2, 4–8, 11, 12, 14*). In the immediate region of the critical point the experimental studies (*6*, 7, *11, 14*) indicate unusual heat transfer coefficients which have not been satisfactorily explained.[25]

And in the same issue W. R. Wilcox and C. R. Wilke quickly summarize two points in the literature:

In the derivation of theoretical expressions for separation in zone melting it is usually assumed that the bulk of the molten zone is well mixed (*5*). Under some conditions, and especially in capillary tubes below about 3-mm. I.D., this is not true (*10*).[26]

Brevity, clarity, and interesting information make these background beginnings effective. But an overlong presentation of a detailed background is one that readers skip. Too often a writer seems reluctant to throw away any of his preliminary research and so imposes all of it

[24] "The German V-2" IV (Fall, 1963), 393.
[25] X (March, 1964), 180.
[26] "Pure Diffusional Mass Transfer in Zone Melting," p. 160.

upon his readers by beginning with it. Like a bather who puts first one toe and then another into cold water, he seems reluctant to start swimming. Many such timid, halting effects are due, I think, either to over-conscientious presentation of more explanations in more detail than the reader needs or to failure to study the material well enough to distinguish the main points. The result is a pedestrian beginning that states every detail of the background.

A much better approach places only a few bits of background at the beginning—some vivid details, perhaps, or some points essential to the understanding of the immediately following sentences. Then the rest of the explanation is introduced where it is needed. An article in the *Times* effectively compresses background in these opening sentences:

> Six months ago, in a move to reduce the number of fare schedules and to increase business, United Air Lines introduced one-class jet travel in seven cities. Last week more than 250,000 one-class passengers later. . . .

With admirable brevity Elroy M. Gladrow and Henry G. Ellert skim over background and then flatly state what was lacking in the literature of their field:

> The preparation of titania by simple hydrolysis of various titanium salts has been described numerous times in the literature. However, the heat stability of pure hydrous titania, as measured by surface area and pore volume, has not been adequately described.[27]

Some writers think that only papers for the general reader may abridge and condense background. But the general reader may require more background than one's fellow specialists, who often need little preliminary explanation. Rudolf H. Eisenhardt and Otto Rosenthal, writing for specialists, explain immediately what is lacking in the literature:

> The mechanism by which free energy is transferred during mito-chondrial oxidative phosphorylation from the exergonic electron-transport reaction to the endergonic phosphorylation reaction remains poorly understood.[28]

J. R. Phillips and B. F. Dodge, in the highly technical article "Deviation from the Inverse-Thickness Relation in Gas-Metal Permeation," generalize the background neatly and efficiently and move rapidly to their own material:

[27] "Preparation and Surface Properties of Porous Titania," *Search* (Esso Research and Engineering Company, Linden, N. J., 1961), p. 12.
[28] "2,4-Dinitrophenol: Lack of Interaction with High-Energy Intermediates of Oxidative Phosphorylation," *Science*, CXLIII (January 31, 1964), 476.

The subject of the flow of gases into and through metals is a broad one with many facets. However, it has been the generally harmful effect of certain gases on the mechanical properties of metals that has fostered a desire to understand the fundamental mechanisms by which gases permeate metals.

The present study was designed to shed light on the relative importance of kinetic steps at the gas-metal interface and diffusion through the metal lattice as rate-controlling factors in the permeation process.[29]

Quotation

> Next to the originator of a good sentence is the first quoter of it. By necessity, by proclivity, and by delight, we all quote.
>
> *Emerson*

Beginning with a quotation is popular, perhaps more popular than it should be, for finding appropriate and worthy quotations is not at all easy, even for the well-read with good memories. But a pertinent quotation adroitly used may make a very good opening, as the following writers in the *Times* illustrate. Stewart L. Udall begins an article on conserving wildlife with a quotation from Thoreau. This least subtle use of a quotation depends for its interest on aptness and on Thoreau's current popularity:

> The squirrel has leaped to another tree, the hawk has circled further off, and has now settled upon a new eyrie, but the woodman is preparing to lay his axe to the root of that, also.
>
> *Thoreau's Journal (1851)*

Joe Nichols uses a quotation adroitly in the sports section:

> Wayne Chambers gave a good rundown on today's $125,000 United Nations Handicap when he said before the race: "Just let me catch Carry Back at the head of the stretch, and I'll beat him." The intent of the 27-year-old jockey was to do the catching with Montepelier's 4-year-old Mongo.
>
> That's exactly what happened in the 1¾6-mile race on the turf.

In writings on science and technology a forecast, a prediction, or a boast may be used in this way after the event to launch a discussion of its fulfillment or failure of fulfillment.

A familiar quotation adapted for humor may be an effective beginning: "A rose is a rose and a skunk is a skunk, and the nose easily tells the difference. But it is not so easy to describe or explain this difference." [30]

[29] *A.I.Ch.E. Journal,* IX (January, 1963), 93.
[30] John E. Amoore, James W. Johnston, Jr., and Martin Rubin, "The Stereochemical Theory of Odor," *Scientific American,* CCX (February, 1964), 42.

An oblique reference to a familiar proverb or event may also provide lightness, as it does in Emerson Chapin's lead:

> TOKYO, Sept. 14—That famous chicken that has been having trouble crossing the Atlantic to gain a welcome entry into the Common Market may find a new haven in Japan.

Writers on technical subjects often weave bits of well-known quotations into their opening sentences:

> Trade traditionally follows the flag: but in the new Europe the order is reversed.[31]

> Large companies seem to be fair game these days for critics of the U. S. business scene. The slings and arrows hurled at "bigness" are many and varied.[32]

But a writer who cannot find an appropriate quotation should write some other type of introduction rather than begin with the dull, the hackneyed, or the tacked-on. Certainly writers with poor skills should avoid trite applications of hackneyed quotations such as "A stitch in time saves nine. Early repairs to the heating equipment in X Building would have saved ten thousand dollars." Here the second sentence, which arouses interest and concern, would be a good beginning. But the quotation is an unnecessary and dull prefix.

Direct dialogue that is amusing is an interest-catching opener. Pat Watters begins a *Times* story on houseboats near Atlanta with dialogue skillfully used:

> "Y'all come on over to our house," in the lexicon of the new Georgia lake country surrounding Atlanta, increasingly means Southern hospitality on a houseboat.

Don E. Kaldenberg appropriately uses dialogue to begin a journal article on interviewing:

> "Employment interview? Who, me! That's a job for the Personnel Department. Why pick on me?" This little piece of dialogue may take place sooner than you think, with you doing the talking.[33]

And two journal writers begin with quotations from authorities to bolster their main points:

[31] Richard Mayne, "Economic Integration in the New Europe: A Statistical Approach," *Daedalus* (Winter, 1964), p. 109.
[32] Lyman W. Porter, "Where Is the Organization Man?" *Harvard Business Review,* XLI (November–December, 1963), 53.
[33] "How to Conduct Your Next Interview," *Hydrocarbon Processing & Petroleum Refiner,* XLIII (January, 1964), 136.

More and more of America's business leaders are subscribing to the view that a strong basic research program is the foundation on which a substantial measure of corporate growth is based. James M. Gavin, president of Arthur D. Little, Inc., has stated for example: "Today in its long-range thinking, industry is beginning to recognize the economic impact of fundamental research. . . ." [34]

In the words of the Chairman of the Board of Directors of one of the largest steel companies in the United States, "Oxygen steelmaking represents the first technological break-through in ingot production that has occurred in over fifty years." [35]

Sometimes only a phrase is quoted, and the rest of the quotation is effectively summarized by the writer: "Bache & Co., one of the nation's large security firms, is 'hoping to incorporate,' Harold L. Bache, directing partner, said." [36] Sometimes an indirect quotation is more effective. Although direct quotations carry authority, it may be necessary to rephrase an entire quotation if it mingles thoughts that are pertinent with those that are not, if it is expressed poorly, if it needs compression, or if a writer wants the style of the introduction to blend smoothly with the next few sentences of his own writing. The *Times* compresses two quotations as follows:

Frederick Erroll, president of the British Board of Trade, has told top Soviet trade officials that Russia is not spending enough of her foreign trade pound sterling earnings in Britain.

Amid continued rioting in South Vietnam, President Diem announces that martial law will be lifted tomorrow, that all powers will be returned to civilian hands and that new national elections will be held Sept. 27.

Chemical Week also begins with an indirect quotation:

Nondefense requirements for filament-wound glass-reinforced plastics will increase sharply in the '60s, according to S. W. Keegin, market research analyst at Pittsburgh Plate Glass. Military uses, he said, will not increase, but industrial demand will grow sixfold—from 2.9 million lbs. in '63 to 16.9 million lbs. in '70. Biggest gains, Keegin added, will come in pipe and tubing, much of which is earmarked for chemical processing.[37]

[34] Melville H. Hodge, Jr., "Rate Your Company's Research Productivity," *Harvard Business Review*, XLI (November–December, 1963), 109.
[35] D. Robert Berg, "The Past, Present, and Future of Oxygen Steelmaking," *Recent Advances in Ferrous Metallurgy*, CEP Symposium Series 43 (American Institute of Chemical Engineers, New York, 1963), p. 131.
[36] *The Wall Street Journal* (February 11, 1964), p. 3.
[37] "Filament Windings Spurt," XCIV (February 8, 1964), 67.

The fact that Mr. Keegin was speaking at Chicago at the conference of the Reinforced Plastics Division of the SPI was reserved for a footnote. A writer for industry who wastes his opening on the negligible information that he heard a statement on February 29, 1965, at the meeting of the Antiquotation Section of the Society for the Propagation of Clichés in the Purple Hotel of Lapwing, Laputa, U. S. A., should place these unimportant if not entirely irrelevant details in a footnote, not in the opening sentences.

Question

What easier way to begin a paper than with a question?

> Should people smile at chimpanzees?
> *John C. Devlin*

> If the cost of living reaches a record high and the prices of various industrial materials and products edge up, can inflation be far behind?
> *Richard Rutter*

> Have you got a house yet?
> *Emerson Chapin*

> How long will the current business advance last?
> *Herbert Koshetz*

> Which would be less expensive to build, a 38-story apartment building or two 19-story buildings with the same number of units?
> *Unsigned*

These *Times* writers know that an eager reader does not want to wait long for an answer. Devlin answers his question at once, "No." And so does Rutter: "Yes, it can, according to many observers of the economic scene." Chapin springs a surprise—the circumstances of the questioner, "That is almost invariably the first question asked of a foreigner in Tokyo, and it seldom fails to start a lively conversation." Koshetz presents detailed analysis before he finally indicates the many reasons for optimism. And the unsigned article immediately analyzes the costs even though it does not reach a final answer until the fourth paragraph. None of these writers delay the answer too long; the brevity of a newspaper story discourages delay. But if a report has a hundred pages or more, readers may grow weary of waiting for the answer to a provocative question asked ninety pages back. To prevent annoyance a writer should answer his question briefly no more than a page or two after asking it. Later in the report he may present a more detailed answer. The Honorable Hubert H. Humphrey opens effectively with a question and cites an estimate as his immediate answer:

"How much research and development needlessly duplicates prior work?" This is a crucial question, and no one is sure of the answer. Some estimates are that, in Federally sponsored research and development, unknowing duplication ranges from 10 per cent to as high (in developmental work) as 50 per cent.[38]

Journals of business, science, and technology frequently begin articles with a question:

What is the future of the passenger vehicle gas turbine? [39]

Is space-time only an empty arena within which real fields and particles move; or is it all there is? [40]

How can we learn to manage work that we do only once? [41]

Why should anyone bother to prepare a paper for publication? [42]

Writers should resist the temptation to ask too many questions in the first paragraph. Too many questions at the beginning or frequent repetition of a question becomes dull. And a question gains force and effect when it is concealed with a little subtlety, as in the following example:

If you ask the nearest electronic computer operator for his comments on the use of fluid computers, you'll likely hear: "Why fluid computers? I'm having enough trouble with the one I've got without worrying about one that leaks besides!" Without realizing it, he will have answered the question: "Why Fluid Computers?" Even with the best computer room facilities, air conditioning, and pampering, the maze of electronic components does give seemingly unending trouble. Fluid computers, on the other hand, using any of a number of liquids or gases, have the potential of high reliability even under adverse environments.[43]

Interest

"My subject is very interesting," state wistful writers, doing their best to make it dull. In some issues of scientific and technical journals

[38] "Unknowing Duplication in Research—A Perennial Tragedy," *STWP Review*, VIII (July, 1961), 2.
[39] John Clark, Jr., "The Gas Turbine Vehicle—Is It for You?" *Mechanical Engineering*, LXXXVI (February, 1964), 49.
[40] Seymour Tilson, "In Brief," *International Science and Technology* (December, 1963), p. 62.
[41] Hilliard W. Paige, "How PERT-Cost Helps the General Manager," *Harvard Business Review*, XLI (November–December, 1963), 87.
[42] Merritt A. Williamson, "The Professional Man and the Obligation of Authorship," *Research/Development* (December, 1959), reprinted in *STWP Review*, VII (October, 1960), 12.
[43] O. Lew Wood and Harold L. Fox, "Fluid Computers," *International Science and Technology* (November, 1963), p. 44.

nearly every article starts with a declaration that the subject is interesting or important. Instead of compounding interest, this repetition magnifies the dullness of this one trite beginning. Moreover, no subject is ever made interesting by a writer's calling it so in his opening sentence—unless the writer is a famous critic.

If material is attractive, interest-compelling, or important, it is better to start with that material, as the following beginnings illustrate:

> While the advent of antibiotics for the treatment of infective endo-carditis has changed this condition from one with a very grave prognosis to one which ordinarily can be managed with success, the failure of therapy in perhaps one third of the patients with this condition keeps it in the forefront as a major threat in heart disease.[44]

> The chemical process industries are facing a new threat in thermal pollution—harmful heating of water by industrial waste effluent and spent cooling water. It could become a major consideration in plant location, design and operation.[45]

> The process of being born is one of the most hazardous of medical episodes in America today. Our peak incidence of death and damage, in fact, is in the four-week periods immediately preceding and following birth.[46]

> The reduced number of students entering into the study of engineering is disheartening, particularly after many years of steadily increasing enrollment.[47]

Journal writers succinctly state the interesting points:

> Fluid flow and heat transfer in the entrance region of circular tubes has been the subject of considerable interest, owing primarily to the application of this data to the design of heat exchangers.[48]

> Synthetic zeolites, some of which are known as molecular sieves, are of interest because their adsorptive properties make them suitable for separation processes and catalyst supports.[49]

[44] Simon Rodbard, "Hemodynamic Considerations in Endocarditis," *Medical Science,* XV (January, 1964), 43.
[45] "Heat Poses New Pollution Puzzles," *Chemical Week,* XCIV (February 8, 1964), 29.
[46] Allan C. Barnes, "Reducing the Hazards of Birth," *Harper's Magazine,* CCXXVIII (January, 1964), 31.
[47] Harding Bliss, "Smaller Enrollments: A Brighter Side," *A.I.Ch.E. Journal,* IX (January, 1963), 3.
[48] T. B. Davey, "Entrance Region Heat Transfer Coefficients," *Heat Transfer— Houston,* p. 47.
[49] Joel Selben and R. Burgess Mason, "Preparation of Gallium Containing Molecular Sieves," *Search,* p. 13.

When a writer has a subject that is of interest, he strengthens his beginning by answering: How? Why? To whom? A subject is seldom of interest to everyone in every way for all reasons, and stating specific limitations attracts the right readers for the right reasons. C. P. Costello and E. R. Redeker specify limitations efficiently in *Heat Transfer— Houston:*

> The use of capillary wicking material to aid in providing liquid coolant to a heater surface has interesting possibilities, especially in circumstances where without the wicking material coolant would be unable to reach the heater surface. Such circumstances might arise in aircraft undergoing violent maneuvers, where the accelerations could force liquid away from the surface; expendable coolant systems where the liquid level could drop below the top of the heater; and operations in zero or low gravity regions, where sufficient forces to carry liquid to the heater surface might be unavailable.[50]

Comparison and Contrast

A poet transmits vivid impressions and fresh insights by comparing his subject to some other subject that resembles it only in the characteristic compared:

> Oh, my luve is like a red, red rose,
>   That's newly sprung in June;
> Oh, my luve is like the melodie,
>   That's sweetly played in tune.
>   *Robert Burns*

A writer presenting information also clarifies and vivifies his subject by comparing it to some other subject not usually thought of as similar, or he enlivens his topic by comparing it to some other subject like it in many ways. Molly Price opens her *Times* story on new hybrid daffodils with a comparison of the second kind:

> Just about everyone likes the old-fashioned golden trumpet daffodils. These hardy, dependable bulbs—disease-free, rodent-proof and practically foolproof—have long been garden favorites. Less well known are the new-fashioned hybrid varieties which not only possess the admirable qualities listed above, but are available in an exciting array of color variations and forms.

This comparison moves from the familiar to the unfamiliar—the best order for making a reader feel comfortable with the unfamiliar. For example, an instructor facing a class of timid women students might

[50] "Boiling Heat Transfer and Maximum Heat Flux for a Surface with Coolant Supplied by Capillary Wicking," p. 104.

compare a pottery kiln to the oven in their kitchens at home. Brandan M. Jones of the *Times* uses this technique to explain the International Management Congress:

> The business equivalent of a United Nations General Assembly with concurrent meetings of specialized agencies will be held here this week.

Journal writers beginning with comparisons often place the familiar first. Reviewing *Electron Scattering and Nuclear and Nucleon Structure* in *Science*, Clyde L. Cowan begins with a well-known phenomenon:

> I am told that quite often the blind, deprived of that most ubiquitous of the five senses, develop the remaining four—and especially the sense of touch—to such an extent as to accomplish astonishing things. They literally feel their way back into a detailed experience of the world. But for that vast fraction of the world which lies in the atomic realm, all mankind is blind. So, man has developed his sense of touch, supplementing his fingers of flesh and bone with fingers made of streams of waves—electromagnetic waves and de Broglian waves; and man has felt his way down and down into those secret regions where nature begins.[51]

Ronald G. Neswald begins his summary of "Nuclear Orbital Structure" by Bernard L. Cohen with stress on the familiar in a comparison:

> The translation from quantum mechanics to the pith-balls and wire so familiar to students of elementary atomics has its analogue in the shell theory of nuclear structure. And it's just as appropriate one place as the other.[52]

Contrast is used in the same way. Here, too, when a writer introduces a new concept, he often places the familiar first, as Alvin Shuster does in the *Times:*

> It was easy in the old days to tell the millionaire from the rest of us. He had that private railroad car, courted Lillian Russell and assorted French actresses, imported chefs from Paris to prepare 20-course meals to be served on gold plates, swam in pools of white Venetian tile or Carrara marble, built "cottages" with 110 rooms and 45 baths and owned a Nile steamer just in case he went to Egypt.
>
> Not so the millionaires of today. They live well but, for the most part, quietly, without the flamboyance of their predecessors. A few even live in the house with the 100-foot lot they bought 15 years ago before they hit it big. With a few exceptions, most are a little shy

[51] CXLIII (January 24, 1964), 344.
[52] *International Science and Technology* (November, 1963), p. 65.

about it all. And even though one of their kind reached the White House by popular demand, many still feel ill at ease when publicly identified as "a millionaire."

And similarly Harland Manchester begins a contrast in "Radiation Is Producing Better Vegetables" with the familiar:

> While to most people nuclear radiation is a harbinger of death and destruction, to a small group of botanists and plant breeders in laboratories throughout the world it is a promising new tool. These men are using it to create new and better food plants to feed the earth's burgeoning billions.[53]

G. Edward Pendray opens a historical article, "Pioneer Rocket Development in the United States," by stressing the contrasts in the work of two pioneers:

> The work of Dr. Robert H. Goddard, the American rocket pioneer, and the early experimental work of the American Rocket Society, both of considerable interest in the evolution of modern rocket technology, were quite different and independent. Goddard's was not only of longer duration—beginning about 1898 and ending only a brief time before his death in 1945—but was of incomparably greater fundamental importance as a contribution to the space age. The American Rocket Society's period of experimentation was contemporary with some of Goddard's work, extending as it did from about 1931 through 1941, and also resulted in some notable contributions.[54]

Definition and Classification

Beginning by defining (explaining the precise meaning) and classifying (placing in a group or category on the basis of similarities and differences) is common. It often seems far too common to teachers of composition who read hundreds of freshman themes beginning, "According to *Webster's Dictionary*." Unfortunately, freshmen are usually defining words like *sophomore*, which their readers know well, or words like *love* and *friendship*, which call for more than Webster's definition. But if definitions are helpful to a reader they may be good openers, as in the following examples:

> Fluid energy milling is a method of reducing solids, and in certain cases semi-solids, to powders of very small particle size.[55]

[53] *Think*, XXIX (September, 1963), 23.
[54] *Technology and Culture*, IV (Fall, 1963), 384.
[55] A. G. Pendleton, "Fluid Energy Milling," *Chemical and Process Engineering*, XLIV (December, 1963), 733.

Integration of power systems means the development and use of interconnections between power systems so that their combined loads and resources can be treated as a unit system to achieve the advantage of large-scale operation.[56]

Revetments—permeable or impermeable protective facings for dune slopes, dykes, banks, and the like—are receiving much attention as engineers fight coastline and beach erosion problems.[57]

Because definition is overworked, writers often strive to make it different. J. B. Priestley enlivens the definition introducing a *Punch* article by stating a personal opinion:

To clear the ground a little, let me say that parapsychology—as the *para* suggests—is concerned with what is *beside* or *beyond* ordinary psychology. It is accepted now as a legitimate study and field of research by all but the bigoted. It examines and records the phenomena associated with extra sensory perception, generally known as ESP. It has to take note of telepathy, precognition, clairvoyance, clairaudience, and so forth.[58]

And Harry Levinson presents a switch on hackneyed-definition beginnings: "For all of man's ages-old preoccupation with work, no one has yet been able to come up with a very satisfactory definition of it." [59]

Classifying a subject, a less popular beginning than defining, is frequently a good way to start. A. I. Braude begins "Bacterial Endotoxins" with a clear, simple classification:

Most disease-producing bacteria can be divided into two classes: those that secrete toxin into the surrounding medium and those that harbor the toxin within the bacterial cell.[60]

John C. Chen and Stuart W. Churchill introduce a three-paragraph classification with stress on specific importance:

Radiation is known to be an important mechanism of heat transfer in packed beds, particularly at high temperatures. The many models which have been proposed to describe simultaneous radiation and conduction may be classified into three groups.

The first type is based on those idealized geometrical arrangements

---

[56] Earl Ewald and D. W. Angland, "Regional Integration of Electric Power Systems," *IEEE Spectrum*, I (April, 1964), 96.

[57] Per Bruun, "Today's Trends in Revetment Design," *Consulting Engineer*, XXII (February, 1964), 78.

[58] "The Initial Shock," CCXLV (December 4, 1963), 800.

[59] "What Work Means to a Man," *Think*, XXX (January–February, 1964), 8.

[60] *Scientific American*, CCX (March, 1964), 36.

of the phases which permit direct algebraic formulation of the transfer processes. Musselt (1), Damköhler (2). . . .

The second type is based on a random walk process. Rosseland (3) interpreted. . . .

In the third type of model the packed bed is considered to be a pseudohomogeneous material, permitting description of the heat transfer processes. . . .[61]

In *Science* Howard A. Schneiderman and Lawrence I. Gilbert combine classification and a description of the attention given to the categories:

The postembryonic growth of higher organisms is under hormonal control during most of the organism's life. The best-studied groups are the vertebrates and higher plants, but increasing attention is being paid to invertebrates, especially arthropods.[62]

A variation of classification that is often more interesting than merely naming the categories is a description of characteristics. The engaging description that opens Carl R. Eklund's "The Antarctic Skua" demonstrates how effective this beginning may be:

The Antarctic skua has the distinction of having been seen closer to the South Pole than any other bird. In keeping with its extraordinary choice of dwelling place, the south polar skua is also unusual in physique and habits. It is a giant among birds, with a wingspread of some four and a half feet. Known as "the eagle of the Antarctic," it is one of the boldest and most ferocious defenders of home and family in the avian world. It is monogamous, mating year after year with the same partner. And for its nesting place, where it hatches and raises its young, it chooses the world's coldest climate.

The name "skua" comes from *skúfa*, an old Norse word meaning "to push aside." One of the earliest descriptions of the Antarctic skua was given by. . . .[63]

Illustration and Example

What would you think if a man told you the way to remember the phone company's area code for San Francisco (which happens to be 415) is to picture a gigantic baby's rattle sitting atop San Francisco's Golden Gate Bridge?

And what if he assured you that it would be a cinch to stamp into your memory the German word for mirror by remembering the phrase, spiegel, spiegel on the wall?

[61] "Radiant Heat Transfer in Packed Beds," *A.I.Ch.E. Journal*, IX (January, 1963), 35.
[62] "Control of Growth and Development in Insects," CXLIII (January 24, 1964), 325.
[63] *Scientific American*, CCX (February, 1964), 94.

These striking examples open David C. Smith's story on mnemonics courses in *The Wall Street Journal* of February 6, 1964. A *Times* editorial on bird migration begins with what the writer calls "rather special examples"—the flickers: "The flickers begin to gather for migration and their actions add another facet to the mystery of the birds." A story on car dealers in *The Wall Street Journal* of February 6, 1964 also begins with an interest-arousing example. Jerry Flint writes:

> Harry Green, a Clarksburg, W. Va., Chevrolet dealer, will begin construction this spring on a new building costing $200,000 to $300,000, and will add six or eight people to his 60-man staff. He has no fear he's over-extending himself.
>
> "They're pretty hot," says Mr. Green of the compacts, medium sized and big cars he handles. In January he sold 40, against 22 in the 1963 month. In all 1964 he expects to sell 700, against 538 in 1963.
>
> Such optimism is typical of dealers who attended the National Automobile Dealers Association meeting here this week. Among scores interviewed. . . .

Specific details make these examples vivid and arresting. Such detailed illustrations and examples are particularly useful where a summary would be dull. Flint's article would have a much less appealing start if he had begun with his third paragraph. In fact, details of examples and illustrations can be so moving that many fund-raising articles begin with a poignant example of someone who will be aided by a contribution, preferably some helpless animal, needy aged person, or sick child—a very persuasive beginning for writing that is meant to move a reader to action.

In the prose of information, examples are useful and interesting beginnings:

> Embrittlement failures of 9-chrome, 1-moly furnace tubes were unheard of until a 1½-inch line in a thermal cracking unit ruptured in 1960. This failure occurred during the unit's down period and the 1½-inch line that failed was attached to a 3-inch tar line. It ruptured when the valve was being taken off in order to burn out the coke. The appearance of the fractured pipe is shown in Figure 1. The failure occurred within a few inches of the weld joining it to the 3-inch line. Two features should be especially noted. . . .[64]

> One of the most striking modern buildings in the city of Rome is the Palazzetto dello Sport, a sports arena erected in 1957 for the 1960 Olympic Games and built almost entirely of concrete. One mile and eighteen centuries away stands the classic Pantheon, built in 120 AD

[64] Harry M. Wilten, "Is 9-Cr 1-Mo Steel Temper Brittle?" *Hydrocarbon Processing & Petroleum Refiner*, XLIII (January, 1964), 115.

by the Roman Emperor Hadrian, using concrete as an essential part of its masonry structure.

Although concrete is basic to both buildings, there is clearly a difference in the way it was used to shape each of them.[65]

"CONGRESS SLASHES SPACE BUDGET"
"BUNGLING IN MOON PROGRAM CHARGED"
Headlines such as these—plus many more in the same vein—have convinced many people that the U. S. space program is in serious trouble and that there is a growing feeling the whole effort should be abandoned in order to stop the waste of the taxpayer's money.[66]

Specific examples, particularly interesting details of specific examples, cannot be surpassed as introductions that arouse reader interest and lead neatly into the next step of the paper—summary, problem, background, etc.

Knocking Down an Argument

Many writers in industry are wary of beginning with an idea opposed to their own thinking. Yet setting up an argument merely to knock it down may be an effective beginning. David Halberstram writes in the *Times:*

> The other day the Vietnam Press Agency announced that Dr. Tran Kim Tuyen, director of the Service for Social and Political Studies, was going to Cairo to become his country's Consul General. For an American it had a familiar ring. Egghead rewarded for services and gets diplomatic post. Just like Galbraith in India and Reischauer in Japan.
> Is this true? Not so.

Susan Marsh knocks down an opinion with a gentle shove to get it out of the way:

> Although this country's most crowded national parks and monuments deserve their due recognition, sometimes it is a relief to tour one of the lesser-known sites. One still worth visiting, yet uncrowded and able to handle more visitors than it gets, is Black Canyon of the Gunnison National Monument.

Chemical Engineering, on the other hand, strikes with a sledgehammer to demolish:

[65] Paul Gugliotta, "Modern Concrete Design," *International Science and Technology* (December, 1963), p. 55.
[66] Lee A. Du Bridges, "Earth to Moon—Is the Fare Too High?" *Think,* XXX (March–April, 1964), 2.

Literature references and still-prevalent industry opinion hold that diethanolamine (DEA) solution, used as absorbent to take hydrogen sulfide out of oil-refinery gas streams, can't be regenerated free of contaminant salts without decomposing the DEA.

Nevertheless, Tidewater Oil Co. has been doing this for the past six years at its Avon Refinery, Martinez, Calif.[67]

Citing facts in this way to refute an opening argument results in impressive victory. Frank B. Brady combats with facts more gently but just as successfully:

On September 24, 1929, James H. Doolittle landed a Navy training plane at Mitchel Field on Long Island solely by reference to instruments. Many people thereupon assumed that the problem of "blind landing" had basically been solved. Now, more than three decades later, any experienced air traveler has been delayed often enough by bad weather to know that this conclusion was, to say the least, premature. In spite of the many remarkable advances that have been made in aircraft instrumentation, Doolittle's feat is still not routinely performed.[68]

The advantages of beginning with an argument and knocking it down are (1) a writer disposes early of the argument that may be lurking in his reader's mind, and so the reader may give his full attention to the writer's point of view; (2) it enables a writer to state as ineffectively as he likes the point of view he is opposing; and (3) it can create an impression of a forceful, logical, courageous writer. The related disadvantages are (1) a reader may be annoyed by a vigorous attack on opinions dear to him, particularly if they are refuted only by other opinions; (2) the method gives a position of emphasis to the ideas the writer opposes, and if the writer does not combat them effectively, the reader may accept the argument rather than the counterargument; and (3) for some papers, some writers, and some readers, the atmosphere of contention that this method creates is inappropriate.

Action

Smith of Interdynamic Chemicals sank down on a couch in the magnificent office of his French hosts; smiled at the pretty, chic secretary assigned by them; patted his stomach, where a Michelin five-star meal was contentedly digesting; and began to dictate his account of how he had been received by the French chemical industry. What he dictated was an action beginning—an account of incidents and events, of favors

[67] "Fouled Diethanolamine Solution Comes Clean," LXX (March 4, 1963), 40.
[68] "All-Weather Aircraft Landing," *Scientific American*, CCX (March, 1964), 25.

received and given, of peerless entertainment, and of gestures of warm hospitality. If a writer on science, technology, and business wishes to give a report the flavor of a story, this action beginning is a good choice. Like dialogue, it arouses interest and leads readers into a report or article easily. When it is appropriate to the material, it can be pleasing.

Journalists, who frequently report action, favor this type of beginning, but they do not always have events as dramatic as the action in the following *Times* news story:

> The drama conferees at the Edinburgh Festival had been discussing how they might attract audiences to the contemporary theatre. In a burst of inspiration, a girl stood up and took off her clothes.

Dramatic action also begins a journal article well, as in "The Polaris" by Wyndham D. Miles:

> At 12:39 on the afternoon of July 20, 1960, thirty miles off the coast of Florida, a tall, bottle-shaped Polaris missile leaped out of the ocean, erupted flame from its base, and rocketed upward. Higher and higher it climbed, smaller and smaller it appeared, until it faded into the heavens, leaving behind a tenuous trail of white smoke and vapor.
>
> At the spot where the missile had emerged the ocean was empty. It was as though the object had popped magically from the deep. But below the surface a submarine, *George Washington*, hovered silently. Within the vessel a happy crowd of officers, seamen, and civilian scientists congratulated each other on the first undersea launch of a ballistic missile.[69]

The narrative beginning used by A. Theodore Forrester and Stanton L. Eilenberg in "Ion Rockets," published in *International Science and Technology*, will remind some readers of science fiction:

> Sometime in the not-too-distant future a package containing a new kind of rocket engine will be strapped to the nose of a conventional booster and lofted out into space. Once the package has coasted beyond the rim of the earth's atmosphere, the wraps will come off the engine and a blue-white beam of ions will begin to spew out the exhaust.[70]

But action beginnings are not necessarily dramatic; a tone of quiet, leisurely reminiscence may be achieved, as in R. K. MacCrone's "Plastic Deformation":

> I vividly remember being confronted as a student with the stress-strain curves of metals beyond their elastic limit. My reaction to endless curves with various kinks and bends was completely and utterly

[69] *Technology and Culture*, IV (Fall, 1963), 478.
[70] January, 1964, p. 52.

negative. Yet only a few years later, these very same curves took on a new meaning; they became alive and fascinating.

My reaction changed because I began to look at the curves from a new point of view, one in which I was mentally inside the metal wondering about the microscopic atomic processes that give the curves their characteristic shape.[71]

Even more informally autobiographical is J. E. Troyan's introduction to "Using Common Sense in Plant Operations." Here the personal-narrative approach is particularly appropriate to the subject:

Recently one morning, while nearing the chemical plant where I work as a production manager, I recalled the old adage that one good picture is worth a thousand words. It occurred to me that the panorama of process units and equipment, marked by flares, smoke, plumes of steam, and other evidences of operating activity, presented a fairly good profile of what was going on if one viewed it analytically.[72]

The action beginning has many advantages. From earliest times tales have captured man's attention, and action still gains and holds it. Many TV westerns, for example, offer little else. And a narrative opening is one of the easiest to read. If the action is inherent in the ideas of the article, as in Troyan's, a reader does not notice the shift from events to thoughts. The disadvantage of this method exists only for a writer with poor judgment. He may attach a story to his report even though there is no close relationship. Then the beginning of his report, being merely decorative, will seem tacked on. The other disadvantage is minor: this beginning occupies more space than a summary of the ideas would. But the length is not truly a disadvantage because one can usually read an action beginning fast. Therefore many skillful writers and many advertisers favor it.

Forecast and Hypothesis

The forecast beginning will appear more frequently in writing for industry as scientists and technologists discover the advantages of contributing their background and judgment to the making of company decisions. The timid and overly self-protective will avoid forecasting, but other writers will use their information and their experience to interpret and predict coming events. And even the timid may quote the predictions of others.

Sports writers, for example, are adept at forecasting without taking responsibility. Gordon S. White, Jr., begins with a forecast in the *Times*:

[71] *International Science and Technology* (November, 1963), p. 36.
[72] *Chemical Engineering*, LXX (March 4, 1963), 120.

> If Villanova's football team is to play in a bowl game for the third consecutive year this winter, it will have to play far above current estimates of its potential.

Articles in journals sometimes predict impersonally. Walter Fagan's "Heating of a Cannon in Rapid Fire with External Cooling" opens with a prediction:

> Present tendencies are to increase the firing rate of heavy guns. A point will be reached when natural convection cooling with ambient air will be insufficient, and stronger cooling methods must be employed. This paper develops simple methods of calculating maximum bore surface temperature and maximum value of the average gun wall temperature due to firing single round, single burst, and series of bursts.[73]

An article in *Science* begins effectively with a hypothesis:

> Sufficient evidence is available to indicate that antibodies are formed from the pool of free amino acids in the cell and that such synthesis requires a full complement of amino acids (1). It would appear that interference with this pool may have serious consequences on the antibody-forming system.[74]

Another beginning in this issue states and corrects a hypothesis:

> Neurosecretory centers in the insect brain are thought to initiate the complex physiological processes leading to growth and molting. Diapause, as a state of arrested growth, is considered to be caused by an endocrine failure, usually that of neurosecretion; and the resumption of neurosecretory activity signals the termination of the diapause state (1). There is increasing evidence, however, that diapause is not invariably produced by a direct effect of genetic and environmental factors on the neurosecretory cells, but may be the result of changes in unidentified physiological processes to which neurosecretory processes are coupled (2).[75]

A hypothesis may follow and answer an introductory question:

> Is the physical universe made of matter, or is it made of mathematics? To put the question another way—is space-time only an empty arena within which real fields and particles play out their drama; or is the four-dimensional continuum of space-time all there is? No questions

[73] *Heat Transfer—Houston*, p. 25.
[74] Wayne L. Ryan and Michael J. Carver, "Inhibition of Antibody Synthesis by L-Phenylalanine," CXLIII (January 31, 1964), 479.
[75] Stanley D. Beck and Nancy Alexander, "Hormonal Activation of the Insect Brain," p. 478.

are more central than these to the master plan of physics, the plan which seeks to unify into one harmonious whole phenomena so apparently diverse in scale and kind as elementary particles, neutrinos, electromagnetic fields, gravitation, and galaxies.

The answer to such questions suggested by striking new developments in general relativity is that empty space may indeed be all there is.[76]

Hypotheses and forecasts interest readers because they stimulate and satisfy curiosity. Sometimes they also have the appeal of novelty. In government and industry, where many writers admit their reluctance to take responsibility for a prediction, such a beginning is unusual; therefore it attracts attention by being different. Because the remark "I don't want to stick my neck out" is a favorite of writers in government and industry, it is hardly necessary to warn them against rash and ill-founded forecasting. Other writers may need to be cautioned that a writer beginning with a forecast or a hypothesis should be sure that his crystal ball is not cloudy and that it is not reflecting an image of a writer's wishes rather than his objective estimates.

Wit and Humor

If, as Meredith said, "The well of true wit is truth itself," then wit is certainly an appropriate beginning for a scientific paper. But stale jokes are not to be confused with dry wit. Although ancient jokes have ancient sanction, it is better if a writer of informational prose does not wonder, like the character in Aristophanes, ". . . shall I begin with the usual joke/That the audience always laughs at?"

Howard Taubman uses wit and the most successful device of humor—turning the joke on oneself—in the introduction of his *Times* drama criticism:

> Trust the readers to be a critic's best friends. Their attentions are as constant and tender as a lover's, as firm and demanding as a non-permissive parent's, as dependent and appealing as a child's, and as reproving and corrective as a stern master's.
>
> Let him express an opinion—and what else has the wretch to express? —and they hasten to react. If they chance to meet him face to face, they may plunge in after the introductions—or they may hold back until after the first martini. If they catch him on the telephone, they may administer a quick, verbal thrust. If he is not within sound of their voices, presumably he can read, even if it's a moot point whether he can write.

[76] John A. Wheeler and Seymour Tilson, "The Dynamics of Space-Time," *International Science and Technology* (December, 1963), p. 62.

Writing in the same key, Clarence B. Randall, former president of the Inland Steel Company, is wittily rueful about himself in an article in *The New York Times Magazine:* "One of the great new freedoms that comes to a man in retirement is the right to stick his neck out." Sometimes the humor is a surprise twist, like Sal R. Nuccio's opening sentence in the *Times:* "In the last few months, an increasing number of people have decided they need life insurance—in their investment portfolios."

A writer for industry who has a sense of humor can find many opportunities to make effective use of his light touch. The rare humorous beginnings gain extra sparkle from contrast with many tired serious openings. In letters to an appreciative recipient, humor is particularly welcome. Even in those difficult letters that refuse a favor, it can be used winningly. For example, one of my students wrote:

> How I'd like to address the alumni banquet as you requested. For an hour or two or three I could tell all those jokes that are usually stopped by your, "I've heard that one before." What an opportunity! If only the wife didn't have to eat and the kids didn't have to pay tuition, I'd tell the boss to go to Chicago himself this week. . . .

At least that letter did not lose him a friend. Instead, it won him an invitation the next year. Another student, faced with writing a tactful memorandum, also solved his problem with humor. He had been asked to offer review conferences to writers in a medical research and development group who had taken a writing course a year before. But he had been cautioned not to press the writers to have the conferences and not to give the impression that the administration was assigning conferences. A light touch helped him to do this:

> Memo to Patients of Dr. Doe's Spring Writing Clinic
> From John W. Jordan, also one of the patients
> Subject ℞: Booster Shots
>   Since the end of Dr. John Doe's clinic last March, have you wondered at all about the health of your writing? Have you noticed a waning of your exercise of unity, coherence, and emphasis? Has your resistance weakened to dangling modifiers, remote antecedents, and incomplete comparisons? In short, has your titer of effective writing techniques declined?
>   Booster shots are now available!

Wit and good humor are often successful when one is defending an unpopular position. Herbert B. Michaelson, presenting the affirmative view of the topic "Should a Talk Be Read from a Prepared Manuscript?" begins effectively with humor:

Reading a technical paper is referred to disdainfully by some engineers as "being *wedded* to a manuscript." Appropriately, my discussion might well be entitled, "How to be Happy Though Married." [77]

Laughter at oneself or one's subject is so rare in the journals of science and technology that Robert Schmidt, finding some in the "Letters" section of *Science,* was moved to write to the editors:

> If the editors continue to exercise, or, still better, even improve a little, their present judgment in selecting the very best morsels for publication, they might even succeed in overthrowing my pet hypothesis: the principal reason for the abysmal distance between scientists and humanists is found in the inability of the former to laugh at themselves.[78]

Not all scientists and technologists are so intently earnest that humor has no place in their writing. In *Scientific American* Benton J. Underwood begins his article "Forgetting" with a humorous comparison:

> Rodin's sculpture "The Thinker," modified slightly by the addition of a wrinkled brow and a suggestion of anguish in the facial expression, could represent man in a more familiar aspect that might be labeled "The Forgetter." [79]

International Science and Technology, which is more original in literary presentation than many other journals, introduces a little fun into the headline and summary of "Measuring Temperature" by Lawrence G. Rubin:

> You might suppose it is hard to measure a thermodynamic abstraction on a discontinuous practical scale with instruments that can perturb the variable. You'd be right.

And Ronald B. Neswald begins the abstract of this article wittily:

> The trouble with any measurement is the inevitable mismatch between the messiness of reality and the purity of the abstractions used to describe it. Of this truism, thermometry is the exemplar.[80]

These examples of wit and humor at the beginnings of articles are all the more delightful and effective for their rarity in science and technology.

Taste and judgment are required for the proper use of such humor and wit. A writer who can think of the antithesis "the messiness of

[77] *IRE Transactions on Engineering Writing and Speech,* EWS-1 (March, 1958), 14.
[78] CXLIII (January 31, 1964), 430.
[79] CCX (March, 1964), 91.
[80] January, 1964, p. 74.

reality and the purity of the abstractions used to describe it" will employ it effectively. But sometimes writers are carried away by jokes. They tell them although the jokes are in no way related to their topics; they include them although the jokes present a point of view alien to that of the article; and they begin with them even though the jokes will offend some readers. Good jokes are so irresistible that writers should scrutinize them for objectionable qualities.

Combinations

For easier understanding I have presented the kinds of beginnings separately. But writers often use one or two kinds together, and such combinations are usually easier to write. The reader of this book has probably noticed that I introduced the discussion of each type of beginning by writing that kind. But this is not meant to discourage writers from using combinations. Indeed, I sometimes had to write a combination instead of just the one type I was illustrating. And it was not easy to find illustrations of single types because in the scientific and technological journals many of the longer introductions are combinations. But usually one kind of beginning dominates the combination; for example, an introduction that states purpose may contain a little background, and a brief question may be followed by a long answer.

HOW TO CHOOSE

The single kinds of beginnings and the combinations provide such a wealth of possibilities that writers naturally wonder how to choose the beginnings for their papers. The three considerations that guide the choice are the material, the writer, and the reader.

A writer should avoid forcing his material into an inconvenient or unsuitable introduction. He should not begin with pointless questions, ineffective quotations, or unnecessary details just to get started. The best beginnings emphasize the main thoughts of papers or at least suggest the main thoughts. And the introduction of a paper should be harmonious with the rest of it. Some after-dinner speakers may consider it necessary to start even praise of the dead with a joke, but effective beginnings do not clash with the mood of the rest of the paper or speech so sharply. Once in a while a journal errs by prefacing a scholarly paper written in a formal style with a colloquial or slangy abstract. The only readers not jolted by the jump in style between the introduction and the paper are those who omit one or the other. The material of an introduction should not lead to disappointment in the subject of a paper; and thus it is unwise to begin with material that may capture a reader's interest and then to drop that material. If a paper begins by comparing two plant sites but then studies only the one near Boston, it may disappoint and annoy readers who, while reading the introduction, developed an interest in the site near Chicago. An introduction suitable to the subject matter of a paper prepares a reader for what lies before him and enlists his interest in that subject.

In choosing a beginning for his paper a good writer weighs his own strengths and weaknesses. If he has little sense of humor, he avoids beginning with humor; if he quickly becomes unpleasantly contentious, he rejects a beginning that knocks down an argument; and if he is inclined to be longwinded or overconscientious in discussing background, he may prefer another type. Although a beginner should practice writing a few of the easier kinds of introductions before attempting to write complex combinations, an experienced writer may increase his own as well as his reader's interest in his work by experimenting with beginnings that are new to him.

But the dominant consideration in the choice is his readers. Careful attention to their interests, background, education, and reading habits is essential. It enables a writer to avoid quoting authorities that they will distrust, using technical language that they do not understand, and reviewing boring background familiar to them. His consideration of his readers helps a writer to answer important questions about the beginning: Should he use a tried-and-true beginning well known to them or a new, imaginative, daring beginning? The answer depends on how conservative they may be, on how they would respond to striking originality. How many details of background should the writer include? Enough to show the thoroughness of his research? Enough to build a beginning that looks impressive to him? No, he should include in his introduction the details of background that his readers need at the beginning and that will lead them easily into the paper. From the introductions that suit his material and his writing skills and his personality, a writer should select the beginning appropriate to his readers. Then his choice will be a sound one.

Chapter V

Effective Organizing

> Order and simplification are the first steps
> toward the mastering of a subject.
>
> *Mann*

Chaos is so frightening and repugnant to man that he associates it with his most terrible experiences. Job speaks of death not only as a land of darkness but as a land "without any order." Many equate the word *disorder* with *sickness* and *disordered* with *deranged.* Perhaps that accounts for the extreme irritation and dislike that readers show when literature lacks plan. No other writing defect arouses so much anger and aversion.

Although writers generally work hard to avoid arousing the antipathy of readers, sometimes writers in business, government, and industry invite this repugnance by neglecting organization. Supervisors notice with surprise that professional men trained in logical thinking write disorganized reports, and they wonder why. One reason is lack of practice. Some of these professional men are used to following blindly an organization required by a school, department, or professor; by industry or government; or by their profession. No one criticized their organizing as long as they placed material under the required main divisions. This made them careless of everything except the outline of the whole, gave them no acquaintance with variety in organization, and, worst of all, led them to consider themselves logical thinkers without any need to plan a paper. When such writers must depart from familiar organizations, they are at a loss. Other writers fail to plan long papers because they are deceived by their success with short papers that require little organization, and they do not realize that a long work requires careful and detailed planning.

Whatever the reason, those who write illogically are seldom familiar with methods of organizing papers. Even when they attempt to plan, their chances of success are limited by their ignorance of the advantages and disadvantages of various organizations. A writer chooses well only when he has a reasonable number of choices and knows something about each.

Planning a work is like planning a journey. On some journeys a traveler may start without a plan or a goal because he intends to wander as the fancy strikes him. But those are not business journeys. A business traveler plans his journey—chooses his transportation, his connections, his stops. He knows what he expects to accomplish at each place, whom he has appointments to see, what he expects to say, and what influence he wishes to exert. He sends letters announcing his coming and reinforcing his visit. He knows when and how he will end his travels. He is no idle wanderer, aimless and unfettered. A good writer of the prose of information also chooses his method of development, his connections, his stops. He knows what each paragraph should accomplish and how that accomplishment is related to his goal. He sends warnings as he approaches new points and reminds his readers of what he has accomplished whenever they need reminding. He is no aimless writer moving from topic to topic as the fancy of the moment dictates and caring only about his own convenience.

The first step in successful planning is a consideration of organizations with a view to eliminating those unsuited to the material. This selection is usually simple. For example, a writer rejects chronological order if there is no time sequence in his subject, geographical divisions if his topic has none, and climactic order if his main ideas have no suitable variations in importance.

Second, a thoughtful writer considers his readers and does his best to select the organization that will be most helpful to them. This choice may involve more deliberation than does the selection of a plan suitable to the material, but it is not necessarily more difficult.

If his readers know less about the subject than he does, a writer should make certain that any explanations that they need are placed at the point where they need them or just before that point. If readers would find Section II of the paper easier to understand after reading the descriptions and definitions in Section IV, the writer moves this explanatory material or even the whole of Section IV to a position before Section II—an easier shift in an outline than in a completed paper. As he examines his outline, the writer is likely to find other ways to help readers who may find the material difficult—comparing the unfamiliar with the familiar, supplying illustrations and examples, explaining abstruse concepts in more detail. Different adjustments may be desirable for other readers. For fellow specialists a writer should be careful to remove unnecessary explanations and to use technical language to achieve brevity. And if busy executives are likely to skim over only a page or two, a wise writer places his most important points first. When a long report contains material for many departments of a company and each reader wants only what concerns his division, the writer may choose to organize his report by departments—manufacturing, packaging, marketing, advertising, etc. He may supply such helps as informative subheads, a detailed table of contents, and an index to guide a reader to the section he wants.

If he has two groups of readers—for example, some with technical training and some without—a writer must try to satisfy both. For his nontechnical readers he may provide a summary of the main points of his report and a detailed table of contents that will enable them to find easily any parts that they want to read. But he may organize the main body of his report to please his technical readers. If it is impossible to suit one presentation to two groups of readers (a review for college freshmen of recent developments in the writer's field, for example, and the same topic for a meeting of industrial chemists) he may have to write two reports, each with its own material, organization, and style. It is better to face this necessity at once than to struggle unsuccessfully to prepare one paper for both groups.

When he has just one reader, a writer should be particular about the preferences of his reader. For a supervisor of sales who usually thinks about sales by areas of the United States, he plans a report by geographical sections to save his reader the labor of extracting this material and reorganizing it. The report on a problem to a man who usually considers first a precise definition of the problem, second the recommended solution, and third the reasons for the recommendation courteously follows that order. If a supervisor has turned down a suggestion twice, an astute outliner begins with new evidence of the value of the suggestion; he does not open with the twice-rejected suggestion. Within the limits imposed by the material, the reader is king. A writer will find it easier to please a monarch, even a constitutional one, if he plans to please him.

When an outliner does not know his readers, he considers the principles of emphasis that make writing more effective for all readers. He asks: Do the first and final topics contain major ideas? If they do not, he reshuffles to improve his organization. A writer with several topics of varied importance should consider the advantages of climactic or reverse-climactic order. In a short report he may arrange topics in

the order of increasing importance to hold his readers' interest. In a
long report he may place his topics in the order of decreasing importance
to ensure that readers have the main points even if they do not read the
whole report.

Planning also enables a writer to estimate the proportion of space
assigned to each idea. When he finds that he has devoted too much
space to minor ideas, he tries to remove some details or to express the
unimportant ideas more succinctly. If that is not possible, he may compensate in one of the following ways for the emphasis that length of
presentation gives to minor ideas:

1. He may give to major ideas the positions of strongest emphasis—
the beginning and the end.

2. He may use strong and vigorous language for the main ideas and
less emphatic language for his bulky minor ideas.

3. He may present vivid illustrations of his major points.

Thus a recognition of the poor emphasis in his first plan helps a writer
to organize better. But a writer who does not discover until his final
draft that he has given only a little space in an unstressed position to
his main ideas seldom has time to reorganize. If he attempts to correct
the poor emphasis by labeling his main points *important, major,* or
significant, he finds that proper emphasis demands more than hastily
inserted adjectives.

As he considers plans for his whole work, a writer may note that
one section of his paper should be organized chronologically, that another
has place relationships suitable for organization by geography, and that
a third lends itself to arrangement in steps of increasing importance.
Thus selecting a plan for the whole work may lead him to assign plans
for some of the parts.

Consideration of his reader may also suggest organizations for parts.
Planning a memorandum for a supervisor who likes only papers that
start with a problem and end with a solution, a writer may find that
comparison is better than problem-and-solution for his presentation of
a new method. To satisfy his supervisor he begins with a statement of
the problem, but in discussing the solving of the problem, he compares
old and new methods.

Good organization is as essential to good style as good structure is
to a beautiful face. When a plan has a spark of appropriate novelty or
freshness, readers are delighted. They may not say so because they may
not analyze why they find reading easy or think a report good. Sometimes, indeed, they may praise the style when they mean the organization,

as when we say that a model who has good facial bone structure has a beautiful photographic face. In his classic address before the French Academy in 1703, Georges Louis Leclerc de Buffon commented on this close relationship of organization and style:

> Style is but the order and the movement that one gives to one's thoughts. If a writer connects his thoughts closely, if he presses them together, the style will be firm, nervous, and concise; if he lets them follow one another leisurely and at the suggestion of the words, however elegant these may be, the style will be diffuse, incoherent, and languid.[1]

A good plan helps a writer. Even the act of choosing a plan is salutary, for it makes a writer think about his subject as a unit. While considering the limits of his subject and the best order for his thoughts, a writer begins to evaluate his material. He sees new facets and relationships. To organize his thoughts, he must shape them, compress or extend them, weigh them, relate them to others, and see them in the perspective of the whole. A writer who has planned his work and outlined is usually ready to write. His preliminary thinking is complete, and his main ideas are expressed. He is quite different from a writer who moans that he cannot begin and from a writer who without thinking rushes to dictate and composes one beginning after another but never touches upon his subject.

A writer of functional prose can begin to plan as soon as he knows his readers and the main points of his paper. He seldom has to pull ideas from the air: a scientist, technologist, or manager usually knows what ideas and information he must convey. Thus he considers his readers and his subject in relation to many plans, like those below. He need never stare at a blank page blankly.

ORDER OF TIME

Suitable Subjects

Chronological order is often desirable and sometimes necessary in writing for industry. Insurance companies, for example, usually request that accidents be reported in the order in which the events happened. And day-to-day reports on the progress of construction are reports in the order of time. Factory procedures or processes like distillation are clear to readers when presented in the order in which the steps occur.

[1] "Discourse on Style," trans. Rollo W. Brown, in *The Writer's Art* (Harvard University Press, Cambridge, 1932), p. 279.

Histories of a study, a company, a society, an industry, a life are usually presented chronologically, as are experimental sections of reports. Detailed instructions, such as those for a machine operator or a laboratory technician, are clearest when written in the exact order in which they are to be carried out. When such instructions are completed, they should be an accurate checklist of the steps performed.

Advantages

The order of time is used so frequently because it has many advantages. It is easy to keep a chronological account coherent. Time words and phrases are excellent connectives: *four years later, the next day, the following step, after this, then, before, until,* and similar words and phrases denoting the passage of time come readily to a writer's mind, even for the first draft. When such natural connectives mark the order, a reader does not become confused about the sequence of events. Moreover, it is easy to record events in the order of occurrence and easy to check for omissions. This makes chronological order desirable whenever an account must be written and checked quickly and whenever every event or the exact order of events is important, as in writing instructions (Chapter XV).

Disadvantages

Though unsurpassed for instructions, chronological order is not desirable for all subjects. It does not necessarily provide proper emphasis. Chronological order may assign to unimportant material the best positions of emphasis—the beginning and the ending—and bury important subjects in the unemphatic middle.

To correct this weakness, historians often disturb the order of time by beginning and ending with important subjects. Thus the writers of epics begin at a critical point in the middle of the action. A writer of functional prose might open an article on the medical uses of nuclear energy with a description of the treatments of patients today at Brookhaven National Laboratory and then shift to the earliest medical use, the first step in his chronological discussion. Or he might open with an imaginative picture of the medical uses of nuclear energy in 1984, shift to the first medical use, recount the history thereafter chronologically, and conclude with the situation today. This provides a strong beginning and ending and, except for the opening, a chronological sequence.

Chronological order, no matter how well it suits the material, is a poor choice if it buries information that a busy reader in management wants to find quickly and easily. Sometimes this buried matter is all that such a person wants to read. For instance, the following chronological organization of a progress report buries the accomplishments of the "current period" so thoroughly that a hurried reader might have difficulty finding them:

Background
Summary of earlier progress
Report on current period
    Problems
    Methods
    Accomplishments
Forecast of future work
    Description
    Projected dates

For such a reader a reporter should select a better organization, perhaps order of importance, which is described later in this chapter. If he must use chronological order, he should at least help his reader by placing first a brief summary of current work and a reference to the page on which the detailed account of current work begins.

A serious disadvantage of time order is that it tends to become monotonous. To keep their readers' attention, writers sometimes introduce other organizations when boredom seems imminent. They may set up and knock down an opposing argument, organize by climax, describe by position, or introduce any other plan that will combine with the chronological. The difficulty is to switch without confusing readers. An experienced writer can move his readers from a time sequence to a climactic presentation effectively, but a beginner may have to work hard to achieve smooth transitions.

A minor monotony of chronological order—the tendency to place time words at the beginning of nearly every sentence—is easily corrected by one of two methods. The simpler remedy is to move the time words: *On that day the first patient was lowered into the reactor* may be changed to *The first patient was lowered into the reactor on that day*. The second method is the substitution of other thought connections for the chronological. This often requires some rewriting of the preceding or following sentences. The example above might become *The first patient was therefore lowered into the reactor*. A sensitive or self-conscious writer may notice time connections and worry unnecessarily about their monotony. Writers of short works need not be concerned about having too many time connections if they vary the positions of the time references and thus avoid calling them to a reader's attention.

ORDER OF PLACE

Suitable Subjects

Organization by place—sometimes called space order, spatial order, or geographical order—is frequent in business writing. Reports may be organized by the divisions of a company; sales and market research reports may be organized by geographical areas; details of a description may be organized from top to bottom, near to distant, east to west, left to right, etc. Place may be important to a reader, for example to a sales manager comparing his districts. It clarifies a concept, as viewing the outside of apparatus and then the inside does. It gives a prospective purchaser a good picture: a description of the community and of the exterior, then of the interior, and finally of the contents of the factory buildings. Spatial order suits many readers because they are visual minded; a picture helps them to understand.

Drawings and photographs may be combined with words for effective presentation. It would hardly seem necessary to mention that the numbering of parts in drawings and photographs should be related to their use in the text, but many illustrations seem to have been numbered by artists ignorant of the order of use. The writer then jumps in his text from *8* to *3* to *5* although the parts might just as easily have been numbered *1*, *2*, *3* for the convenience of both the reader and the writer. Also, if a writer uses numbers for space concepts, it is wise to avoid other numbers in that passage. Two sets of numbers, even when expertly handled by a writer, may confuse a reader temporarily and necessitate rereading. Handled inexpertly, they may confuse permanently.

Advantages

Organization by place has many of the advantages of chronological organization. Spatial words and phrases provide connections between sentences and paragraphs: *where, wherever, farther left, on top of, directly north, two inches below,* etc. Another advantage shared with chronological order is that a writer does not have to spend thought and judgment on what should come next; once he has established spatial order, what comes next is out of his hands, and he can devote himself to phrasing and sentence structure. This order, moreover, presents a clear, logical picture to the reader and enables him to find a part of the work easily.

Disadvantages

Spatial order does not, however, stress points of interest or by itself hold a reader's attention. In a short paper a reader may be carried from place to place by the transitions and the logical arrangement, but in a longer paper these devices are likely to become monotonous unless other plans are introduced within sections for emphasis and variety. A writer employing organization by place has, moreover, the same problem with introductory phrases that a writer employing a chronological organization has; he will find the techniques recommended on page 70 useful in meeting this problem.

ORDER OF INCREASING IMPORTANCE

Suitable Subjects

Arranging thoughts and events in the order of increasing importance, an ancient organization for storytelling, is popular in business, scientific, and technological writings today. In analyzing fiction, critics usually diagram this ladderlike arrangement simply (Figure 1). Writers of functional prose used to regard climactic or nearly climactic order as the best and perhaps the only order for reports on experimental work:

> Statement of problem
> Description of equipment
> Discussion of procedure
> Statement of results
> Discussion of results
> Conclusions and recommendations

Journal articles were traditionally organized this way, with a history of the art or a discussion of the background of the problem preceding either the statement of the problem or the description of the equipment:

> Background and history
> Statement of problem
> Description of equipment
> Discussion of procedure
> Statement of results
> Discussion of results
> Conclusions and recommendations

Writers also arranged reports on other work in a crescendo of interest:

> Statement of problem
> Analysis of problem
> Description of solutions proposed

Advantages and disadvantages of these solutions
Conclusions and recommendations

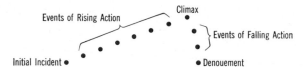

Figure 1. Climactic order in storytelling.

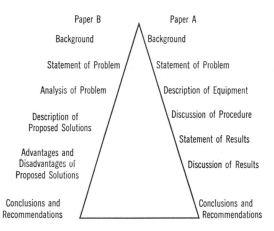

Figure 2. Climactic order in two papers.

Critics and teachers diagram the method as a triangle with the apex representing the least important point and the base the most important material (Figure 2). Because a triangle suggests bulk more than it suggests rising interest, many students find a shaded diagram more meaningful. In Figure 3 the light areas are the least important. The gradual darkening indicates the increasing significance of the material, and the darkest section represents the material of greatest interest, placed at the end of the report.

Advantages

The great advantage of arranging material in a crescendo of importance is that the gradually increasing importance holds a reader's attention. If material has the proper degrees of interest, a reader progresses always to more significant material and thus, according to the theory of climax, the material lures him to the next page and the next.

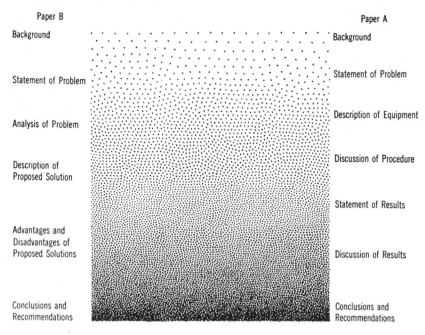

Figure 3. Climactic order in two papers.

Another advantage is that this order is traditional in science and technology, and readers find it familiar and safe. If the many surveys that reveal technologists as predominantly conservative are accurate, then a traditional order has an appeal for them.

Disadvantages

Climactic order has disadvantages when topics do not have suitable degrees of interest. In many papers the ladder is shaky here and there; the crescendo is imperfect. The analysis of the problem, for example, may not be less interesting or less important than the description of the solutions, or the description of solutions may be more interesting than the advantages and disadvantages of the solutions. Even the description of equipment may be the most important topic in some experimental papers. And sometimes the importance of a topic may vary with the reader. When interest does not increase gradually as it should but is now small and now great or is always even, the principal advantage of climactic order—the holding of the reader's attention—is lost.

Moreover a paper cannot hold a reader's interest until it has engaged it, and the first material in an informational paper organized by climax is the least important and often the least interesting. A story writer easily overcomes this disadvantage by choosing for his first incident some event that attracts his reader's interest. To ask a writer of functional prose to do this is to ignore the nature of his material, the difference in his freedom of choice, and the waste of his time on what may be an uncongenial exercise.

This traditional organization of scientific and technological papers meets a more formidable obstacle in the attitude of the reader. A reader of informational prose is not in the mood of a reader of fiction, who is delighted by suspense, pleased to spend leisure time reading, and entertained by effective dilatory presentation. A reader of informational prose is busy and hurried; he wants to grasp as much as possible in as little time as possible. If the organization of a report places the material he wants at the end, he thumbs through the pages to find it. And turning pages of tables and charts does not put him in good temper. When he finally comes upon the conclusions and recommendations, he may have little time left to read them. And even if he does have time, he may no longer have the patience and energy required to understand the full statement of conclusions and recommendations when he has not read the rest of the report.

ORDER OF DECREASING IMPORTANCE

Suitable Subjects

Busy readers complained so much about the inconvenience of climactic organization that writers in government and industry reversed this organization and placed the important material first for such readers (Figures 4 and 5). This order of diminishing interest or decreasing importance suits subjects with adequate variations in importance.

Advantages

For a hurried reader organization in a diminuendo of importance has the advantage of the front-page stories in his morning newspapers; he gets the most important material first. When he stops reading he has covered all the main thoughts that he can grasp in that much time. Like a newspaper reader, he knows that the material at the end is least necessary to him, and he can in good conscience put it aside for later reading, or he can forget about it.

And a report organized in the order of reverse climax makes a strong initial impression because it begins with the material that interests readers most. Managers and other busy readers welcome such a presentation.

Disadvantages

The interest of anyone reading an entire report organized in the order of decreasing importance gradually diminishes. Sometimes a writer can stimulate dying interest by an adroit placement of material of concern to the specialist, but more often he can do little to recapture his reader's close attention.

And this order may fail to arouse the interest of some readers. It demands, of course, that readers be able to understand difficult material, like conclusions and recommendations, before they have read the rest of the report. This organization is, therefore, obviously ill suited to many readers and many subjects.

ORDER OF EMPHASIS BY POSITION

Because of the disadvantages of organizing by the increasing or decreasing importance of subject matter, writers sought a plan that would

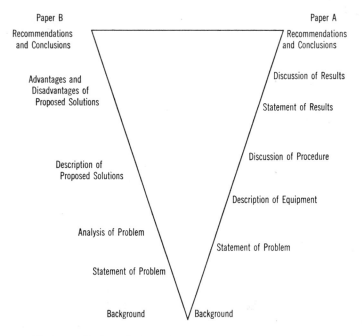

Figure 4. Order of decreasing importance in two papers.

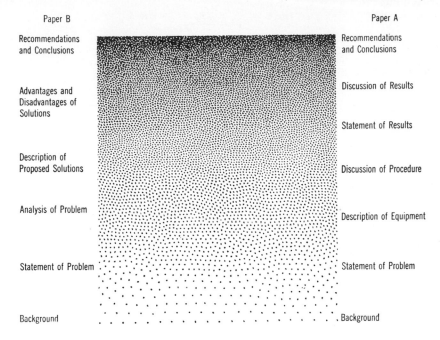

Paper B

Recommendations and Conclusions

Advantages and Disadvantages of Solutions

Description of Proposed Solutions

Analysis of Problem

Statement of Problem

Background

Paper A

Recommendations and Conclusions

Discussion of Results

Statement of Results

Discussion of Procedure

Description of Equipment

Statement of Problem

Background

Figure 5. Order of decreasing importance in two papers.

eliminate some of the undesirable features and retain the advantages. They evolved the organization presented in Figures 6, 7, 8, and 9. Because of its appearance, men sometimes call Figure 6 the hourglass; women, knowing the hourglass figure to be hopelessly dated, call it the wine flask. The term *hourglass* is misleading because a summary, if it is as short as it should be, does not provide a proportionate top for the lower triangle, as Figures 6 and 8 show. A writer inclined to write the long summary suggested by the word *hourglass* should visualize the method as it is shown in Figures 7, 8, and 9 and think of it as the short-summary-first plan. For that is exactly what it is—a short summary of main points prefixed to a report which is organized in the order of increasing importance.

Usually this summary is the beginning of a report, as in Figures 6 and 7; sometimes it is a separate work, as in Figures 8 and 9. It may be a separate work sent without the report to certain readers; it may be part of a letter of transmittal accompanying the report; or it may be a separate page that accompanies the report but is not part of it. One danger of presenting the summary as an individual work is that it may soon be detached physically from the report, which then becomes a

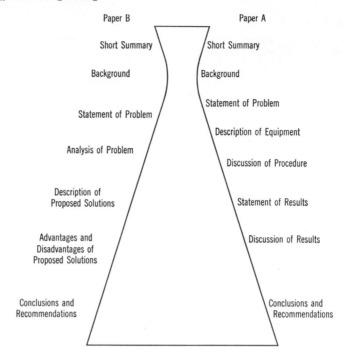

Figure 6. Emphatic organization of two papers.

report organized in the order of increasing importance with a weak beginning instead of the strong one the writer intended. Even a summary that is not physically detached from a report may become separated from it in a reader's mind. An executive may read a letter of transmittal and postpone his study of a report. When he eventually does begin to study the report, he may think, "I've read that," skip the letter of transmittal, and begin his reading of the report with the next topic, the point of lowest interest.

The prefixed summary should always be brief: a sentence or two suffice for a memorandum of a few pages; as much as a page may be necessary for a long report of one hundred pages or more, the limit being one page. This brief epitome may be (1) a summary of the significant ideas, which may be scattered in the report, (2) a summary of the results or conclusions or recommendations, or even (3) a summary of one result or conclusion or recommendation. (Chapter IV discusses this epitome in more detail.) A writer must consider his readers carefully in order to select judiciously the thoughts of his paper that are needed by those who read only the summary; he must express these thoughts

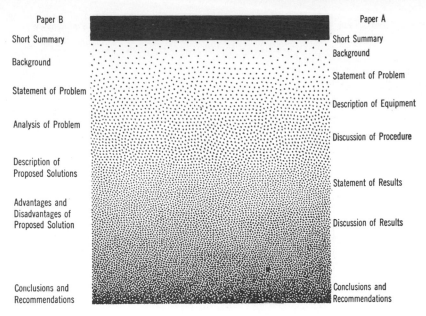

Figure 7. Emphatic organization of two papers.

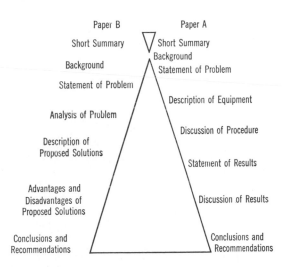

Figure 8. Separate summary and climactic organization—two papers.

Short Summary   Short Summary

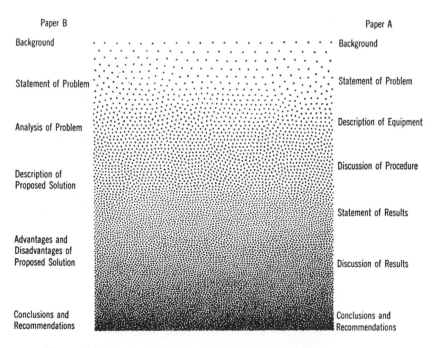

Paper B   Paper A

Background   Background

Statement of Problem   Statement of Problem

Analysis of Problem   Description of Equipment

Description of   Discussion of Procedure
Proposed Solution

                                                          Statement of Results

Advantages and
Disadvantages of
Proposed Solution   Discussion of Results

Conclusions and   Conclusions and
Recommendations   Recommendations

Figure 9. Separate summary and climactic organization—two papers.

in language intelligible to his readers and must bring all the concepts within their understanding.

Advantages

When a writer can do all this, he will find this plan a superior choice. Its popularity is well founded, for it enables a busy vice president to read a few sentences of a memorandum with confidence that he will find in those sentences the information he needs. He can read one page of a report of two hundred pages, know that he has the gist of the matter, and judge on the basis of the summary whether he will read more of the report. Even the specialist benefits. Glancing quickly through the summaries of a number of reports guides him to the reports he should read immediately and to those he may put aside for later reading. If the summaries are well written and he is well informed on the subjects, he can read ten or fifteen summaries and arrange the reports in the exact sequence in which he should read them. The value of this procedure to a busy specialist should not be overlooked. And other readers are also happy with the initial summary and with the rising interest of the rest of the report.

This organization (Figures 6, 7, 8, and 9) uses the positions of emphasis to great advantage. It opens with a short summary of the significant thinking of the paper, then presents the material in the order of increasing interest, and ends with a full presentation of the material most important to the reader. By thus combining the desirable stress of a beginning and an ending that contain important material with the effectiveness of climactic presentation, it offers advantages to many kinds of readers.

Disadvantages

In government and industry the popularity of this organization has created a disadvantage. The initial summaries, especially in letters and memorandums, tend to become monotonous formulas (Chapter IV). Once a writer is aware of this danger, he can avoid it by remembering that his readers know from the format of his writing that they are reading a letter or memorandum or report. They do not need to be told so in the first sentence: "This memo summarizes . . . ." It is usually equally obvious without a statement that they are reading a summary or a recommendation. A writer who starts with a main idea of his report rather than with a statement that this is a report writes more interesting and more varied first sentences because the different ideas of various reports suggest different constructions.

Supervisors who demand these formula beginnings should remember that although a reader does not object to them at first, after he has read dozens of them, he is irritated by the routine sameness and finally he does not read them at all. They become like the inside address, the salutation, and the complimentary close of a business letter—words that even careful readers skip.

Some material should not be organized by this plan because the initial presentation of the main point of the paper may antagonize a reader. If the main point is a recommendation that has been considered carefully several times and rejected, a weary reader may become annoyed. "Not that again," he protests and throws the paper aside. If a reader is stubbornly opposed to an idea, only a foolish writer waves that red flag in the opening sentence unless the writer wishes the bull to snort, paw the ground, and attack. Another beginning—the reason that led the writer to recommend again a much rejected or strongly opposed idea—will prove more successful.

Occasionally an initial summary presents difficulties that are not insurmountable: (1) a reader needs some slight background or explanatory material to understand the summary or (2) a writer is immersed in his final research and cannot take the general view of his material that is necessary for the writing of a summary.

If there is no acceptable way to incorporate slight background or explanatory material in the summary, it may precede it. But a writer should carefully limit this material to the minimum that his readers require, should rigorously revise it to achieve succinct expression, and should, by one method or another, strongly emphasize his summary when he finally presents it. The best way to achieve emphasis is to use strong, vivid expression in the summary. If this does not highlight it sufficiently, a writer may use devices of format. One or more of the following devices will stress summary beginnings that do not stand first:

> Larger type
> Different type
> White space around a centered summary
> A single line around the summary to box it
> Indention of the main points of the summary
> Indention and the use of numbers, dots, dashes, or other devices to mark
>   each main point of the summary

An initial summary is sometimes difficult to compose when a writer's mind is concerned with the details of a long research project. He has lost his general view of his subject and cannot recapture it while parts of the work dominate his thinking or while he is pressing hard to meet a time schedule. Some research groups assign the summary to another person whenever a report writer meets such a difficulty. A person more remote from the current work views the entire project more objectively and isolates the main points more easily than the writer can at that time.

SOME PROBLEMS IN ORGANIZATION

Knocking Down an Argument

Stating an opinion, conclusion, decision, or belief and then knocking it down is a technique often used when a writer is combatting a popular or entrenched opinion, when a reader may present the opposing argument if the writer does not mention it, or when only an opinion stands in the way of the idea a writer is advancing. This can be an effective method of organizing argument, but a writer who chooses it must be sure that he will not become contentious. This order requires judgment and taste. One major problem is to set up the opposing argument fairly, but not so firmly that it cannot be knocked down. Only when his arguments are more persuasive than his opponent's should a writer choose this order.

A supervisor who has excellent reasons for recommending changes in a shipping department may start with the advantages of the present methods and then prove that changes would retain these advantages, provide other advantages, and eliminate some defects of the present system. This would be tactful and convincing.

But if one is suggesting marketing a drug that has been withdrawn for seemingly good reasons and that has been reconsidered at intervals and again rejected, it would be tactless and weak to begin by rehashing the old arguments for rejection and then answering them. A more effective beginning might be some new market information about requests for the drug and about complaints from doctors and hospitals that could not obtain it. If these details are impressive, a reader will continue and may be persuaded by the information and by answers to familiar arguments.

When a writer begins by knocking down an argument, he must also use other plans. For example, he must organize the arguments he expects to combat. Some suitable orders are climactic, reverse climactic, and chronological. He may wish to organize his own arguments more effectively than his opponent's. Here, of course, is an opportunity for subtle deception. It is possible to organize an opponent's arguments ineffectively for poor emphasis and to organize one's own arguments to achieve convincing emphasis. Only careful readers experienced in organizing will detect the deception. This trick is common in political oratory and writing because it deceives well and is difficult to combat. Any writer for industry who is honestly concerned with presenting the truth seldom uses it. However, a writer in government and industry should know that the practice exists, for he is also a reader who must beware of such tricks.

Some writers of argument organize all their paragraphs by presenting the opposing point of view first and then knocking it down, the harder the better. Their organization becomes a constant seesawing from an opponent's point of view to the arguments against it, and readers grow tired of switching back and forth. If such a paper does not conclude with a strong statement of the writer's best point or a summary of the writer's point of view, the conclusion will stress the opponent's arguments, not the writer's.

To a writer who has selected a pro-and-con organization, transitional expressions come naturally: *but, yet, still, however, on the other hand, on the contrary, nevertheless, notwithstanding, in opposition to this, in contrast with that, at the same time, although that is true, but then, but after all, conceding that point; moreover, further, besides, in addition, also, too, furthermore, again, first, second, third, finally, hence, therefore, consequently, thus, as a result, because of this, in short, in brief, in fact, indeed, to be sure.*

Comparisons and Contrasts

Organizing comparisons and contrasts defeats many writers of technical information, as their circuitous and repetitious papers show.

Sometimes the defeat is due to their attempts to express in words material that belongs in tables and graphs. Whenever he finds himself struggling with expressing the details of a comparison, a writer should consider using a table or graph. Even in a memorandum or in a letter, presenting a table or a graph is better than trying to express the information in sentences—better not merely because it lightens the writer's task but because it makes reading and understanding easier. It leaves a writer free to comment as he wishes on information without detailing all of it in his text. If he thinks that it will assist the reader, he may place a representative table or graph in the text, the detailed table or graph appearing in an appendix. Whatever arrangement he chooses, he should try to help readers by expressing in sentences the details that may be understood best in this form and placing in tables or graphs the details suited to such presentation.

Another weakness in many comparisons is the choice of an organization that encourages and demands repetition. The first outline on the next page, the plan of a paper comparing two drugs, shows that a poorly organized comparison drags on interminably.

Information about Drug A
- Price
- Manufacturing costs
- Other costs
- Relief
  - Remarks of patients
    - After one dose
    - After four doses
    - After eight doses
  - Relief measured by objective tests
    - Test I
      - After one dose
      - After four doses
      - After eight doses
    - Test II
      - After one dose
      - After four doses
      - After eight doses

Information about Drug B
- Price
- Manufacturing costs
- Other costs
- Relief
  - Remarks of patients
    - After one dose
    - After four doses
    - After eight doses
  - Relief measured by objective tests
    - Test I
      - After one dose
      - After four doses
      - After eight doses
    - Test II
      - After one dose
      - After four doses
      - After eight doses

Advantages of Drug A
- Price
- Costs
- Patients' testimony after one dose

Advantages of Drug B
- Patients' remarks after four and eight doses
- Relief measured by objective tests

Disadvantages of Drug A
- Patients' remarks after four and eight doses
- Relief measured by objective tests

Disadvantages of Drug B
- Price
- Costs
- Patients' remarks after one dose

Comparison of Drugs A and B
- A more economical
- A more immediately efficacious after one dose according to patients' remarks
- B more efficacious after four and eight doses according to patients' remarks
- B more efficacious after one, four, and eight doses according to objective tests

Recommendation: That B be studied further with a view to reducing manufacturing and other costs

A paper such as the one outlined here makes a reader feel that he has been riding on a merry-go-round. The comparison is less repetitive and much clearer when organized as a unit:

Comparison of Drugs A and B
- Prices
- Manufacturing costs
- Other costs
- Patients' remarks
  - After one dose
  - After four doses
  - After eight doses
- Results of objective tests of relief
  - After one dose
  - After four doses
  - After eight doses

Summary of advantages of B (if the paper is long enough or the material complex enough to require a summary)

Recommendation: That B be studied further with a view to reducing manufacturing and other costs

Outlining before writing would have made the excessive repetition obvious, but the writer had no outline. He doggedly expressed all the topics and even strove valiantly to make them sound different. Such overlapping discussions should be avoided.

A writer presenting

1. The characteristics, advantages, and disadvantages of fractionating tray x
2. The characteristics, advantages, and disadvantages of fractionating tray y
3. The characteristics, advantages, and disadvantages of fractionating tray z

still requires additional sections to compare the three. He will probably find that varying the phraseology for these discussions is a strain and leads to artificiality, whereas failing to vary leads to monotony. And his paper will tend to become three papers, one on each tray, with the comparative study at the end not strong enough to pull the three together. Unless he has readers who are interested in only one tray, he should organize by some other plan, such as the following:

1. A comparison of the advantages of fractionating trays x, y, and z
2. A comparison of the disadvantages of fractionating trays x, y, and z
3. Recommendation

Whether a writer should place advantages or disadvantages first depends on where he wants the emphasis to fall. Many writers prefer to place last the points that bolster the recommendation. Thus a writer recommending Computer I rather than Computer II ends with the comparisons most favorable to Computer I; a writer comparing two factory sites ends with the material that favors the site that he has selected; and a supervisor discussing the promotion of one of his two assistants compares the two in the order that places last the strong points of the assistant he wishes to promote. If this climactic order does not suit his material, a writer should choose some other order—for example, chronological or geographical. Antonio Ferri in his article "Hypersonic Flight Testing" gives similarities and then differences in two paragraphs arranged chronologically:

> In the early stages of high-speed aerodynamics, we described what we observed by means of three interchangeable adjectives: hyperacoustic, supersonic, and hypersonic. All three meant but one thing— that the observed phenomenon had occurred at a speed above the speed of sound. They differed only in their etymology; the first is all Greek, the second all Roman, and the last is Greco-Roman.

Today, however, the word hypersonic is used only in conjunction with flight speeds above 5 to 6 times the speed of sound, while supersonic now defines the flight velocity range above the speed of sound but below these values. The word hyperacoustic has become an anachronism.[2]

It is sometimes more effective to present one subject separately and then to compare it with another or with others. If the first subject is more familiar to readers or if the first subject is the only familiar one, then to progress from the known to the less well known or from the known to the unknown is sensible because these plans assist readers. The familiar material may clarify the unfamiliar material and thus prepare readers, as the following example from the same issue shows:

> If you or I had invented the world, chances are we'd have botched the job. For eventually we would get around to inventing a way to hold the solid stuff of our world together. This is too all-encompassing a job to entrust to the selective interactions of chemical bonds. So it is likely that we would cook up some kind of "universal intermolecular force" and let it go at that. But in our haste to keep the world from falling apart, we would no doubt forget to invent some means, at the same time, to keep these universal forces of adhesion in check. That would be disastrous: Before our home-made world was ten seconds old, all its moving parts would lock solid, stuck fast with the universal glue of our own inventiveness.
>
> Now nature has been somewhat less reckless than we would have been, and somewhat more cunning too. She did invent a "universal intermolecular force" to keep the solid matter of her world together, but she made it an exquisitely refined and well-controlled force. Not that it's a weak one; it is, after all, the force that holds the atoms of a steel building together at the places where they are not held together by covalent, metallic or other chemical bonds, and it often accounts for more than 80% of the binding forces in solids.[3]

Induction or Deduction

"Shall I use induction or deduction?" asks the writer of informational prose and sometimes wastes his time writing a section of a paper both ways to see which he prefers. Whether to move from the particulars to the general or from the general to the particulars, from proof to proposition or from proposition to proof, may usually be decided by considering one's readers. Which order will be clearer, more convincing, more helpful to them? If a generalization will help readers to understand the details,

[2] *International Science and Technology* (April, 1964), p. 64.
[3] Louis H. Sharpe, Harold Schonhorn, and Charles J. Lynch, "Adhesives," p. 26.

examples, or illustrations, then it should stand before them. If the details, examples, or illustrations will help readers to understand the generalization, they should stand first. Occasionally a writer places a generalization in the middle of a discussion if readers who have become familiar with the preceding particulars can grasp the generalization. This order reserves the position of final stress at the end of a paragraph, section, or paper for a striking example. The example is frequently a more effective ending than a proposition that a reader grasped earlier in the paragraph. If, after readers know the details, a generalization is so simple and obvious that it must come as an insult to their intelligence, it should stand before the particulars, or it should be omitted.

Sometimes a simple proposition may be introduced successfully by a question. Walter C. Michels uses such a question and answer and follows them with particulars of proof in his talk on the occasion of receiving the Oersted Medal of the American Association of Physics Teachers:

> Who is to be blamed for the increasing confusion between science and technology, for the short-sighted policy that seems to be emerging? I submit that the fault lies largely with us, the community of physicists. We have not used the past eighteen years to accomplish the educational job that the relative freedom of that period made possible. A public that does not understand science and the role that science plays in our rapidly moving, technologically dependent civilization cannot be expected to act intelligently in its own self interests. The understanding necessary for a continued national interest in science cannot be brought about by advertising or by propaganda; it can result only from a serious and long term educational program.[4]

Explanation of the Plan

The question of whether a writer should announce or describe his organization for his reader is answered best by consideration of the reader. If a plan is simple and easy to follow, discussing it may be oversimplification; for example, if a reader is familiar with a plan because it is traditional in a profession or because it is used frequently by those reporting to him, he needs no preliminary description. But if a complex plan is new to him, he may find a description of it helpful. This description may be given in a table of contents or in a descriptive abstract. Meaningful headings and subheadings keep a reader apprised of the steps of an organization, and transitional words and phrases make a plan clear. Although a reader should not be uncertain about the plan of a work, it is generally not desirable to explain it at length. If an organization is so difficult that a reader cannot follow it without explanations, the writer should search for an order that

[4] "Men with Ideas," *International Science and Technology* (April, 1964), p. 98.

is easier for his reader to understand. Prolonged elucidation of a plan of development stresses the plan at the expense of the ideas, but more subtle guides to a plan clarify it without shifting the emphasis from the ideas. Finding an organization that does not require much clarification and finding methods of directing a reader without subtracting emphasis from ideas are both easier before a paper has been written. Outlining, which is discussed in the next chapter, provides a writer with a general view of a work and its parts while the organization is still flexible.

Chapter VI

Easy Outlining

If a man can group his ideas, he is a good writer.

Stevenson

A writer can move and change parts of an outline easily. But once a paper has been written, the parts are closely woven into a whole. And a writer is naturally reluctant to destroy this whole. Thinking of the labor involved in reassembling a completed paper discourages change. But an outline encourages a writer to improve the organization of a paper. Because an outline prevents thoughts from prematurely hardening, shifting the parts of an outline is easy. It is like shaking a kaleidoscope: another design emerges, new possibilities reveal themselves, fresh relationships appear. I do not know any way for a writer working by himself to shake up his thinking and shape his paper as successfully as by outlining. Outlining encourages forethought instead of afterthoughts.

GENERAL ADVANTAGES OF OUTLINING

Most writers outline by listing their main ideas on sheets of paper (one sheet for a short work) and then numbering and renumbering as they experiment with various organizations. When they have settled upon a plan, they supply divisions of main ideas and then divisions of divisions; later they select a plan for each set of subdivisions. Some writers find an even more flexible method helpful. They jot each main idea on a card and then lay out the cards and move them about to try various plans. Laying out this game of solitaire is most helpful to those who have difficulty finding and accepting any order but that in which their ideas first come to them. Sometimes accidental placing of the cards suggests relationships that writers had not noticed.

In whatever form it is written, an outline is a trial, a pattern to try on and refit and redesign as necessary. It is a skeleton with movable parts.

If a writer has placed a finger where a toe should be, he can change this easily; if a bone is missing, he can supply one; if the skeleton has two heads, he can discard one. But once the bones are fleshed, it is difficult to detect skeletal errors, let alone to correct them. Few writers have x-ray eyes and osteopathic techniques. But any writer can improve his outline.

Unity

Working on an outline improves a writer's thinking. Outlining forces him to define his thesis clearly, and once a thesis has been clearly stated, departures from it become obvious. A writer who cannot see that a section of his finished report destroys the unity would have spotted such a digression in an outline and could have removed it easily.

Coherence

Errors in coherence are also more obvious in an outline than in a completed report. A writer who does not plan before writing may struggle long and hard to connect sections of his writing because he does not know what is wrong until someone points out that he is trying to connect two parts that do not belong together.

A safety chairman, for example, placed the four following recommendations in the order in which they had occurred to him while he was dictating a memorandum:

1. That black lines be painted at eye level on all glass doors
2. That supervisors enforce regulations about safety eyeglasses
3. That temporary black tape be placed on glass doors until the black lines can be painted
4. That caution signs be placed on the temporary scaffolding at the entrance to Building A

An accident to a chemist who had tried to walk through a glass door and had nearly succeeded prompted point 1. That accident reminded the writer of an accident to a laboratory assistant who had neglected to wear safety glasses. Then he thought of the time that it would take for the black lines to be painted, and he decided to order temporary tape. This reminded him of the temporary scaffolding and the need for warning signs.

When he wrote in that order, he could not connect the topics. But as soon as he had jotted an outline, the safety chairman telephoned the maintenance department and ordered 3 and 4. Then he sent that department a memorandum of confirmation and an order for 1. He also saw immediately that regulations about safety glasses belonged in a separate memorandum to the supervisors of a few laboratories. Thus he wrote less, secured prompter service, and saved the reading time of supervisors. Yet when writers are busiest, they tend to ignore planning and to rush immediately to a final draft of what came to mind. Because writing by free association wastes time, planning is most necessary when a writer is most hurried.

Emphasis

An outline is thus useful for improving unity and coherence, and it is also useful for more advanced work—the achievement of good emphasis. An outline gives the general view of the whole paper and the specific view of the parts that a writer needs when he considers emphasis. Outlining shows which subjects are in the positions of importance, which subjects will receive stress because their presentation will be lengthy, which organization will emphasize important ideas, and which parts of the paper need attention because the chosen plan stresses them too much or too little.

Few writers can see all this without outlining. And even fewer have the time and energy and patience to move parts of a completed paper, compensate for lengthy development of minor ideas, change the organization, and rephrase sections to improve emphasis. Such strenuous revision is not always possible without a complete rewriting. Writers of functional prose who rewrite to strengthen the unity and coherence are frequently reluctant to rewrite to improve the emphasis. Therefore the only way for them to achieve better emphasis is to outline their papers before writing them. Then they can experiment with organizations to find the best one for their material, their objectives, and their readers (Chapter V). Then they can experiment imaginatively with that plan, adapt it as they desire, and thus attain effective emphasis.

SPECIAL ADVANTAGES OF OUTLINING

Help to Busy Writers

Outlining offers special advantages to anyone who is interrupted frequently—sometimes for long periods. After a long interruption a writer might spend an hour or more reading preceding pages and finding his way back into his work. Consulting an outline enables him to do this in much less time; sometimes the bird's-eye view offered by an outline helps him to orient himself in a few minutes. For anyone who can work only at intervals, an outline is essential. He may write an outline piecemeal by filling in missing sections as he thinks of them or as he completes his research. The outline will help to keep him informed of progress in his research, for omissions will be obvious. And when, as he is writing his paper, annoying interruptions drive ideas from a writer's mind, his outline often helps him to recall them or at least to find his place quickly and begin rephrasing.

His outline also reinforces his memory at other times. It reminds him what his next topic is, whether he has already covered a point, and how important one topic is in relation to other topics and to the whole work. And outlining helps him to avoid repetition, digression, omission, and poor emphasis. A completed outline is a boon to him when he has been doing other work and is suddenly asked a question about the subject of a report. Many a writer has told me that when his mind went blank and he did not have time to search his report for the answer, his outline supplied it quickly. A man who can refer to an outline will never seem confused or ill-informed about his work. And the usefulness of the phrasing in an outline has won the blessing of many a man trying to write on one of his bad days. When words just will not come, it is a boon to find phrases and sentences ready in an outline.

Help to Co-Writers

Another advantage of the outline is its usefulness when several men are writing one report. Each writer can see the position assigned to his work; can establish relationships between his sections and the other sections, especially those immediately preceding and following; and can think more easily of his work in relation to the whole. When one person writes a report and others approve it, the altering of an outline until it is approved prevents much tiresome rewriting. Thus outlining helps to eliminate some of the irritations and dissatisfactions of the writing by groups or committees that is necessary in government and industry.

Help with Progress Reports

Outlining is also useful to writers of progress reports, for it keeps them aware of goals, warns them against attractive but insignificant digressions, and keeps them alert to the relative importance of ideas. Reading outlines of preceding reports and then outlining the current one can help writers to avoid losing sight of the main objectives of a long study and overemphasizing the minor details of recent research.

Help with Abstracts, Summaries, Tables of Contents

An outline is most useful in the preparation of an abstract or summary, especially if one is required before a paper is completed. Writers of abstracts or summaries who have no written plan of the whole work may emphasize minor points at the expense of major, include material that will not appear in the final paper, or omit main points. But the writer with an outline has a much better general view of his subject and probably has ready in his outline some of the wording for his abstract or summary.

An outline may also provide the wording for the descriptive table of contents and for the subject headings of a paper, for a table of contents and subject headings are often little more than expanded or contracted outlines.

Help with Short Works and Dictation

Letters, memorandums, and two- or three-page reports benefit from outlining. Many a man, especially one who dictates easily and fluently, fails to plan these works. Although he always outlines lengthy works, he rushes without a plan to dictate short ones. As he dictates, he is expressing one idea while he is trying to remember the three ideas that should come next. He fills in with unnecessary words while he gropes for the next thought, expresses himself with halting ineptness while he tries to remember what he has just finished saying, and in his frustration even becomes angry with his secretary or his reader because the memorandum or letter is not progressing well.

Of course it is not. When he combines phrasing the dictation of the moment with developing or recalling the next thought, his mind is likely to rebel and perform only one of the tasks, and that one indifferently. The man who dictates without a plan usually breaks most of the rules of coherence and emphasis and tends to be turgid and verbose. Good and even adequate impromptu speakers are tempted to dictate impromptu. But what is acceptable to an audience, which has the advantage of a speaker's personality, gesture, voice, and phrasing and even of the atmosphere of the occasion, is a far different matter on paper. A sensible man realizes later that the works he dictated without a plan are his poorest. Unfortunately he sometimes mails or distributes them immediately and regrets his costly haste later.

Anyone who doubts that this applies to him—and some successful impromptu speakers stubbornly resist the truth—should try dictating from informal outlines for a week and should compare the results with the results of impromptu dictation. Reading one's own hasty dictation is a useful revelation. It makes strong men shudder, especially after they have complained about the letters and memorandums of other writers, and leads even stubborn doubters to the realization that they dictate best from an outline.

Writers in my courses who dictated or wrote hastily and carelessly and scorned all kinds of planning were amazed at the improvement that resulted from a few moments spent outlining. Some writers had been using one letter plan for ten years or more, regardless of the contents and the readers. They found much to improve when they spent a few moments thinking; they often developed better organizations for some types of letters and some kinds of readers. Thus many letters benefitted from a few minutes spent planning one letter. These writers were surprised too at how their outlining suggested a new idea, located an annoying digression, and pinpointed unconscious, unnecessary repetition in even the shortest work. No wonder that the secretaries commented that the bosses had become better and happier writers. Every secretary knows that the dictation of a man who has not planned is marked by omissions, awkward insertions, time-consuming backtracking, and separation of related ideas. Much incoherence in brief works is due not to inability or failure to recognize related ideas but to lack of organization.

One supervisor, planning a memorandum to give to an assistant, wrote four points:

1. Lack of aggressiveness
    Two examples when leadership might have prevented errors
2. Need for courses in new methods
    Two suggestions
3. Good team work
    Getting along well
    Doing his share of routine work
4. A new assignment—his teaching new workers

He had placed last his main point—his wish to have his assistant spend most of the next four months teaching other workers.

As he looked over the points, he decided that the unfavorable point, 1, would make a poor beginning. If he started with 4 and related his first and second points to it as necessary improvements, then 3 would follow as a concluding reason for expecting success in the teaching. He also considered starting with good teamwork as one reason for selecting his assistant to teach new workers. Then 1 and 2 would become improvements for the assistant to make in preparation for the teaching. As the supervisor considered other organizations, the main point of his writing dominated, and his other thoughts related themselves to that main point. His final memorandum, which had more focus than if he had discussed points 1, 2, 3, 4 in that order, influenced his assistant as the writer wished.

Outlining a short paper also helps in other ways. I have seen executives study their jottings, divide them into two memorandums, and then direct them to different readers. Their readers responded better when they did not have to wade through what did not concern them to find what did. I have also seen an executive examine his outline of a letter, telephone to discuss three possibilities, and write a confirmation of the action selected. That saved the energy and time involved in a long letter and a long reply. The most common improvement is the removal of unnecessary material. Apparently writers tend to expand a short work when they first think of the contents, and if they do not examine and plan, they dictate much more material than a reader needs. Outlining helps them to keep short works to proper length.

KINDS OF OUTLINES

The outline form that a writer should use to achieve these good results is determined by his own preference. Whatever form helps him the most is the best form for him. Many writers avoid formal outlines except when they write outline reports. Having to struggle with carefully numbered parallel topics distracts them from their ideas and irritates them. They evolve satisfactory systems of their own. Many of them indent to mark the relative importance of topics and do not number topics until they have reached a final decision about order. Others use cards for the outline of a short report, but for a long report they number the cards and have their secretaries type an outline from them. And some outliners use colored pencils, strips of paper, or blackboards. Whatever suits each writer is best for the outlines he prepares for his own use.

But for outline reports submitted to readers, standard forms are necessary because a reader can understand them more easily than he can understand a writer's idiosyncratic outlining. The principal types are the sentence outline, the topic outline, and the paragraph outline.

The example of a sentence outline (1, below) illustrates closed (or close) punctuation, which may be used in any of the outline forms; the example of a topic outline (2, below) illustrates open punctuation, which is also suitable for any outline form; and the example of an outline that combines forms (4, below) uses periods after sentences but no punctuation after topics that are not sentences. Writing for an old-fashioned reader, I would use closed punctuation; for a modern reader, open or a combination.

1—*Sentence Outline*

  I. In a sentence outline, each division is one complete sentence.
  II. The use of complete sentences has advantages.
    A. An outliner is forced to formulate and analyze his thoughts thoroughly.

B. Information is conveyed fully and clearly in a form familiar to a reader.

    1. A reader does not have to expand incomplete sentences to understand the meaning.

    2. A reader is not distracted by the choppiness of the topic outline.

C. The thought relationships are expressed more exactly than in a paragraph outline.

D. Should the outliner wish to expand his outline into a paper, he will find many sentences ready for use.

III. The use of complete sentences has disadvantages.

    A. Repetition of sentence patterns is likely, as in topics III *B* 2 *a* and *b* of this outline.

    B. When subdividing is thorough, the sentences for minor subdivisions may be awkward, inappropriate, and cumbersome.

        1. Subdivisions in many outline reports, particularly scientific and technical reports, may be numerous.

        2. Many subdivisions lend themselves better to expression as phrases or single words.

           a. This is true of lists.

           b. This is true of details.

               (1) Subdivisions after the fourth are frequently unsuited to expression in sentences.

                  (a) Sections *a* and *b* of this outline would be clear as single words.

                  (b) Scientific and technological information, like a reading of temperature or pressure, belongs in phrases.

               (2) Expressing details in sentences gives them too much emphasis.

                  (a) This is illustrated in topics (*a*) and (*b*) of the preceding section.

                  (b) Indented material easily extends to so many lines that the bulkiness emphasizes minor information.

                  (c) A sentence is the most important grammatical form in an outline.

2—*Topic Outline*

I. Each division in a topic outline a clause or phrase

II. Advantages of topic outline

    A. Thought relationships clear

    B. Minor topics in minor grammatical forms

III. Disadvantages of topic outline

    A. Ambiguity more possible than in sentence outline

    B. Writer not forced to formulate ideas fully

    C. Form not familiar to all readers

    D. Need to achieve parallelism

    1. Writing parallel constructions (Chapter XIII) more difficult than writing sentences
    2. Under one topic, divisions of equal rank in parallel form
      a. Topics *A, B, C, D*, etc., under III
      b. Topics 1 and 2 under *D*

3—*Paragraph Outline*

    I. In a paragraph outline each division is a summary of a paragraph.
    II. The paragraph outline, which may be difficult to prepare for long papers, is particularly useful for short papers.
  III. It exhibits paragraph structure but not necessarily thought relationships.
  IV. It provides topic sentences that are useful when a writer expands his outline into a paper.
    V. It is not useful as a report form.
  VI. The thought is often less complete in a paragraph outline than in a sentence or topic outline.

4—*An Outline That Combines Forms*

Many writers combine the sentence and the topic outline to obtain the best advantages of each. They express major topics in sentences and minor topics in clauses, phrases, or single words. This requires attention to parallel construction if an outline is written for any reader besides the writer himself. The following partial outline combines forms:

    I. Some writers use sentences, phrases, clauses, and single words in an outline.
    A. Sentences for main topics following
      1. Roman numerals
      2. Roman numerals and capital letters
      3. Roman numerals, capital letters, and Arabic numerals
    B. Phrases, clauses, and single words for minor topics
      1. Under such topics equal divisions to be parallel in expression
        a. Nouns and their modifiers, as in topics 1, 2, and 3 under *A* in this outline
        b. Single words, as in topics (1), (2), (3), and (4)
          (1) Nouns
          (2) Verbs
          (3) Adjectives
          (4) Adverbs
    II. Combining grammatical forms offers some of the advantages of the sentence outline and of the topic outline.

USES OF OUTLINE FORMS

Outline forms are usually employed as follows: sentence outlines or sentence outlines with minor subdivisions in phrases or single words—

for outlines to be submitted to readers instead of complete reports, for outlines to be used only by the writer, and for outlines to be used by several writers in planning a paper; topic outlines—for a writer's own use and for the use of several writers in planning a paper; paragraph outlines or paragraph outlines with some subdivisions in clauses, phrases, or single words—for a writer's own use in planning short papers.

The paragraph outline is a very useful but neglected form. Many writers would benefit from outlining by paragraphs when they plan a letter:

1. Thank him for hospitality at convention
    Dinner and theater
    Flowers for Helen
2. Request samples of polymers discussed with him at convention
3. Ask him to serve on Hospitality Committee next year
    Four national conventions
    Three regional meetings
4. Send copy of article on heat transfer he requested

Looking this over, an outliner may decide to interchange 2 and 3. The two items on hospitality may be easily connected, and the two professional courtesies (of sending an article and requesting samples) belong together. According to the amount of development given the ideas, the division of the material into paragraphs may be one paragraph for convention hospitality and one for the professional courtesies, either paragraph standing first; or the division may be four paragraphs in one of the following orders:

I

Thank him for convention hospitality
Invite him to serve on hospitality committee
Mention that requested article is in mail
Request samples

II

Tell him I'm sending article
Request samples
Invite him to serve on hospitality committee
Thank him for hospitality

III

Thank him for hospitality
Tell him I'm sending article
Request samples
Invite him to serve on hospitality committee

Order I provides a pleasant beginning suited to a reader who is pleased by social grace, as the correspondent seems to be; it separates the thoughts on hospitality and on technical matters. Order II also separates these but starts with the technical article, a good beginning if the request was urgent. This plan ends with gracious thanks. Order III groups at the end the two requests, a necessary precaution if the reader is absentminded enough to overlook one request if the two are separated. Thus consideration of the reader determines the choice of plan.

Of major importance for busy executives is the simplicity of such outlining, the ease with which one can change the order by renumbering or inserting arrows, and the help to an executive who may be interrupted while dictating or writing. The paragraph outline of a letter, memorandum, or short report is almost too obviously useful. This outline resembles the papers that one searches the office for while they are lying on top of the pile in the middle of one's desk. It is easy to overlook.

However, once a writer uses it, he is less likely to overlook it again. In fact, one executive became so enthusiastic about the value of the paragraph outline in improving his writing and so eager to recommend it repeatedly that his harassed colleagues wished I had not enlightened him.

Chapter VII

Some Fallacies to Forget:
Misconceptions and Misinterpretations

> An old tutor of a college said to one of his
> pupils: Read over your compositions, and
> wherever you meet with a passage which
> you think is particularly fine, strike it out.
>
> *Boswell*

Misunderstandings about writing are common and stubborn. As a consultant on writing for industry and as a teacher of English, I hear many misconceptions so often that I begin to think I have entered some looking-glass world of writing, where all the principles are upside-down or greatly distorted. Those who impose ritualistic instruction on writers seem to be characters in a Victorian nonsense tale. There Miss Mouldypate incants, "Never end with a preposition; never end with a preposition; never, never end with a preposition," as her ball misses a wicket. Mr. Chipson-Shoulder pleads as he hands out straitjackets, "But it is the best way to say it, the only way to say it, my way to say it. And besides, the vice president–elect says it that way." And little Adam Panacea takes his thumb out of his ear long enough to recite,

> Please use a small word.
> Small words are good
> For you—and me.

Bits of advice from this Never-English land have a strong influence on writing. If cooking were controlled by such misconceptions, then indigestion and poisoning would threaten at every meal. Style in professional writing has been poisoned by erring precepts that are no more accurate or truthful than a word passed around a circle is when it reaches the last listener. But people do accept these misconceptions, act upon them, and even insist that their subordinates act upon them too; therefore the misconceptions are too virulent to be ignored.

ON DULL STYLE

A misconception that plagues me is the belief of many writers, editors, and supervisors that writing on professional subjects cannot be easy, interesting reading. Such writing is by its nature dull and heavy, they insist, and they cite scholarly journals as proof. True, journals are often hard reading, even for scholars who are used to reading them; and some articles come as close to being unreadable as anything published today with the exception of a few textbooks and many doctoral dissertations. The writers of turgid prose either do not know how to write better or, like the residents of Laputa, they scorn to cast light on the world and would rather cast a shadow. Some of them condescendingly assume that their readers are so stupid as to admire only what cannot be read and understood easily. But few readers are duped by unintelligibility. Even the greenest undergraduate views skeptically an incomprehensible professor: "Well, maybe he knows his subject, but you'd never guess it from the way he explains it."

The lively lucidity of many scholars proves that poor style is not inevitable in the professions. The writers of the journal articles from which I have quoted in Chapter IV use words to convey sense, not to impede understanding. In my experience there is a marked correlation between the excellence of a writer's understanding of his subject and the clarity and grace of his expression.

ON THE LONG AND SHORT OF IT

A related misunderstanding is that there is only one style suited to writings on professional subjects. The error of this belief is shown by the confusion of those who try to describe that style. One believer states that unless a writer uses long words, long sentences, and long paragraphs, his style will not seem professional; another insists that there is only one way to make writing clear and readable—the use of short words, short sentences, and short paragraphs. Equally contradictory admonitions are offered for the lengths of works: the longer the work, the more the readers will be impressed; the shorter the work, the more the readers will admire it. To listen to the long and short of it, one would think that no words, sentences, paragraphs, or entire works were ever of medium length.

The length of a work depends on the material and the readers. The lengths of paragraphs and sentences depend on many considerations, one of the most important being variety (Chapters XIII and XIV). And length is a misleading criterion to apply to words because words are chosen for other reasons—for denotation, connotation, suitability to the reader, concrete and specific qualities, tone, etc. (Chapter XII). The English language has developed what it needs—words, sentences, and paragraphs of great variety. To select from this variety with judgment and skill is interesting and challenging. Advisers and writers who would substitute counting for judgment and skill can be replaced by adding machines.

ON REPEATING AND REPEATING AND REPEATING

Another fallacy that misleads writers is the advice to repeat ideas three times. In an anthology on technical writing one contributor assigns to a "Navy publication friend" the recommendation "that first you tell them what you are going to tell them; then you tell them; and then you tell them what you have told them." Another contributor to the same volume attributes this advice to a preacher who developed his sermons by such repetition. And according to my students, high school teachers strongly recommend that paragraphs be developed this way.

Yet few writers can repeat ideas three times effectively. A paragraph that begins by telling readers that a drug has three side effects and cites convincing proof certainly does not benefit from two more statements that the drug has three side effects. Perhaps poor students benefit from repeating the main idea three times in each paragraph; at least they may achieve some paragraph unity by reminding themselves of their main subject. But experienced readers and writers do not need three reminders of the topic of each paragraph.

ON NEVER ENDING WITH A PREPOSITION

The taboo against ending with a preposition is a dimly perceived point of emphasis incorrectly applied. Near the end of an English sentence a major stress falls, sometimes on the last word, sometimes on a word just before the last word, sometimes on the final phrase. For effective emphasis, the word or phrase stressed should be important.

EXAMPLES

He authorized us to spend ten thousand dollars. (The stress is on *ten thousand dollars*.)

He emphasized the final point. (The stress is on *final point* or *final*.)

> She said that she would complete the work on Monday. (The stress
> is on *Monday*.)

Careful writers avoid stressing an unimportant word, like a preposition
or adverb, particularly an unnecessary word.

EXAMPLES

> These pipes are difficult to connect up. (*Up* is unnecessary and should
> be deleted.)
> Everyone thought it a poor way for the speech to end up. (The stress
> falls on the unnecessary *up*.)
> This is the drawer to put cancelled checks in. (The stress falls on *in*.
> *This is the drawer for cancelled checks* stresses *cancelled checks*, and
> *Put cancelled checks in this drawer* stresses *this drawer*.)
> He said that after he returned from California he would contribute
> two hundred dollars however. (The stress falls on *however*. If *however*
> is placed after *he said*, it performs its proper function of connecting
> sentences—which it cannot perform well at the end of a sentence—and
> the final stress falls on *two hundred dollars*. *He said, however, that
> after he returned from California he would contribute two hundred
> dollars*.)
> Baton Rouge is the division of the company that he is coming from
> and Seattle is the division he is going to. (This might be sensible
> emphasis if there had been a disagreement as to whether he was coming
> from or going to Baton Rouge or Seattle. The *to* would be stressed,
> and *to* would be important. Otherwise the sentence has better emphasis
> if it is rephrased: *He is coming from the Baton Rouge division of the
> company and going to the division at Seattle*.)

But in many a sentence that ends with a preposition, the stress falls on
the word before the preposition. If that word is important, there is no
need to avoid ending with a necessary preposition or adverb.

EXAMPLES

> He is a difficult person to disagree with. (The stress falls on *disagree*,
> and *disagree* is an important word in the sentence.)
> Children should have bright objects to play with. (The stress falls on
> *play*, an important word.)

ON NEVER SPLITTING AN INFINITIVE

Another shibboleth—never splitting an infinitive—arises from a similar
misunderstanding. The natural place for the sign of the infinitive is
next to the infinitive, as in *to come, to understand, to demonstrate*.

A word or phrase between the sign of the infinitive and the infinitive disturbs normal word order, and a word out of its usual place in the sentence attracts stress: *to complain surreptitiously* is the normal order, and *to surreptitiously complain* stresses *surreptitiously*. Obviously there are occasions when a writer might want such stress. A supervisor discussing two employees—one who had warned the supervisor that he was taking a complaint to a vice president and another who complained secretly to the vice president—might write that he regretted that the second employee found it necessary to surreptitiously complain to the vice president. Thus he would emphasize the distinction between complaining and surreptitiously complaining.

If a writer does not realize that splitting an infinitive emphasizes the word or phrase after *to,* he may accidentally stress a word that he does not want emphasized and thus confuse or mislead his reader. Good writers split infinitives when splitting is desirable for emphasis and when avoiding it would be awkward. But splitting an infinitive is also awkward sometimes, particularly when several words come between *to* and the infinitive.

EXAMPLE

> He attempted to by every means gain promotion.
> *Improved*: He attempted to gain promotion by every means.
> By every means he attempted to gain promotion.
> His motion to carefully for three months examine these findings was passed immediately.
> *Improved*: His motion to examine these findings carefully for three months was passed immediately.

Some split infinitives are redundant. Careless writers tend to insert trite intensifiers or qualifiers between *to* and the infinitive, as in the following examples: *to actually realize, to better know, to clearly understand, to definitely believe, to really comprehend,* and *to virtually have.* Unnecessary adverbs, like other unnecessary words, should be deleted during revision (Chapter VIII).

ON NEVER BEGINNING WITH . . .

To avoid beginning sentences with certain words is another common taboo. A writer may begin a sentence with any word that he likes. The first word or words in a sentence are usually stressed, and they should be important words. But occasionally even the much maligned *however* may be important because a writer wishes to emphasize for a reader or listener that an unexpected shift in thought follows. *But* and *and,* which are also listed as forbidden first words by some teachers who teach *don't's* instead of *do's,* seldom are stressed when they introduce a sentence; and they are, therefore, useful, unobtrusive initial conjunctions.

Writers who have been avoiding them should notice how often and how effectively *and, but, for,* and other short conjunctions introduce good sentences in modern prose. Writers in the professions might use them more often to begin sentences. They should take care, however, to avoid placing the same unimportant word at the beginning of so many sentences that it becomes monotonous. Sentence variety, essential for an interesting style, may be defeated by monotonous sentence beginnings (Chapter XIII).

ON NEVER REPEATING A WORD

It is usually wise to avoid repeating unimportant words. But important words may, and even should, be repeated. Skillful repetition is useful and effective: it provides coherence and emphasis. The naysayers would have writers avoid repetition by using synonyms and synonymous phrases. This technique, known as *elegant variation,* is, in spite of its pleasant name, undesirable. It soon leads a writer to high-sounding terms. A *horse* in the first sentence becomes in later sentences *a stallion, a brute creature, a steed, an equine creature,* and *equus caballus.* Thus elegant variation encourages pseudoelegant, flowery, and extravagant diction. If a writer wishes to avoid repeating a word or phrase, he should know that pronouns serve better than roundabout expressions and inexact synonyms.

The preceding objections to awkward avoidance of the repetition of words and phrases concern mainly taste and judgment, but writers of functional prose have another objection to elegant variation—the shortage of exact synonyms. Using an inexact synonym may mislead readers. Even a more general or a more specific term is undesirable when, as often happens, it confuses. If an engineer writes about Experiment A taking place in a tank and Experiment B in a unit, readers assume that he is using different equipment when he is using elegant variation.

ON THAT PRECIOUS FIRST DRAFT

Another old saw is that one must write correctly enough to write a paper only once. Such a belief makes the first writing slow, difficult, and painfully unsatisfactory (Chapter III). It also leads to the notion that the first phrasing of ideas is sacred and immutable; second thoughts are taboo. If for a good reason, like awkwardness or lack of clarity, a passage needs rewriting, the writers who believe that expression is sacred in the form that it first came to them try to change the passage as little as possible, rather than to improve it as much as possible. They do this even when common sense demands that they throw the sentences out and start again. Such writers also object to removing from a paragraph a sentence on another subject. And if anyone suggests cutting a section from a report, they bleed. The belief that every idea is expressed best as it first comes to a writer makes revision painful and unsuccessful. A writer works better if he is convinced that he is blessed when his first expression of an idea is satisfactory, that he is lucky when a first revision succeeds, and that such good fortune in writing is rare. Successful revision demands a measure of ruthlessness. If a writer tries to revise and cut his work as calmly and thoroughly as he would the work of someone else, he will, after a time, revise less painfully. And his readers will read less painfully.

ON PUTTING YOURSELF IN THE READER'S PLACE

Another old saw about writing is, "Put yourself in the reader's place." Some writers do this all too well.

Once when a chemist persisted in sending unnecessary details of his research to a vice president who was not interested, I advised, "Before you write you ought to consider how much of this information Mr. Jones wants and needs. After all, he is a busy man, and his desk is loaded with reading. Surely you don't think that he wants all these details."

"But I did consider it," the chemist protested. "My writing teacher told me to put myself in the reader's place, and I did. I said to myself, 'O.K., Joe, you are now in Jones's place; you are a vice president. How much of this material do you want?' And I wanted it all."

A better admonition than "Put yourself in the reader's place" is "Forget yourself and become your reader." When Joe was told this, he said, "Oh, well, if you mean I am Jones without any scientific training and interested only in results and using them for company decisions, why then I have to cut out these details. But that's not putting myself in the reader's place."

Joe managed easily to take Jones's point of view, but some people never see any point of view but their own. Concentration on self is often laughable, like the remark of an actor, "I've had a rough time with *The Hostage;* I get thrown about a bit. One time I broke the leading lady's ankle."

The ability to take the reader's point of view is essential in writing functional prose. It is essential to the selection and rejection of material, to the choice of an organization (Chapter V), to the style of paragraphs and sentences (Chapters XIII and XIV), and to the choice of words (Chapter XII). It aids every decision that a writer makes when he is revising. It influences every facet of a paper. If readers are varied, a good writer weighs and considers them and adjusts his paper to their variety. This is a more difficult and a far more useful process than mentally promoting himself to vice president and deciding what he as vice president would like.

A writer's success in assuming another point of view depends on his flexibility and on his knowledge of the world. Going to the theater, reading about the lives of others, and perceptively observing people— these provide a basic understanding for writing. This is one major similarity between the good writer of expository prose and the good executive: they use their understanding of people, and their understanding of people is good. The relationship is so close that I consider good young writers in my classes to be potentially good administrators; and if they are offered and take the chance to become administrators, they do not disappoint me. It is also true that I have observed poor writers become better writers after holding an administrative position that forced them to work with people and to learn more about them. A good writer is a good practicing psychologist.

ON WRITING THE WAY YOU TALK

A common cause of misunderstanding that leads to poor writing is the advice, "Write the way you talk." Writing and speech are different in vocabulary, in grammar, in sentence structure, and in organization. Sometimes a few sentences can be retrieved from the taped discussion of a committee, but who would have the patience to read the repetitive and discursive whole? There is a vast difference between actual conversation, dialogue in a book or play, and other writing. As Chapter II illustrates, the professional writing that sounds easiest and most natural has been worked over the most, for writing that is easy to read is a long way from talk. Some few novelists have good enough ears to catch the nuances of talk and to use them skillfully in writing dialogue that reads like talk. But unedited talk is confusing and boring reading.

Some years ago a professional society received complaints about the recording of discussion at its meetings. Irate speakers accused the stenographers of inaccuracy, the editor of incompetence, and the publishers of dishonesty. The society had been recording discussion stenographically, editing it into some semblance of meaning, and sending typed copies to speakers for correction. After many complaints the society recorded the discussion on tape, transcribed it in the pure form in which it had been uttered, and sent the speakers their verbatim comments. They screamed. In fact, they could not have shrieked louder had they been told to give up wine, women, and golf. The talk of government officials at press conferences also illustrates the unsuitability of talk for print—the rambling verbosity, the tendency to backtrack, the inadequate vocabularies, and the failure to state clearly what is meant. Such poor talk does not make good writing.

This is not to say that a writer cannot benefit from thinking of his reader in order to direct his writing to his reader. Considering how one would explain a process to a particular mechanic, to a known professor, or to a certain administrator may help in selecting material, in planning the paper, and in expressing the ideas, as the preceding chapters show.

The reason behind the admonition, "Write the way you talk," is often sound; the adviser wants the writer to adjust his material and his expression to his reader. And the question, "How would you explain this to Jones?" is sometimes useful to a writer who has failed repeatedly to explain a thought and is weary of revising his paper: it may free him from his typed sentences and enable him to start fresh. And this may be what he needs when a particularly knotty passage will not untangle.

But if writers think that "Write the way you talk" is an invitation to use the vernacular of the shop and the cafeteria, to employ sentence fragments and incorrect grammar, and to wander and repeat as they might in conversation, what they produce is not writing or talk or dialogue. Unfortunately, writing that gives the impression of being talk is not achieved that easily, even by the best novelists and dramatists.

Chapter VIII

Brevity: The Soul of It

> Words are like leaves; and where they most abound
> Much fruit of sense beneath is rarely found.
>
> *Pope*

Writing too much is a common fault. An overload of reading is the obvious result. A chemist grumbles that if during every working hour of a year he were to read the articles published that year in his special field, he would at the end of the twelve months be behind in his reading by ten years. A college professor complains that he receives a pound a day of notices, reports, book advertising, and articles—not only more than he can read but more than his wastebasket can hold. And a vice president estimates that skimming the material that a day brings to his desk would take him forty-eight hours. Exhausted readers take courses to improve their reading speeds, delegate to others the task of sifting the towering piles of written matter, and curse the easy and inexpensive methods of reproduction that encourage the deluge.

It used to be feasible just to tell a porter to supply more towels to the company lavatories. Now memorandums on the subject are dictated, typed, reproduced, distributed, read (by some recipients), filed, stored, and sometimes even retrieved. In industry few people talk; they write instead. In fact, some companies supply pads inscribed, "Don't say it; write it." And everyone does—at length. Speeches are preprinted, printed, and reprinted. Inexhaustible writers on science and technology stretch their articles to the utmost even for journals known to be as much as a year behind in publishing. Writers vie at dashing off the windiest letters, the longest memorandums, and the most diffuse reports—and at addressing them to the most people.

Some writers broadcast every paper as though they must convince the whole company that they are working. Supervisors should prevent this discourtesy to busy readers and should themselves avoid the error of telling their whole business world what only a few people need to know. Writers can show consideration for others by selecting judiciously the readers to whom they address their pages.

An even more successful way to reduce the flood of words is to delete unnecessary material. The amount of detail in any writing for industry should depend not on a writer's infatuation with his subject but on his reader's needs. As Schopenhauer wrote, "True brevity of expression consists in everywhere saying only what is worth saying, and in avoiding tedious detail about things which everyone can supply for himself." The specialist who has written an overlong report has catered to his own interests, and in doing so he has wasted his reader's time. Though suffering readers may doubt it, this writer usually knows that much of his material is of interest to no one but himself—and possibly his doting mother. He also knows that most of his report is suitable only for fellow specialists, that those educated in science and technology can read some of it, but that only a small part is of general interest in his company. If he is pressed hard, he can identify this material accurately.

First he should discard the material of personal interest. Even the files do not need detailed reports of his unsuccessful attempts to build equipment or to find pure chemicals if there is nothing to be learned from those attempts. Then he should place in appendices a large part of the material that interests only specialists. Detailed graphs and tables, for example, belong there, and only representative data need appear in the body of the report. But some writers are reluctant to relegate any material to appendices. When a national engineering society began publishing only representative data, loud screams and groans haunted the editors, who had sent the details to the American Documentation Institute, from which they could be retrieved easily if anyone needed them. But only the writers screamed and groaned—and only about their own articles; each writer saw clearly the advantage of printing only representative data in the articles of other engineers. And readers expressed pleasure. The material filed with the A.D.I. was seldom requested, yet for many years this society had published the superfluous data on pages needed for other articles.

The more material a writer can place in appendices the better. He saves the time of busy readers who try to skip such material. He gains readers because his shortened report is more attractive. And he achieves a reputation for thinking clearly and knowing his subject well because his readers, freed from the clutter of unnecessary details, can understand his main points more easily.

A writer should be careful not to supply background and explanation that his reader knows, especially after telling the reader that he knows it. Experienced scholars are less prone to this weakness than are recent products of graduate schools. A little learning can make a very tiring writer. A reader of a medical report written by a new M.D. is lucky if it mentions a BMR without supplying an introduction to all the ductless glands. A young botanist may summarize the general information about nuclear reactors before even hinting at what happened to his irradiated stringbeans. And the new Ph.D. in chemistry will not only explain everything mentioned in his paper but will regale his readers with his favorite professor's theories—even those only remotely connected with the subject. This tendency to squeeze out all the information one knows is probably left over from taking college examinations.

In functional prose, explanations are most useful where they are needed. If the explanations relate to point three of the paper, they should appear at point three. If a few sentences will make result two easier to understand, the writer should place those few sentences just where the reader needs them. When a writer places explanations where they are helpful, he is less likely to explain more than is necessary. When a writer is discussing point three or result two, he shares his reader's eagerness to get on with the subject, and he explains briefly. But if his introduction is a blank in his mind, he may seize this explanatory material and detail it until his introduction seems long enough. Such long-windedness is a disfavor to one's subject and a discourtesy to readers. As Jerome B. Wiesner points out, "More information does not automatically mean better information. . . . The user should be informed, not overwhelmed." [1]

Even after a writer has reduced his subject matter, his report may still be too long because of a wordy style. Therefore, after discarding unnecessary details and adapting his material to his readers, he should examine his writing for verbosity and rigorously delete unnecessary words.

Much informational prose expresses a single thought in words enough for ten thoughts. In many reports words obscure the sense so thoroughly that readers have to unearth the meaning and rephrase it to understand it. One supervisor wrote the following instruction, "Prior to proceeding to the further and succeeding step of written communication, make every reasonable effort to plan ahead in orderly fashion and to place your plan in a written form that clearly marks major and minor divisions." His readers eventually translated this as "Before writing, outline." But they felt that they had winnowed the meaning in spite of the writer.

[1] *Where Science and Politics Meet* (McGraw-Hill Book Company, New York, 1965), p. 158.

Readers of professional journals, government documents, textbooks, and industrial reports develop, through practice, a facility for this kind of translation. But I never heard of anyone who grew to like it. Being forced to sift a paragraph of words to get one sentence of meaning is always annoying, and when a reader is busy or tired, it is exasperating. Yet writers, showing no consideration for their readers, dilute their meaning in oceans of words. The only extenuation that I have ever found for them is that they are totally unaware of the windiness of their writing. Among the most verbose writings in government and industry are complaints about wordiness. No one, apparently, minds his own prolixity, but everyone objects to the prolixity of others.

The first step, then, in acquiring a brief style is self-consciousness. I have seen instructors force this upon students by eliminating one third of the words on a page without sacrificing any thoughts. A public demonstration leaves a lasting impression on the victim whose page was reduced, but many in the amused audience do not apply the lesson to their own work. Like the verbose complainers, they see only the wordiness of others.

A less painful way to learn brevity is to study examples of common kinds of wordiness and to eliminate those kinds from one's writing. Functional prose is prone to seven kinds of wordiness, which I discuss under the headings *Tautology, Dilute Verbs, Hiccups, Roundabout Constructions, Hedging and Intensifying, Pointless Words and Phrases,* and *False Elegance.* These seven faults of style are not unrelated to the seven deadly sins, particularly Pride, Envy, and Sloth.

If a writer guilty of these principal kinds of wordiness eliminates them from his writing, he gains effectiveness. Cogency is a Siamese twin of brevity. Some verbiage may be struck out as soon as it is found; removing other kinds requires rephrasing. At first writers may spend hours revising for brevity. But shortly wordiness disappears from their first drafts because after they have repeatedly taken out unnecessary words and phrases, they will avoid them. Finally wordiness will disappear even in their speech, the improvement in speech being, as those master tautologists the advertisers write, "an extra added bonus."

TAUTOLOGY

Tautology—the unnecessary repetition of an idea in other words— results from failure to consider meaning. If he who writes *round in shape, twelve feet by twenty feet in size, beige in color,* and *in the range of ten to seventy-five pages* will think about meanings, he will write instead *round, twelve by twenty feet, beige,* and *ten to seventy-five pages.* Examining the following common examples of tautology should increase a writer's sensitivity to the fault.

EXAMPLE	DISCUSSION AND ILLUSTRATION
about	If *about* precedes what is clearly stated as an estimate or approximation, omit *about.*

> *Wordy:* He estimated the profits as about one million dollars.
>
> *Improved:* He estimated the profits as one million dollars.
>
> *Wordy:* He reads about twenty to thirty articles each week.
>
> *Improved:* He reads twenty to thirty articles each week.

a.c. current d.c. current	Use *a.c.* and *d.c.* or *alternating current* and *direct current* to avoid the repetition of *current.*
adequate enough	Use either of these words, but not both.
advance forward	Use *advance.*
advance planning advance warning	Omit *advance* because the meaning is contained in *planning* and *warning.*
and etc.	*Et cetera* means *and other things, and so forth.* Omit *and.*
any and all	Use *any* or *all.*

> *Wordy:* Any and all employees are invited to the picnic.
>
> *Improved:* All employees are invited to the picnic.
>
> *Wordy:* Any and all accidents should be reported on form A.
>
> *Improved:* Any accidents should be reported on form A.

as a usual rule
  as a general rule
  generally as a rule
  as a rule usually
	Use *as a rule, generally,* or *usually.*

at an early date	Avoid this wordy business cliché. There are many acceptable words that mean *soon.* And a specific date is helpful to a reader.
at hand, in hand	These are business clichés.

> *Commercial and wordy:* I have your letter of July second at hand (*or* in hand). I am sending the samples you requested.
>
> *Correct:* I am sending the samples you requested in your letter of July second.

EXAMPLE	DISCUSSION AND ILLUSTRATION

at present, at the present time

Omit these business clichés when the verb indicates present time. If a time word is needed, the simple word *now* is useful.

Commercial and wordy: He is reviewing the matter at the present time.

Improved: He is reviewing the matter.

attached hereto

Use *attached* alone.

Redundant: Please file the notices attached hereto.

Improved: Please file the attached notices.

When it is feasible to omit *attached*, do so for brevity and simplicity: *Please file these notices.*

attach together

Use *attach*.

basic fundamentals

What other kind?

be in receipt of

In many sentences this business cliché is unnecessary; in others it should be replaced by a simple reference to what the writer has received.

Commercial: I am in receipt of the samples I requested. Thank you for sending them promptly.

We are in receipt of your letter of March 16. We will ship the order therein immediately.

Correct: Thank you for sending promptly the samples I requested.

We are shipping your order of March 16 today.

before in the past

Use *before* or *in the past* or neither.

Wordy: This division has never before in the past used form B.

Improved (1): This division has never before used form B.

Improved (2): This division has never used form B.

(Note the difference in meaning. Improved sentence 1 implies that form B is being used or will be used. Improved sentence 2 does not imply this.)

brief in duration

Use *brief, quick,* or *fast* without *duration*.

by return mail

This business cliché comes from an era of infrequent mails, when *return mail* meant something. Today it is meaningless. If an indication of time is necessary, use *today, next week,* or a specific date.

but that

Redundant: I had no doubt but that he would fail.

Improved: I had no doubt that he would fail.

EXAMPLE	DISCUSSION AND ILLUSTRATION

by the use of

Use *by* when it conveys the meaning.

> *Redundant:* He proved his point by the use of examples from his experience.
>
> *Improved:* He proved his point by examples from his experience.

circle around

Use *circle.*

circulate around

Use *circulate.*

collect together
  combine together
  connect together
  consolidate together
  cooperate together
  couple together

There is no other way to *collect, combine, connect, consolidate, cooperate, couple.*

> *Redundant:* He combined their suggestions together in his report.
>
> *Improved:* He combined their suggestions in his report.

consensus of opinion

Consensus means a collective opinion; therefore this popular phrase is redundant.

> *Redundant:* The consensus of opinion was that we should act immediately.
>
> *Improved:* The consensus was that we should act immediately.

consequent results

Results are consequential.

> *Redundant:* The consequent results are discussed on page twenty.
>
> *Improved:* The results are discussed on page twenty.
>
> *or*
>
> The consequences are discussed on page twenty.

contents duly noted

Omit this business cliché. Your correspondent assumes that you have read the letter you are answering.

continue to remain

Remain conveys the idea of continuing.

> *Redundant:* Regardless of the treatment, the spot continued to remain.
>
> *Improved:* Regardless of the treatment, the spot remained.
>
> *Redundant:* The report indicated that the problem continued to remain unsolved
>
> *Improved:* The report indicated that the problem remained unsolved.

desirable benefits

Because a benefit is usually desirable, the adjective is unnecessary; however a writer may wish to describe undesirable benefits: *He refused the demeaning benefits offered by the Society for the Assistance of the Incompetent Needy.*

EXAMPLE

DISCUSSION AND ILLUSTRATION

disappear from sight

Omit *from sight* unless there is a need to distinguish sight from sound or taste.

early beginnings

Because a beginning is the earliest step, the start, or the first stage, the word *early* is unnecessary.

> *Redundant:*   He discussed the early beginnings of the company.
>
> *Improved:*   He discussed the beginnings of the company.
>
>   *or*
>
>   He discussed the founding of the company.

enclosed herein
   enclosed herewith

Enclosed means that something is sent in the same envelope or package.

> *Redundant:*   Enclosed herewith is the report of the meeting. You will be interested in page three.
>
> *Improved:*   You will be interested in page three of the enclosed report of the meeting.

(Note: *Enclosed* is nearly always unnecessary in business letters because enclosures are listed at the end. *Enclosed please find* is a hackneyed beginning.)

end result
   final result

Use *result* unless there is a need to distinguish.

endorse on the back

Endorse means to write on the back.

equally as good as

As good as and *equally good* are the same.

> *Redundant:*   Our machine is equally as good as this one.
>
> *Improved:*   Our machine is as good as this one.
>
>   *or*
>
>   The machines are equally good.

fast in action

The attribute *fast* implies action unless the context indicates that *secure* is meant.

> *Redundant:*   We need not worry about his completing the job on time because he is fast in action.
>
> *Improved:*   We need not worry about his completing the job on time because he works fast.
>
>   We need not worry about his completing the job on time because he is fast.

EXAMPLE	DISCUSSION AND ILLUSTRATION

few in number Use *few*.

> *Redundant:* The samples were too few in number for the experiment.
>
> *Improved:* The samples were too few for the experiment.

final completion
final ending
final upshot

The many steps involved in completing legal and financial procedures do make one long occasionally for the *final completion, final ending,* or *final upshot.* But because whatever is completed or ended is wholly finished, the adjective should be omitted. An *upshot* is a final outcome.

first beginnings See *early beginnings.*

> *Redundant:* He discussed the first beginnings of his plan.
>
> *Improved:* He discussed the conception of his plan.
>
> *or*
>
> He discussed the first step in his plan.

following after Use *following* or *after*.

> *Redundant:* Following after the dinner came the reception for honored guests.
>
> *Improved:* After the dinner came the reception for honored guests.

funeral obsequies Use *funeral rites* or *obsequies.*

hopeful optimism Use *hope* or *optimism.*

if and when Use *if* or *when.*

important essentials Essentials are important, vital, indispensable.

> *Redundant:* The important essentials of this plan are . . .
>
> *Improved:* The essentials of this plan are . . .
>
> *or*
>
> The important aspects of this plan are . . .

in my opinion I think Use *in my opinion* or *I think.*

in the course of Use *during* or *in* when it conveys your meaning.

in the form of This phrase is usually unnecessary.

> *Wordy:* They get their profits in the form of tax rebates.
>
> *Improved:* They get their profits as tax rebates.
>
> *Acceptable:* He referred to energy in the form of heat.

EXAMPLE	DISCUSSION AND ILLUSTRATION

in the range of ten to twenty million

As *ten to twenty million* is a range, there is no need to say so.

Redundant: He has in the range of ten to twenty million dollars in cash.

Improved: He has ten to twenty million dollars in cash.

in the same way as described

Use *in the same way* or *as described*, but not both.

Redundant: The second group was injected in the same way as described.

Improved: The second group was injected in the same way.

or

The second group was injected as described.

in the shape of

This is usually unnecessary.

Redundant: He gets his recreation in the shape of fishing.

Improved: He gets his recreation fishing.

Acceptable: He ordered a cake in the shape of a horseshoe.

in this day and age   Use *today*.
join together   Use *join*.
joint cooperation

Cooperation is a joint effort.

Redundant: The work represents their joint cooperation.

Improved: The work represents their joint efforts.

or

They cooperated on this work.

joint partnership   Use *partnership*.
just exactly

Use one or the other.

Redundant: Their solution looks just exactly like ours.

Improved: Their solution looks exactly like ours.

Their solution looks just like ours.

large in size

See *larger-sized*.

Redundant: The samples were large in size.

Improved: The samples were large.

larger-sized
** smaller-sized**

Larger and *smaller* usually clearly indicate size.

Wordy: a larger-sized beaker, a smaller-sized package

Improved: a larger beaker, a smaller package

EXAMPLE	DISCUSSION AND ILLUSTRATION

main essentials   See *important essentials.*

melt down   Use *melt.*
  melt up

merge together   Use *merge* or *mingle* or *mix.*
  mingle together
  mix together

minimize as far as possible   Use *minimize.*

modern methods of today   Use *modern methods* or *methods of today.*

more preferable   Use *preferable.*

mutual cooperation   *Cooperation* is mutual.

> *Redundant:* He asked the divisions to give their mutual cooperation to the project.
>
> *Improved:* He asked the divisions to cooperate on the project.

necessary requisite   There is no other kind of requisite.

> *Redundant:* The bachelor's degree is a necessary requisite for matriculation.
>
> *Improved:* The bachelor's degree is a requisite for matriculation.
>
> *or*
>
> The bachelor's degree is required for matriculation.
>
> *Redundant:* Larger equipment is a necessary requisite for the experiment.
>
> *Improved:* Larger equipment is necessary for the experiment.
>
> *or*
>
> The experiment requires larger equipment.

neurogenic in orgin   Use *neurogenic.*

9 A.M. in the morning   Use *9 A.M.* or *nine o'clock in the morning.*

obsequies for the dead   For anyone else?

one and the same   Use *the same.*

personal friend   Use *friend* unless it is necessary to distinguish.

plan ahead   Use *plan.* Futurity is inherent in *plan.*
  plan in advance
  plan for the future

prolong the duration   Use *prolong.*

reason is because   Use *reason is that* or *because.*

> *Incorrect:* The reason for making the change is because . . .
>
> *Improved:* The reason for making the change is that . . .

EXAMPLE
DISCUSSION AND ILLUSTRATION

> *or*
> The change will be made because . . .

remand back	Use *remand.*
repeat the same (story, idea, etc.)	Use *repeat the* (story, idea, etc.).
resultant effect	Use *effect.*
seems apparent	Use *seems* or *is apparent.*
separate and distinct	One is enough or too much. *The seven steps* is usually better than *the seven separate and distinct steps.*
state the point that stress the point that	Omit *the point.*
surrounding circumstances	*Circumstances* are surrounding conditions.

> *Redundant:* The circumstances surrounding his dismissal were the basis of the union complaint.
>
> *Improved:* The circumstances of his dismissal . . .

single unit	Use *unit.*
still continue	Use *continue.*
summer months	Use *summer* or *June, July, and August.*
ten miles distant from	Use *ten miles from.*
three hours of time	Use *three hours.*
throughout the entire	Use *throughout* or *in the entire.*
to the northward	Use *to the north* or *northward.*
total effect of all this	Use *total effect* or *effect of all this.*
true facts	Use *facts* or *truths.*
ultimate end	Use *end.*
veritable	Omit it when it is unnecessary. It usually is.
ways and means	Writers usually mean one or the other, not this tired combination, unless it is the name of a committee.

Some writers do not even bother to repeat a meaning in other words; they use the same words. This strange use occurs when advertisers, having destroyed the meaning of a word, repeat the word in an attempt to restore its meaning. If they had not used *portable*, for example, to describe what only a derrick can lift, they would not need the phrase *portable portable TV sets.* And if *small* and *compact* had not been used for *large*, advertisers of cars would not need the *small small car* and the *small compact.* Writers of functional prose should not mangle language in this ridiculous way, which makes them sound like tellers of children's stories: "And so then the teensy, weensy, tiny Little Bear said. . . ."

Ineffective repetition of words also occurs through failure to revise carefully. The first *made* should have been deleted from the following newspaper sentence:

> However, it is expected that new laboratory made variants on the antibiotic molecule can be made.

If a writer who has a propensity for careless repetition does not train himself to find and eliminate it in revision, he will write sentences like this one from a chapter news letter of a technical writing society:

> Before we meet to check a rough draft or to brief you on developments, try to have your questions ready beforehand.

The repetition and the tautology illustrated in this section are pitfalls for teachers and public speakers, who necessarily repeat when lecturing. When they write, they should revise carefully to avoid such tautology as appeared in Jack Paar's letter to a network executive: "If I have acted hastily on an impulse. . . ."

DILUTE VERBS

Common in functional prose is the weakened or dilute verb. Some writers avoid a specific verb like *consider;* they choose instead a general verb of little meaning like *take* or *give* and add the noun *consideration* with the necessary prepositions, as in *take into consideration* and *give consideration to, devote consideration to,* and *expend consideration on.* Thus they not only use three words to do the work of one, but they also take the meaning from the strongest word in a sentence, the verb, and place the meaning in a noun that has a subordinate position. They flout the nature of the English sentence, and this results in wordiness and poor emphasis. Such writers never *study* a subject; they *make a study of* a subject. Or when they want to impress readers, they *undertake a study of* a subject. They do not *analyze;* they *make an analysis* (or *analyzation*) *of;* they never *prove;* they *give proof of;* they do not *measure;* they *take the measurements of;* they never *approximate;* they *make approximations of;* their data do not *agree* but *are found to be in agreement* (they put the dilute verb in the passive voice and thus achieve more awkwardness and poorer emphasis); they do not *examine;* they *make* or *perform examinations of;* and they never *purify* but in their pompous, long-winded way *achieve purification of.*

Dilute verbs and the use of the passive voice instead of the active voice (Chapter XI) give to scientific and technological writing its characteristic verbose, awkward, and vague style. Using specific active verbs, one might write, "The members of the committee agreed to examine secretarial salaries and report to the president by March first." But this is too simple, direct, and clear for a recording secretary who translates it into dilute passive verbs: "The members of the committee were found to be in agreement that an examination of secretarial salaries should be made by the committee and a report should be submitted to the president by or on March first." Weak as a jigger of Scotch in a pitcher of water, this is neither good liquor nor good water.

Such dilute verbs as the following weaken style or, in the words of this debilitated style, *give a weakness to it.*

DILUTE VERB	SUGGESTION	EXAMPLE	
achieve purification	Use *purify.*	*Wordy:*	An expert will achieve purification of this water.
		Improved:	An expert will purify this water.
are found to be in agreement	Use *agree.*	*Wordy:*	The values are found to be in agreement.
		Improved:	The values agree.
analyses were made	Use *analyze.*	*Wordy:*	Analyses were made of each sample.
		Improved:	Each sample was analyzed.
is applicable	Use *applies.*		
carry on the work of developing	Use *develop.*		
connection is made	Use *connects.*	*Wordy:*	The connection is made by pipes. . . .
		Improved:	Pipes connect. . . .
carry out, has been carried out	Avoid this phrase when nothing is carried.	*Wordy:*	The installation of the television station has been carried out.
		Improved:	The television station was installed.
carry out experiments	Use *experiment.*		
carry out mixing	Use *mix.*		
carry out purification	Use *purify.*		
is characterized by has the character of	Use *be* or *have* or *resemble* or *look like* when suitable.	*Wordy:*	Her work is characterized by errors.
		Improved:	Her work has many errors. Her work is inaccurate.
		Wordy:	This element has the character of several less common elements.
		Improved:	This element resembles several less common ones.

DILUTE VERB	SUGGESTION	EXAMPLE	
bring to a conclusion	Use *conclude, complete, end, finish.*		
is corrective of	Use *corrects.*		
arrive at a decision	Use *decide,* at least sometimes. Occasionally one must decide without the delay suggested by *arrive at.*		
determine detection	Use *detect* or *determine.*	*Wordy:*	The detection of x is determined by the method.
		Improved:	We detect x by the method. The method determines x.
failed to find	Use the negative, at least occasionally.	*Wordy:*	They have failed to find an answer.
		Improved:	They have not found an answer.
is found to be	Use *be.*	*Wordy:*	The recommendation is found to be preferable.
		Improved:	This recommendation is preferable.
give an indication of	Use *indicate.*		
give proof of	Use *prove.*		
give a weakness to	Use *weaken.*	*Wordy:*	This finding gives a weakness to his conclusions.
		Improved:	This finding weakens his conclusions.
is indicative of	Use *indicate.*	*Wordy:*	This is indicative of carelessness.
		Improved:	This indicates carelessness.
institute an improvement in	Use *improve.*	*Wordy:*	His method would institute an improvement in the process.
		Improved:	His method would improve the process.
are known to be, is known to be	Use *are* or *is* except in rare instances.	*Wordy:*	The reaction time is known to be unreliable.
		Improved:	The reaction time is unreliable.
		Exception:	Although the readings of this operator are known to be reliable, he insists upon checking them.

DILUTE VERB	SUGGESTION	EXAMPLE
make adjustments to	Use *adjust.*	
make an approximation of	Use *approximate.*	
make an examination of	Use *examine.*	
make an exception of	Use *except.*	
make mention of	Use *mention.*	
make out a list	Use *list.*	
make a study of	Use *study.*	
obtain an increase or decrease in temperature	Use *raise* or *lower* temperature.	
are of the opinion that	*Think that* and *believe that* are briefer.	*Wordy:* We are of the opinion that the process is economical. *Improved:* We think that the process is economical.
perform an examination of	Use *examine.*	
proceed to separate	Use *separate.*	
present a conclusion	Use *conclude* if that is what you mean.	
present a report	Use *report.*	
present a summary	Use *summarize.*	
put to use in (building, measuring, purifying, etc.)	Use *build, measure, purify; used for building, measuring, purifying.*	*Wordy:* The old wood was put to use in building the garage. *Improved:* The old wood was used to build the garage. *or* He built the garage of the old wood.
was seen, was noted	In many sentences these are unnecessary and weak.	*Wordy:* A large increase in volume was seen. *Improved:* Volume increased by 2,500 sales. *Wordy and weak:* The temperature was noted to be 103°F. This suggested that . . . . *Improved:* The temperature of 103°F suggested that . . . .
succeed in doing, in making, in measuring, in estimating, etc.	Omit *succeed in.* Use *do, make, measure, estimate,* etc.	
is suggestive of	Use *suggests.*	
take cognizance of	Use *note, notice, heed.*	
take into consideration	Use *consider.*	
undertake a study of	Use *study.*	

HICCUPS

Closely related to the dilution of verbs is the insertion of unnecessary prepositions and adverbs. This clutters writing with useless words and creates a jumpy effect as though the writer had the hiccups. "Up to the time he came out from the office to follow up the problems outside of the plant, we never met up. Later on we cooperated together checking up on speeding up the sealing off of pipes, and the number of problems was reduced down. And every job ended up with a good write-up when we were paid off." Such speech or writing sounds uneducated in some sections of the United States, and in other sections it suggests a movie gangster. A study of the following examples should help writers to avoid some of these hiccups.

PHRASE WITH UNNECESSARY PREPOSITION OR ADVERB	SUGGESTED IMPROVEMENT	EXAMPLE	

as to
  as regards
  in regard to
	Use *about* or some other simple preposition.	*Poor:*	Will they question him in regard to the patent?

		Improved:	Will they question him about the patent?
		Poor:	He will speak as regards taxes.
		Improved:	He will speak on taxes.
as to whether	Omit *as to* whenever possible.	*Poor:*	They will decide as to whether the experiment will continue.
		Improved:	They will decide whether the experiment will continue.
at about eight o'clock	Use *about eight o'clock*.	*Poor:*	They will meet in the auditorium at about eight o'clock.
		Improved:	They will meet in the auditorium about eight o'clock.
at above, at below	Use *above, below*.	*Poor:*	This reaction occurs at above 97°F.
		Improved:	This occurs above 97°F
back of	Use *behind* when that is the meaning.	*Poor:*	The garage is back of the research building.
		Improved:	The garage is behind the research building.

PHRASE WITH UNNECESSARY PREPOSITION OR ADVERB	SUGGESTED IMPROVEMENT	EXAMPLE	
call for	Use *demand, require*.	*Poor:*	The project calls for $5,000.
		Improved:	The project requires $5,000.
check into, check upon, check on	Use *check*.		
climb up, close down, close up	Use *climb* and *close*.		
connect up	Use *connect*.	*Poor:*	He will connect Pipe A up with Pipe B.
		Improved:	He will connect Pipe A with Pipe B.
		Poor:	He will connect the two small pipes up with the pump.
		Improved:	He will connect the two small pipes with the pump.
		Poor:	He connects this response up with a neurosis.
		Improved:	He connects this response with a neurosis.
count up	Do not use *for count*.	*Poor:*	He counted up the money in the till.
		Improved:	He counted the money in the till.
debate about	Use *debate*.		
decide on	Use *decide, select*.		
descend down	Use *descend*.		
divide up	Use *divide*.		
empty out	Use *empty*. A tank is just as empty when it is emptied as when it is emptied out.		
end up	Use *end*.		
enter in, enter into	Use *enter*.	*Poor:*	The wires enter into the thermocouple at B.
		Improved:	The wires enter the thermocouple at B.
face up to	Use *face*.	*Poor:*	He faced up to his shortcomings.
		Improved:	He faced his shortcomings.

PHRASE WITH UNNECESSARY PREPOSITION OR ADVERB	SUGGESTED IMPROVEMENT	EXAMPLE	
figure out	Use *understand*.	Poor:	He could not figure out the meaning.
		Improved:	He could not understand the meaning.
file away	Use *file*. The redundancy may reflect the common experience that any wanted paper seems to be filed far away, probably in Outer Mongolia.	Poor:	Please file away this report.
		Improved:	Please file this report.
first initiated	Use *initiated*.		
follow after follow up	Use *follow*. There is no escaping the doctor's *follow-up treatment* and the *follow-up form* of the Personnel Department, but otherwise avoid the unnecessary *up*.		
generally agreed	Use *agreed*.		
go into	Prefer *investigate* or *examine* if that is what you mean.		
go on with	Use *continue*.		
head up	Use *head*.		
hoist up	Use *hoist*.		
in between	Use *between*.		
inside of	Use *inside* or *within*.	Poor:	He placed the wires inside of the housing.
		Improved:	He placed the wires inside the housing.
		Poor:	He will leave inside of three hours.
		Improved:	He will leave within three hours.
join up	Use *join*.		
know about	Use *know*.	Poor:	He knows about carpentry.
		Improved:	He knows carpentry.
later on	Use *later*.		
level off	Use *level*.		
link up	Use *link*.		
lose out on	Use *lose*.		

PHRASE WITH UNNECESSARY PREPOSITION OR ADVERB	SUGGESTED IMPROVEMENT	EXAMPLE	
meet up with	Use *meet*.		
miss out on	Use *miss*.		
of between	Use *to* instead of *between*.	*Poor:*	widths of between two and three inches, speeds of between sixty and eighty
		Improved:	widths of two to three inches, speeds of sixty to eighty miles
of from	Omit *from*.	*Poor:*	heights of from fifty to sixty feet, distances of from ten to twenty miles
		Improved:	heights of fifty to sixty feet, distances of ten to twenty miles
off of	Omit *of*.	*Poor:*	He took the apparatus off of the table.
		Improved:	He took the apparatus off the table *or* from the table.
		Poor:	He removed the name off of his accounts.
		Improved:	He removed the name from his accounts.
open up	Use *open*.		
out of	Use *of*.	*Poor:*	Only two out of the five drugs were approved.
		Improved:	Only two of the five drugs were approved.
outside of	Use *outside* or *besides* or *except*.	*Poor:*	He placed the extinguisher outside of the laboratory.
		Improved:	He placed the extinguisher outside the laboratory.
		Poor:	No one outside of my supervisor knows that I am leaving.
		Improved:	No one besides my supervisor knows that I am leaving. No one except my supervisor knows that I am leaving.

PHRASE WITH UNNECESSARY PREPOSITION OR ADVERB	SUGGESTED IMPROVEMENT	EXAMPLE	
over with	Use *over* or *ended*.	*Poor:*	The recruiting is over with.
		Improved:	The recruiting is over. The recruiting is ended.
take off	Use *remove*.	*Poor:*	He took off the extra charge.
		Improved:	He removed the extra charge.
pay up	Use *pay*.		
penetrate into	Use *penetrate*.		
plan on	Use *plan*.		
protrude out	Use *protrude*.		
raise up	Use *raise*.		
recall back	Use *recall*.		
recur again	Use *recur*.		
reduce down, refer back, remand back, repeat again, return again, return back, revert back	Use *reduce, refer, remand, repeat, return, revert*.		
rest up	Use *rest*.		
resume again	Use *resume*.		
retreat back	Use *retreat*.		
seal off	Use *seal*.		
speed up	Use *speed, accelerate,* or *hasten*.		
spell out	Use *explain, detail*.		
still remain	Use *remain*.		
succeed in doing	Use *do*.		
termed as	Use *termed*.		
try out	Use *test* except for the theatre and sports.		
weigh out	Use *weigh*.		
win out	Use *win*.		
up to this time	Use *before*.		
write up (*verb*)	Use *write*.		

ROUNDABOUT CONSTRUCTIONS

Weak indirect constructions and circuitous phrasing waste a reader's time. Even worse, they weaken thoughts, frequently the very thoughts that the writer wishes to stress. "There is a treatment available. It consists of . . ." is a typical example, for many roundabout constructions begin with *there is* or *there are* and waste a sentence to state that something exists. Most of these constructions are easily improved; the eight words become four words: "The treatment consists of. . . ." The following examples also illustrate the gain in directness and strength achieved by eliminating weak indirect constructions. (The poor example is the first one in each numbered group.)

1. There are three active ingredients in these tablets. They are . . . .
   The three active ingredients in these tablets are . . . .
2. There are six causes that produce poor morale in our division. They are . . . .
   The six causes of poor morale in our divisions are . . . .
3. There were at least a hundred chemicals that were added to the list.
   At least a hundred chemicals were added to the list.
4. It is with the third process that this paper is concerned.
   This paper concerns the third process.
   The third process, the subject of this paper, reveals that . . . .
5. This is a most important section of your proposal and it should be prepared carefully.
   This most important section of your proposal should be prepared carefully.
   Prepare carefully this most important section of your proposal.
6. It might be expected that there would be some exceptions to this treatment.
   Some exceptions to this treatment might be expected.
7. It appears that the new formulation is better than the old.
   The new formulation seems better than the old.
8. In the case of polymer studies it was shown that . . . .
   Polymer studies showed . . . .
9. In the case of experiments with dogs it was proved that . . . .
   Experiments with dogs proved that . . . .
10. The fact that the chemicals were impure caused the delay.
    The impurity of the chemicals caused the delay.
11. If the chemical is not one listed on the chart . . . .
    If the chemical is not listed on the chart . . . .
12. There is no doubt that he will be promoted.
    Doubtless he will be promoted.
13. It is obvious that the law will pass.
    Obviously the law will pass.
    The law will pass.
14. In a previous article by Cope and Dodge (1), it was shown that . . . .
    Cope and Dodge (1) showed that . . . .

The writers of indirect constructions 1 to 5 stated the existence or importance of their subjects in main clauses and stated their principal thoughts in other sentences or clauses. Presenting the main thought succinctly in the main clause is a more effective and a neater construction.

Examples 6 and 7, which have oblique wording, waste the main construction on unimportant thoughts and bury the main thoughts in subordinate constructions.

Examples 8 and 9 begin with the unnecessary and somewhat misleading phrase *in the case of*, a common cause of wordiness, as are its counterparts *the fact that* (sentence 10), *in this respect, with regard to, from the point of view of, in regard to, with reference to, in reference to, insofar as . . . is concerned, because of the fact that*, and *with relation to*.

The writer of sentence 11 subordinated the main verb *listed* by introducing an unnecessary *one* and by employing *listed* as a participle. These examples illustrate upside-down subordination as well as wordiness, as do sentences 12 and 13, in which a main clause performs the work of an adverb.

Sentence 14 contains the cumbersome main clause *it was shown that*, which has some equally burdensome relatives: *it was stated that, it was proved that, it was argued that, it was thought that* (or *felt that*), *the statement was made that*. Some writers even use *the thing that I have in mind* for *goal* or *plan*. Such wordy and awkward constructions are so common in journals of science and engineering that a reader receives the impression that no one ever states anything although the book or article has an author: "In Bacon's essay the statement is made that . . ."; "In Van Antwerpen's column the point is made that . . . ." Apparently gremlins place these statements, arguments, and points in the writings of innocent authors, who incidentally are never mentioned except in the possessive case, as though they owned the articles or books but had not written them. One suspects that the next step will be: "In Wiley's new book on designing servomechanisms and regulating systems it is stated that . . ."; and the names of Harold Chestnut and Robert W. Mayer, the authors, will not be mentioned. Some writers in industry and government have evaded responsibility so often in their writing that they now evade for other writers too.

HEDGING AND INTENSIFYING

"It seems that it might possibly be very wise to follow this procedure if no better one is proposed," states (if I may use so strong a word about so noncommittal a sentence) a writer. He not only adds hedge to hedge (*seems, might, possibly, if*), but then ironically intensifies the idea by *very*. The best advice for the writer of such a passage is—"Cut those hedges; prune those intensifiers."

An antipathy to forthright statements may reflect a scientist's honest caution. But placing hedge after hedge in a single sentence suggests a timid, self-protective, indecisive writer. This Milquetoast returns from a meeting that voted unanimously for a holiday on October twelfth and tells his secretary, "We may perhaps have a holiday on October twelfth if nothing happens to interfere." He writes to his supervisor, "We expect to complete the runs on the new machine tomorrow if there are no absences or unanticipated interruptions." I knew one writer who qualified even the inevitable. Asked to name his beneficiaries, he wrote, "If by some chance I should die, distribute my company benefits as follows . . . ."

Like other kinds of wordiness, hedging is contagious. An aggressive, self-confident executive who was used to making decisions for his own company took an important post in a large corporation. He conferred with me weekly about his writing.

At the end of our second meeting he said, "Well, I'll see you at the same time next week if nothing interferes."

"Do you expect something to interfere?"

He banged his fist on the desk. "No I don't expect anything to interfere." Because of my sex he followed this with only mild profanity. "I'm beginning to hedge and qualify like everyone else around here. I sound like a green kid. It's all that stuff I read and listen to. I'll see you next week—without fail."

Some of the most prolific hedgers in industry are not timid. One of them was the most aggressive person I have ever taught. But as soon as he wrote, he sounded as awkward and unsure as a shy boy at his first party. Later he told me that he had been taught to hedge by a timid supervisor. Writing without excessive hedging would have cost him his job. By the time he left that supervisor, the hedging that he had practiced for years had become a deep-seated habit. When I met him he was about to lose an important position because of lack of forcefulness in his writing.

Overuse of intensives is also contagious, and it too creates a poor impression. Qualifying absolutes—*most unique, absolutely perfect, more paramount, very essential*—gives an impression of illogic or carelessness (Chapter X). Conversational intensives, which are inappropriate in formal writing, make writers sound too casual and relaxed. For example, "The color did not change" is preferable to "The color did not change at all." And "It was impossible to obtain results" is clear and strong, but "It was quite impossible to obtain results" suggests to some readers that the writer is attempting to conceal that he did not try hard enough.

Sometimes intensives worn out by use retaliate by weakening instead of strengthening the meaning. Hollywood has so overworked *colossal*, *supercolossal,* and *epic* that when a theatre advertises the coming of a supercolossal epic, movie-goers note the date to avoid a B minus picture. In the same way *very* and *extremely* may weaken the words they modify. When a high school English teacher tells her students that an assigned book is *interesting,* they accept her statement with only slight reservations about the peculiar reading tastes of English teachers. But when she says that a book is *very interesting* or *extremely interesting,* their eyes glaze with the resistance of a customer being told by a dealer in secondhand cars, "This 1944 Dodge is just like new." Writers of informational prose should use words like *very* and *extremely* cautiously. The sentence "His work is of a very uneven character" does not mean more than "His work is uneven." "The work was extremely difficult and . . ." may antagonize a supervisor, for he suspects that if the work has not been completed the writer is concealing incompetence or laziness and that if it has been completed, the writer is bragging.

The indiscriminate use of intensives and superlatives has another disadvantage. It injects into a business or scientific atmosphere a touch of girlish gushiness—middle-aged girlish gushiness; it suggests several idle middle-aged women admiring a new dessert: "Too, too divine," "Really perfectly darling," "Perfectly heavenly actually."

POINTLESS WORDS AND PHRASES

Many words and phrases are just fillers: they fill time and space until an idea appears. And their sedative effects on writer and reader are great. The writer dictates them without thinking, and the reader skims them with an equal lack of attention. Some common examples are

> It may be said that
> It might be stated that
> In this connection the statement may be made that
> It is interesting that
> It is interesting to note that
> You will find it interesting to know
> You will be interested to learn

Not all of these are tranquillizers for all readers. Tell some readers that they will find information interesting, and their first response is, "What's interesting about that?" Executives reading for the thousandth time "As you may recall," "You may no doubt recall," "You will no doubt remember," and "As you know," may explode. "If he thinks I know it, why is he taking two paragraphs to tell me about it?" demanded one busy executive. I have heard many faculty treasurers read reports like,

"As you may remember, our balance a year ago was $1,129.64." The faculty was delighted when one treasurer reported, "As you may remember, though I doubt that you do, our balance a year ago was $473.26." Meaningless fillers become so irritating that harassed readers wish writers would think about what they are writing and interpret it literally, particularly that common phrase "needless to say," which usually introduces a long, unnecessary discussion.

More treacherous are time-wasters like *angle, aspect, case, character, element, field, situation, type,* and *nature* used pointlessly. Many sentences containing *in the case where* or *in the case when* are better sentences if *in the case* is omitted. "These examples are taken from the field of chemistry" does not need *the field of*. "He is the type of employee who is frequently late" means nothing more to the Personnel Department than "He is frequently late." The phrase *with respect to* is a favorite filler in writings on science and technology. "The pills with respect to their effects cause headaches" is clearer as "The pills cause headaches." Removing such fillers improves clarity and speeds comprehension.

Teachers and other public speakers are prone to use pointless words and phrases. Afraid of silence, they fill in with such expressions while they are phrasing or planning their next sentences. Such fillers may not be completely undesirable in public speaking, for they do give the audience a chance to catch its breath. (However, a transitional phrase would be more useful.) In writing, fillers serve no useful purpose; and if they are frequent, they may ruin an otherwise good style.

FALSE ELEGANCE

Many writers attempt to impress with their learning, efficiency, or intellect by substituting words for thoughts. Their simplest ideas emerge in jargon, business clichés, gobbledygook, or bookish terms. To them *pretentious* and *impressive* are synonymous. The poorly educated who admire false elegance in diction are pathetic. One man asked me, "But who'll know I'm educated if I use easy words?" Other offenders are well educated—but too recently. After interviewing a new Ph.D., an executive said to me, "Well, I suppose we'll hire him, and he'll be unbearable for a couple of years until he's displayed every term he learned in graduate school. And then after two years he'll begin to talk and write like a normal human being and we'll begin to think that maybe we can live with him after all. You know what will happen then? He'll get another job." As a suffering reader of many long dissertations, I am often inclined to think that Ph.D. stands for Phony Diction.

Like a fully inflated balloon, writing puffed up with words tempts critics to prick it into ludicrous collapse. The pin is easy to use. A *New Yorker* writer on teenagers quoted a distinguished sociologist on the characteristics of teenage culture as follows:

> 1. Compulsive independence of and antagonism to adult expectations and authority. This involves recalcitrance to adult standards of responsibility.
> 2. Compulsive conformity within the peer groups of age mates. It is intolerable to be "different."
> 3. Romanticism: an unrealistic idealization of emotionally significant objects.

Then the *New Yorker* writer applied the pin: "Practically anybody would agree with this summary, and practically anybody could have made it, though in less stately language: Teenagers are disobedient, group-minded, and unrealistic." [2]

Pretentious professors must be assigned some of the blame for the reverence of young graduates for fancy language. Although college handbooks of writing stress simplicity and brevity, some professors— and this includes English professors—set poor examples in their lectures and in their textbooks and atrocious examples in their articles in learned journals. They foster esoteric cults that make it difficult and sometimes impossible for biologists to talk to sociologists, for chemists to talk to engineers, for specialists in English linguistics to talk to specialists in English literature; indeed for specialists of one school of linguistics to talk to those of another school. Their students complain, "Well, he may be a great scholar, but he can't teach." Their colleagues shrug their shoulders and comment sardonically that wordy, pretentious writing weighs heavier on the scales that measure writings for promotion than clear, brief writing does. And this professorial use of pompous language is carried on by coteries of likewinded students.

Some supervisors in industry have earned an even larger share of the responsibility for the cult of false elegance. They write, "We will endeavor to ascertain" instead of "We will try to find out" even when all they are investigating is whether their staffs want meat or fish at the dinner for retiring members. When they mean *this shows*, they write, "As stated above, observations seem to indicate." They prefer *in the nature of*, *in the neighborhood of*, *in the order of*, and *in the order of magnitude of* when they mean *about*. Every profession has writers of poor style training the young: lawyers use *in view of the fact that*, *in view of the aforementioned*, and *in view of the foregoing circumstances*

---

[2] Dwight Macdonald, "A Caste, a Culture, a Market," XXXIV (November 29, 1958), 76.

instead of *therefore;* and it is better for the sensitive to avoid thinking of the examples presented to the apprentices who are learning to write federal tax laws.

For those who wish to recover from the influence of pompous professors, pretentious supervisors, and falsely elegant reading, I have listed some long-winded phrases and simple replacements for them. Fancy language like *transpire* for *happen*, *methodology* for *methods*, and *hypothesize* for *assume* are poor taste. The words in the false-elegance column below are often used in an attempt to disguise absence of thought. I have never met a writer who could make them sound natural in writing for government or industry. They are fancy dress, and government and industry are not costume parties.

Any writer who consistently uses the words in the left column should strenuously revise his work. Writers who think that they seldom offend by such use should check their writing carefully to be sure that they have not been blind to these faults. Occasional use of a fancy or long-winded phrase may not be the most objectionable characteristic of poor style. But it is one of the most dangerous, for the habit of using such phrases is easily acquired, especially if one reads and hears them. I ask the writers that I coach to try to eliminate fancy language entirely because even then some of it will escape their editing.

FALSE ELEGANCE AND WORDINESS	SUGGESTED IMPROVEMENT
above	the, this, that, those, these
abovementioned	
accounted for by the fact that	due to, caused by
add the point that	add that
advent	coming, arrival
afford an opportunity	allow, permit
after this is accomplished	then
aggregate	total
a great deal of	much
along the line of	like
a majority of	most (when *most* is meant)
analyzation	analysis
an example of this is the fact that	for example, as an example, thus
another aspect of the situation to be considered	as for
answer is in the affirmative (negative)	answer is yes (no)
a number of	several, many, some
approximately	about
as of now	now

FALSE ELEGANCE AND WORDINESS	SUGGESTED IMPROVEMENT
as per	Avoid this phrase.
	Poor: I am sending you the information as per your letter.
	Improved: I am sending you the information requested in your letter.
as regards	about
as related to	for, about
assist	help
assistance	help
assuming that	if
at this time	now
based on the fact that	due to, because
beg leave to say, beg to differ, beg to say	Omit.
by means of by the use of	by } when *by* is clear by }
come to an end	end
commence	begin. Save *commence* for official ceremonies and procedures.
communicate	Prefer a specific verb like *write, telephone, telegraph, cable.*
compensation	pay
concerning	about
conclude	end
construct	build
contemplate	intend
demonstrate	show, prove
due to the fact that	because, due to
duly noted	noted
during the time that	while
dwell	live
effect, effectuate, institute a change	change (when *change* is meant)
encounter	meet
endeavor	try
eventuate	happen
except in a small number of cases	usually
exhibit a tendency to	tend to
firstly	first
floral offering	flowers
for the purpose of	for, to
for the reason that	because, since
for the simple reason that	because, since

FALSE ELEGANCE AND WORDINESS	SUGGESTED IMPROVEMENT
forward	send (when *send* is meant)
for your information	This is usually superfluous.
having reference to this	for, about
if at all possible	if possible
in case, in case of	if
in close proximity	near
in conjunction with	Use *with* alone whenever *in conjunction* is unnecessary.
in connection with	Use *about* or *of* whenever possible.
in favor of	for, to
initial	first
initiate	begin
in lieu of	instead of, in place of
in order to	to
in the course of	during
in the first place	first
in the vicinity of	near
inquire	ask
in rare cases	rarely
in reference to, with reference to	about
in regard to	about
in relation with	with
in short supply	scarce
intermingle	mingle
in terms of	in
in the amount of	of, for
in the case of	for, by, in, if
in the event of, in the event that	if
in the instance of	for
in the light of the fact that	because
in the majority of instances	usually
in the matter of	about
in the neighborhood of	about (except in descriptions of a locality)
in the not-too-distant future	soon
in the proximity of	near, nearly, or about
in view of the above, in view of the foregoing circumstances, in view of the fact that	therefore
involve the necessity of	require
is defined as	is (at least occasionally)
it is incumbent on me	I must
it is often the case that	often
it stands to reason	Omit.

FALSE ELEGANCE AND WORDINESS	SUGGESTED IMPROVEMENT
it was noted that if	if
it would not be unreasonable to assume	I (we) assume; I (we) think
kindly (in a request)	please
leaving out of consideration	disregarding
make the acquaintance of	meet
modification	change
necessitate	require, need
not of a high order of accuracy	inaccurate
notwithstanding the fact that	although
nuptials	wedding, marriage
objective	aim, goal
obligation	debt (when *debt* is meant)
of a dangerous character	dangerous
of considerable magnitude	big, large, great
of very minor importance	unimportant
on account of the fact that	because
on a few occasions	occasionally
on behalf of	for
on the grounds that	because
one and the same	one *or* the same (whenever possible)
presently	now
prior to	before
proceed	go
proceed to investigate, study, analyze, etc.	Omit the unnecessary *proceed to.*
reimburse	repay
relative to this	about this
remains	body (when that is the meaning)
remuneration	pay
ruination	ruin
spells	is (when that is the meaning)
subsequent	next
subsequent to	after
sufficient	enough
take appropriate measures	act
taking this factor into consideration, it is apparent that	therefore, therefore it seems
terminate	end
termination	end
the foregoing	the, this, that, these, those
the fullest possible extent	Omit or use *most, completely,* or *fully.*
the only difference being that	except that

FALSE ELEGANCE AND WORDINESS	SUGGESTED IMPROVEMENT
the question as to whether or not	whether
there are not many who	few
there is very little doubt that	doubtless, no doubt
to be cognizant of	to know
to summarize the above	in summary
transmit	send
transpire	happen, occur
usage	use (except for other meanings such as *custom, practice in language*)
within the realm of possibility	possible, possibly
with reference to	Omit (or use *about*).
with the exception of	except
with this in mind, it is clear that	therefore

See also pp. 114–121.

Chapter IX

The Standard of Grammar for the Professions

Let school-masters puzzle their brain,
    With grammar, and nonsense, and learning;
Good liquor, I stoutly maintain,
    Gives *genus* a better discerning.

Goldsmith

When he connects grammar with schoolteachers, the roistering play-boy of *She Stoops to Conquer* voices an association familiar today. And even teetotal writers in industry and government have been known to echo the sentiments of his first two lines. Today grammar is both a sacred subject and the subject of much profanity. In government and industry arguments about grammar generate more heat than a discussion of politics does—even office politics.

It is almost impossible to discuss any other phase of writing for an audience of businessmen, scientists, or technologists without meeting extraneous questions like, "But does it matter if my grammar is wrong?" and "Why don't the colleges teach engineering students some grammar?" At a reception during an engineering convention, an elderly engineer asked to meet me solely in order to tell me, "There are two things I learned at my mother's knee—to read the Bible and not to use *ain't*. And I want you to know that I won't use *ain't* no matter what the dictionaries and you English teachers say."

No less heated are the reviewers of books on technical writing who praise with rejoicing all authors who omit instruction in grammar and the reviewers who greet with excessive praise all authors who devote at least two thirds of their pages to grammar. Some reviewers state that technical writers do not need instruction in grammar, but unfortunately the language of these statements often proves that the reviewers, who are also technical writers, do. Other reviewers state that what a technical writer needs most is grammar correction, but they state this in paragraphs that demonstrate unmistakably that what the reviewers need most is instruction in how to shape sentences and paragraphs. A reader is likely to conclude that technical writers need everything, but do not know that they need it.

All this fire and smoke comes from misunderstandings. Grammar is not a set of rules arbitrarily imposed upon writers by dictionary-makers, schoolteachers, or anyone else. The grammar of writings on professional subjects should be the grammar that educated writers use and that educated readers expect. Ideas about this grammar change—sometimes rapidly, sometimes slowly. What was regarded as incorrect twenty years ago may not be considered incorrect today. Moreover, the grammar of speech is not necessarily that of writing. In answer to "Who's there?" Americans answer today, "Me" or "It's me." "It's I," which was preferred, now sounds affected, pompous, pedantic. But in writing, educated Americans use "It's I," as in the sentence "It is I alone who recommend this change; the committee has said nothing about it."

Incorrect writing annoys readers of functional prose. It is ironical that even those who write incorrectly complain about the incorrect writing of others. Readers want to be free to move along a page without the distraction of errors. They want to grasp information and ideas as rapidly as possible. All readers resent having to rephrase or recast or even reread sentences in order to understand them; they balk at bringing their knowledge to bear in order to discover what a writer meant to say but did not say. Readers want to read, not edit or interpret. They are entitled to clear, correct exposition. They would like it to be brief and interesting also. But it must be clear and correct.

Some writers are deterred from attempting to achieve correctness because they think that they must undertake a complete study of English grammar. I consider such a study unnecessarily burdensome for professional men, who have better ways to spend their time. Worrying about dozens of rules that one has never broken may be harmful. It is like teaching a grown man to correct his walk by having him study in detail all the muscle and nerve action involved in walking.

Teaching all the rules of grammar to busy professional men can be a disservice. Writers who never had trouble with *who, which,* and *that* memorize all the rules for the use of those pronouns and then find *who, which,* and *that* stumbling blocks whenever they write. A busy man does not have time to learn all the rules and to practice applying them until the correct use becomes automatic.

A professional man should concentrate on the rules that he needs— those he breaks. The rules in this chapter have been selected carefully to spare him the tedium of a complete study. They concern the errors and weaknesses that appear most often in the writing of accountants, of lawyers, of scientists, of technologists, and of other administrators in government and industry. These are the errors that editors and supervisors grow weary of correcting. They are the errors that writers in my classes ask about most often. They are the errors that any professional man is likely to make. If he does not make one of them now, he probably will make it later unless he carefully avoids it, for he will read it many times in the writing of his colleagues. And errors are contagious.

A writer is fortunate if he can ask a competent editor or supervisor or teacher to read five or six pages of his work to find and mark errors. The writer can study the correction of the errors, look for them when he revises his next papers, and correct them. After a time the errors will no longer appear in his first drafts, and he will be ready to ask his mentor to correct for him again. When the corrector finds no errors and weaknesses, the writer is ready for the next steps in revision (Chapter II). But an annual check on errors is advisable because writers are likely to acquire new bad habits or revert to old ones.

Many professional men using this book do not have available the help of competent editors or supervisors, and some men prefer to work without such assistance. They should read the sections on grammar that follow and should mark for study any rules that they break or might break. Those a writer might break will be revealed by his experience with the examples: the correct examples sound wrong, and the incorrect examples occur frequently in his reading. After studying the explanations of the rules that he breaks or might break, a writer should search for examples of broken rules when he revises his papers, not while he is writing (Chapter II). Very likely he will find some error that he thought he never made. He should practice correcting the errors he finds until correct usage becomes automatic, as shown by the disappearance of mistakes from his first drafts. After that an annual skimming through the following examples of common errors should enable him to spot the mistakes in his writing.

Many writers enjoy striving for effectiveness because the study of language interests intelligent people and provides occasional entertainment and amusement. But the study of common errors is not always entertaining and cannot be made so. A writer must discipline himself to continue when he finds study or correction dull. Then he should remind himself that the ability to write correctly will be useful all his life. Tedium should not be great, for the following errors are probably all he need examine. These errors are made so often that an editor of an engineering journal expects to use the list to train new technical editors.

THE AGREEMENT OF SUBJECT AND PREDICATE VERB

Errors in agreement between subject and predicate are common in the prose of information. True, one seldom finds "These methods is recommended" or "The mixture are boiled"; but writers—and editors too—often err in less simple constructions. For example, a medical journal published this opening sentence, "Experience with two antidepressant agents which are known as monoamine oxidase inhibitors are presented in the following." *The New York Times* printed, "From this work has come improved antibiotics." And writers in industry often publish sentences like "The recommendation for salary increases were examined."

Because blunders in agreement occur most commonly in certain constructions, a study of these constructions enables writers to avoid the errors.

Separated Subject and Predicate

Many writers become confused about number when a subject is separated from its predicate verb, particularly if the intervening words introduce another number, as in the following incorrect examples:

> The effective *use* of these machines *require* study and practice.
> A *tabulation* of the animal responses *have* been presented elsewhere.
> *Estimation* of the pressure drop and fluidization characteristics *are* desirable.
> The *esophagus, stomach,* and *duodenum* of each *was* examined.

In the first three examples the subjects are clearly singular—*use, tabulation, estimation*—but the plural words *machines, responses,* and *characteristics* misled the writers, who would not otherwise write or say *use require, tabulation have,* and *estimation are*. The writer of the fourth example would certainly have written *The esophagus, stomach, and duodenum were examined,* but he was misled by the intervening singular *each*. Any writer who thinks that because of the intervening words he too would have made this mistake should remember to make one step of his revision a check of the agreement of subjects and verbs that are separated.

Subject Following Verb

Errors are also frequent when subjects follow verbs. The journalist who wrote, "From this work has come improved antibiotics. . . ." would not write *antibiotics has come*, but the reversed order confused him. "Out of even the best college comes many writers ignorant of the basic principles of English," wrote one of my students and unconsciously offered proof of his generalization by his statement of it. He would have looked condescendingly on anyone who wrote *many writers comes*. If the order of subject and predicate is reversed, this student should place the subject before the predicate to find the correct number. The primary-school device of asking, "Who or what come or comes?" leads to the correct answer, "Writers come." This device is helpful to anyone who would otherwise read the sentence and like the sound of it. For the sentence, "The agreement between the values substantiate the accuracy of the latent heats," the writer would ask, "Who or what substantiate or substantiates?" and answer, "Agreement substantiates." He should not remove the substantive from the prepositional phrase *between the values*, in which it appears, and answer, "The values substantiate."

Some writers become confused when a subject follows a verb in a sentence beginning with *there is, there are, here is, here are*, or *it is*. The last of these is the simplest. *It is* may be followed by a singular or plural noun:

> It is this book that I need.
> It is these books that I need.

But when a sentence begins with *there is, there are, here is*, or *here are*, a writer should take special care. Usually the question, "Who or what is or are?" will help a writer who has difficulty distinguishing the subject.

> There (*is* or *are*) at least three treatments for this condition.
>   (Q. What is or are? A. Three treatments are.)
> There (*is* or *are*) an x missing in the equations.
>   (Q. What is or are missing? A. An x is missing.)

Many indirect statements have poor emphasis; they should be direct statements (page 130). The second example, for instance, is a stronger sentence without *there is:*

> An x is missing in the equations.

The first example is better if the writer omits *there are* and says something about the treatments instead of just pointing to their existence:

> At least three treatments for this condition were demonstrated at the conference.

At least three treatments for this condition are inadvisable because of the patient's allergies.

Words Attached to Subjects

Writers should remember that words attached to the subject by such connectives as *accompanied by, along with, as well as, including, in addition to, no less than,* and *together with* do not affect the number of the subject in formal English.

> His secretary, as well as many other members of the division, is attending the meeting on computers.

The singular *is* has as its subject *secretary; members,* introduced by *as well as,* does not make the subject plural.

Collective Nouns

A collective noun (the name applied to a group), such as *band, class, family, jury,* takes a singular verb when the group is regarded as a unit and a plural verb when the members of the group function as individuals.

> The committee *is* in favor of a holiday on June first.
> The committee *are* leaving for vacations.
> The class *is* presenting a scholarship to the college.
> The class *are* going to graduate schools or taking jobs.

Those who do not like the sound of the plural verb after the collective noun should remember that they may dislike the sound because the correct form is strange to them. If they think their readers will be distracted, they may rephrase. In the preceding examples they may substitute *members of the committee* and *members of the class.*

Writers on finance, science, and technology, who use amounts frequently, should check their manuscripts to make sure that they have used a singular verb whenever the expression of quantity is thought of as a unit and a plural verb otherwise.

> Three grains diluted in sterile water *was* injected.
> Ten and a half ounces *is* added to the solution.
> Two teaspoonfuls *is* a large dose.
> Add water until there *is* three pints of solution.
> Twenty stamps *are* scattered on the table.
> Twenty stamps *is* a small number to collect in a year.

Foreign Singulars and Plurals

Some singulars and plurals, such as the following, have been taken into English from other languages:

SINGULAR	PLURAL	SINGULAR	PLURAL
alumna	alumnae	media	mediae
alumnus	alumni	medium	media
appendix	appendices	memorandum	memoranda
basis	bases	minimum	minima
crisis	crises	parenthesis	parentheses
cherub	cherubim	phenomenon	phenomena
continuum	continua	radius	radii
datum	data	seraph	seraphim
criterion	criteria	series	series
desideratum	desiderata	species	species
erratum	errata	stamen	stamina
formula	formulae	stimulus	stimuli
fungus	fungi	stratum	strata
index	indices	syllabus	syllabi
maximum	maxima		

Because the English language has a strong tendency to impress its own methods upon borrowed words, many foreign words acquire English plurals: appendixes, cherubs, formulas, funguses, indexes, maximums, mediums, minimums, memorandums, phenomenons, radiuses, seraphs, stamens, stratums, syllabuses.

Often the foreign plural is used in a more technical sense. One can see this most clearly in the words used in the specializations of others. *Cherubs,* for example, is used for beautiful children, but the Hebrew plural *cherubim* is used in theology for one of the nine orders of angels. Either may be used for a representation of a beautiful child with wings. The distinction for *seraphs* and *seraphim* is similar. Less common is the practice of adding an English plural to the foreign plural: *cherubims, seraphims.*

Formulae is used in mathematics and chemistry, although even in these sciences *formulas* is often used. *Funguses* is used more often than *fungi,* although *fungi* is commonly used in medical writing. In mathematics *indices* is used, but elsewhere *indexes* is common. *Maxima* occurs frequently in mathematics and astronomy, but elsewhere *maximums* is used. Although *memorandums* is commonly used, some formal writers and some scientists and technologists prefer *memoranda. Phenomena* is used in philosophy with one meaning and in the sciences with two, but exceptional persons, things, or occurrences are *phenomenons. Radii* is more frequent in the sciences and mathematics than is *radiuses,* but I have noticed an increasing use of *radiuses. Strata* is preferred in biology and geology; *stratums* sometimes appears in general usage. *Syllabuses* is used frequently and might just as well be because the word comes to English from the Latin through a misreading.

A writer who understands the use of the plurals of these words is not likely to make such common errors as the following:

> This formulae is . . .
> The maxima is . . .
> This fungi are found . . .
> The syllabi was used.

Some plural usage varies from the general. One Latin plural—*stamina*—is regularly used as a singular for vigor, and another—*media*—is accepted by many dictionaries as singular when it is used for a means of conveying advertising. *Stamens* is the plural of *stamen* in botany and elsewhere. *Minutia* is seldom used, but *minutiae* is common.

Datum is seldom used in English except in such phrases as *datum line*, *datum plane*, and *datum point*. But *data* perplexes many writers. With more persistence than patience, teachers and supervisors have trained scientists and technologists to use *data* as a plural. No point of grammar or style has received so much emphasis, with the possible exception of the banishment of *ain't*. Some who inveigh most strongly against *data* as a singular have no true plural concept of *data*. They change *This data is* . . . to *This data are*. . . . They write, "Smythe's data are accurate. It proves. . . ." The use of *this* and *it* reveals that they think of *data* as singular despite their preachments that it is plural. Making *data* both singular and plural as in *This data are* and *Considerable recent data show* is worse than the consistent use of one number—even the wrong number.

But the scientist who said, "This data is helpful to me," was not using the wrong number. He was thinking in a collective sense of *data;* to him it meant information, not separate points of information. When *data* is thought of as functioning as a unit, then the singular is sensible and correct: "This data supports my theory"; "The data appears in the appendix." If *data* is thought of as units operating individually, then the plural is sensible and correct: "These data are useful in a number of fields"; "Few data have been accepted in so many fields as these have."

Writers likely to use such constructions as "Much data are . . ." and "Little data are . . ." do not have a concept of *data* as either singular or plural, for they use singular modifiers and plural verbs. They may test their constructions by substituting *information* for *data* when they wish to indicate that the points are to be considered as a unit. Then they will write, "Much (information) data is . . . ," and "Little (information) data is. . . ." When they mean that the points are operating individually, they may experiment by substituting *facts:* "Many (facts) data are . . ." and "Few (facts) data are. . . ." Writers who would never use "Much facts are . . ." become confused by *data* unless they test with another noun —a singular noun when they want a singular concept (*information*) and a plural noun when they want a plural concept (*facts*). These writers are confused not so much about English grammar as about their concept of *data.*

Company Names

Although the British frequently use company names and the official titles of other bodies as plurals, Americans usually prefer them to be singular.

> Corroon, Carroll, Curran & Cooney, Incorporated, *is* mailing the policies this month.
> The Government Printing Office *issues* this document; *it* charges fifty cents a copy.
> The Research Division *submits* quarterly reports. *It* also prepares special reports on request.

Difficulty arises when the company or division does not function as a unit. Then the writer should not awkwardly switch to the plural. "The Research Division is investigating the proposed method. Some of *them* think. . . ." *The Research Division,* established as singular by the verb *is,* may not serve as the antecedent of the plural *them.* The writer may correct by substituting a plural subject word: "The Research Division *is* investigating the proposed method. *Some of the members* think. . . ." The error of switching incorrectly from one number to another is illustrated by the company that advertises in newspaper type nearly an inch high: "A big office furniture company like Itkin doesn't have to be an authority on decorating too. But they are." Is Itkin or are Itkin?

Whether one decides to use the plural or the singular with the titles of companies and other bodies is not important. But being consistent in maintaining the plural or the singular is helpful to readers. If the chosen number is difficult to use for a particular concept, a writer can easily substitute another word. Although the point seems obvious, many writers of company reports do not realize that because one starts to write about "The Medical Illustration Department, which *is* located on the eleventh floor," one does not have to retain the singular throughout the report. Any writer can think of dozens of escapes to the plural, such as *the medical illustrators, the members of the department, the opinions of the department, the methods, the policies, the executives, the artists,* etc.

Mathematical Expressions

In mathematical calculations either a singular or a plural verb is correct:

> Three times three *is* (or *are*) nine.
> Three and three *is* (or *are*) six.
> Three and three *makes* (or *make*) six.

An equation, regardless of the number of terms on either side, is singular:

> In assuming that $x + y(3a/b) = 46$ *is* valid for every case. . . .
> He was certain that $a^2 + b^2 = c^2$ *was* correct.

Singular Indefinite Pronouns as Subjects

Another, anybody, anyone, anything, each, either, everyone, everybody, everything, neither, nobody, nothing, one, somebody, someone, and *something* require singular verbs.

> Neither of the treatments *is* safe.
> *Is* anyone listening?
> One *has* to file *his* copy by Monday.
> Each of us *is* a poor judge of *his* own writing.
> Each of the machines *has* advantages. (But when *each* is an adjective, it does not affect the number of the verb: They each *have* a chance for the nomination.)

None as Subject

When *none* is the subject, the verb is usually plural. *None* may be used with a singular verb if a writer wishes to stress a singular concept, but in such instances *no one* or *not one* is generally used.

> *None* of the animals *are* responding.
> *Not one* of the animals *is* responding.

A writer should of course use the number that the context suggests:

> Every patient improved, but *none has* recovered complete use of *his* damaged limb.

Subjects Connected by Correlative Conjunctions

Singular subjects connected by *either . . . or* or *neither . . . nor* take singular verbs.

> *Either the Purchasing Division or the Manufacturing Division is* responsible.
> *Neither crystallization* caused by pressure *nor slippage* at the capillary walls *causes* this discontinuity in flow behavior.

When the subjects connected by *either . . . or* or *neither . . . nor* differ in number, the verb agrees with the subject nearer it.

> Neither polymeric *substances* nor their physical *behavior is* understood thoroughly.
> Either you or *I am* going. (A writer who does not like this sentence may rephrase: Either *you are* going or *I am.*)
> Neither the doctor nor the *nurses are* to blame.
> Neither the nurses nor the *doctor is* to blame.

THE PRONOUN

Although most writers on professional subjects know that a pronoun agrees with its antecedent in number, gender, and person, many of them have difficulty with the following constructions.

Collective Nouns as Antecedents

Once a writer has decided whether his collective noun is singular or plural, he must use that number not merely for his verb but also for any pronouns that refer to the collective noun and for any words that modify it.

> INCORRECT: The committee *is* planning to submit *their* report before January.
> CORRECT: The committee *is* planning to submit *its* report before January.
> INCORRECT: *These* data for copper deposition *has* been given previously. *They have* been used to prove. . . .
> CORRECT: *This* data for copper deposition *has* been given previously. *It has* been used to prove. . . .
> CORRECT: *These data* for copper deposition *have* been given previously. *They have* been used to prove. . . .

(The singular or plural forms are used with *data* according to whether the writer is indicating that the data functions as a unit or that the data are functioning individually. Discussion of this point appears under Agreement Between Subjects and Predicate Verbs: Collective Nouns, on page 149.)

He or She, Him or Her

Grammar being a man's world, a singular noun that may be either masculine or feminine is followed by a masculine pronoun, not by *he or she, him or her.*

> INCORRECT: *Every employee* must submit *his or her* request for vacation dates by January fifteenth.
> CORRECT: *Every employee* must submit *his* request. . . .

When the noun is feminine, it is followed by *she* or *her*.

> INCORRECT: *Any applicant* from a woman's college usually has *his* mind
> made up about marriage and a career.
> CORRECT: *Any applicant* from a woman's college usually has *her* mind
> made up about marriage and a career.

The combination *he or she, him or her* is used for an antecedent composed
of two members, one masculine and one feminine.

> Every high school *boy and girl* should reach *his or her* own decision
> about entering college.

If such a construction seems awkward, a writer should change the wording:

> *All employees* must submit *their*. . . .
> *High school girls and boys* should reach *their* own decisions.
> *High school students* should reach *their* own decisions.

Ambiguous or Vague Antecedent

Every pronoun should refer unmistakably to a noun or pronoun or
noun phrase. *Unmistakably* means that the antecedent of the pronoun
should be obvious to the reader. He should not have to select from two
antecedents:

> INCORRECT: Miss Jones told Miss Smith that she might receive a raise.
> CORRECT: Miss Jones told Miss Smith, "You may. . . ."
> CORRECT: Miss Jones told Miss Smith, "I may. . . ."
> CORRECT: Miss Jones told Miss Smith that Miss Smith might. . . .
> CORRECT: Miss Jones told Miss Smith that Miss Jones. . . .
> CORRECT: Miss Jones told Miss Smith that she expected a raise. (Miss
> Jones probably did not know what Miss Smith expected and so
> was referring to herself.)

Avoid reference to an idea that is not expressed or not expressed as a
noun:

> INCORRECT: The executive secretary has suggested that I write for your
> files and minutes of Board meetings. I hope it will be convenient
> for you to do this.
> CORRECT: I hope that it will be convenient for you to send them to me.
> INCORRECT: In infections it becomes acidic, the degree of which depends
> on dilution by exudate.
> CORRECT: In infections it becomes acidic; the degree of acidity depends
> on. . . .
> CORRECT: In infections it becomes acidic, the degree of acidity depending
> on. . . .

One

Writers should avoid overworking *one*. In the most formal writing, where *one* must be followed by *one* and *one's*, the pronoun may become monotonous. This error is frequent in technical reports, where it occurs in awkward, wordy statements of writers who are striving to be impersonal.

> AWKWARD: One can see that it is obvious that one can use the tiny David Computer with more speed and accuracy than one can use the massive Goliath Computer.
>
> IMPROVED: Obviously, the tiny David Computer offers more speed and accuracy than the massive Goliath Computer. (The improved sentence avoids personal pronouns but does not use *one*.)
>
> AWKWARD: If one supplies *x* in the first step of one's equation, one will find that one has to spend less time solving and one will find oneself less confused by the complexity of the solution.
>
> IMPROVED: Supplying *x* in the first step speeds and simplifies the solving of the equation.

A common error is confusing *one* with *I, you, we,* or *they*. An unnecessary shift in pronouns is incorrect whether it occurs in a single sentence or in a paragraph.

> INCORRECT: As *one* tours the factory, *one* notices the cleanliness, achieved, you suspect, by little effort.
>
> CORRECT BUT AWKWARD: As *one* tours the factory, *one* notices the cleanliness, achieved, *one* suspects, by little effort.
>
> IMPROVED (Informal): As *one* tours the factory, *he* notices the cleanliness, achieved, *he* suspects, by little effort.
>
> INCORRECT: When *one* applies for employment, *they* should expect long delays.
>
> CORRECT (Formal): When *one* applies for employment, *one* should expect long delays.
>
> CORRECT (Formal): When applying for employment, *one* should expect long delays.

The use of the nominative *he, she, it;* the possessive *his, hers, its;* the objective *him, her, it;* and the reflexive *himself, herself, itself* to refer to a preceding *one* is common in American informal style.

> *One* has a blot on its titlepage.
>
> *One* oils *itself* for six months.
>
> *One* must keep *one's* opinions to *oneself* while working for Scrooge (Formal).
>
> *One* must keep *his* opinions to *himself* while working for Scrooge (Informal).

Many writers have difficulty when a construction containing *one* is followed by a relative clause.

> He is one of the competent students who have been hired for summer work.

The antecedent of *who* is *students;* the meaning is that he is one (but not the only one) of the competent students hired for summer work. When the meaning is *the only one*, the antecedent of the relative pronoun is *one*.

> He is the one of the students who is incompetent.

Usually the meaning is *one*, not *the only one*, and the relative pronoun is plural in agreement with its antecedent, as in the following sentences:

> He is working on one of those research projects that are sponsored by the government.
> He is one of those overambitious executives who are always seeking promotions. (BUT—He is one of those ambitious executives who is ready for promotion. This means that he is *the one*.)
> He made one of those personnel decisions that are hard to change.
> The patient is one of those who suffer nausea and vomiting all through their pregnancies no matter what drugs they are given.
> He made one of those errors in English that are noticed at once.

Although formal usage requires the plural in this construction, a singular is acceptable in informal English. But the singular construction may be ambiguous when a writer does not mean *the one who* or *the one which;* therefore I recommend that writers on business, science, and technology adopt the formal usage.

Cases

Writers sometimes allow a parenthetical expression to attract a pronoun into the objective case.

> INCORRECT: The employees whom he thought were to be assigned to the project were all working on other research.
> CORRECT: The employees who he thought were to be assigned to the project were all working on other research.
> INCORRECT: He rejected the applicants whom he judged might know more than he did.
> CORRECT: He rejected the applicants who he judged might know more than he did.

In the first sentence *who* is the subject of *were to be assigned*. In the second sentence *who* is the subject of *might know*.

A pronoun takes its case from its own function in its own clause, as the following sentences illustrate:

> INCORRECT: They objected because he recommended *whomever* was his friend for the promotion.
> CORRECT: They objected because he recommended *whoever* was his friend for the promotion.
> INCORRECT: The report stating *whom* should be held responsible for the poor shipping record was discussed in detail.
> CORRECT: The report stating *who* should be held responsible for the poor shipping record was discussed in detail.
> INCORRECT: He has a pleasant word for *whomever* comes to his office.
> CORRECT: He has a pleasant word for *whoever* comes to his office.

In the first sentence *whoever* is the subject of *was*. In the second sentence *who* is the subject of *should be held responsible*. In the third sentence *whoever* is the subject of *comes*. In all three sentences the relative pronouns are in the nominative case because they are subjects. The fact that in each sentence the entire relative clause is the object (of *recommended* in the first sentence and of *stating* and of *for* in the second and third sentences) does not affect the case of the relative pronoun: it is still in the nominative case because it is the subject of the relative clause.

The case of a pronoun following *as* or *than* can be determined by completing the construction in one's mind.

> His secretary is taller than he (is).
> My supervisor is more interested in causes than I (am).
> I like his substitute better than (I like) him.
> I like his substitute better than he (does).
> My secretary works harder for him than (for) me.
> I like routine work more than he (does).

Some writers have difficulty distinguishing participles and gerunds because they look alike: *coming, going, seeing, summarizing*. Participles are used as adjectives, and gerunds, as nouns. In *I dislike his scheming ways, scheming* is a participle modifying *ways*. In *His scheming gained him no advantages, scheming* is a gerund used as the subject of *gained*.

A noun or a pronoun modifying a gerund is in the possessive case.

> When *their* sleeping improved, patients reported their delight.
> After examining the animals, he said that he had no doubts about *their* being satisfactory for his experiment.

There is a difference in meaning between a phrase containing a gerund and one with a participle, as well as a difference in grammar.

> GERUND: I observed his *finding* of the lever.
> PARTICIPLE: I observed him *finding* the lever.

GERUND: I remember his *smashing* of the apparatus.
PARTICIPLE: I remember him *smashing* the apparatus.

The use of a gerund and of a noun or pronoun in the possessive case emphasizes the act. The use of a participle and of a noun or pronoun in the objective case emphasizes the actor.

GERUND: I have been worrying about his scheming ever since I hired him.
PARTICIPLE: I have been worrying about him scheming ever since I hired him.

Because of these differences in meaning, writers should carefully avoid confusing gerunds and participles.

COMPARISONS

If comparisons are correctly employed, they clarify and vivify. In functional prose, they are frequently the foundation of the thought. The subject of a report may be a comparison of two chemicals, of methods of controlling pressure, of several computers, of several designs for a bridge, of the side effects of three drugs. And even when comparison is not the central idea of a paper, comparisons frequently appear. Errors unfortunately are also frequent: ambiguous and incomplete comparisons, omission of necessary restrictive words, omission of a standard, use of a vague standard, confusion of classes and constructions.

Incorrect comparisons are often published. An advertisement for a book states: "She has seen further into this difficult and rewarding man than anyone else." Does this mean that she has seen further than anyone else has or that she has seen further into this man than into anyone else? Another advertisement for a book compares earnings with professional men: "Today her earnings are comparable to the top doctors, attorneys, and professional men of the nation."

Ambiguous and Incomplete Comparison

When *than* completes a comparison, a careful writer checks to be sure that he has used the words necessary for clear construction.

INCOMPLETE: The shop steward condemned the supervisor more than the operator.
COMPLETE: The shop steward condemned the supervisor more than the operator did.
COMPLETE: The shop steward condemned the supervisor more than he condemned the operator.
AMBIGUOUS: In the overlapping areas Wilip's results were given more

weight because they were in better agreement with Beattie's than those of Ramsey and Young.

CLEAR: In the overlapping areas Wilip's results were given more weight because they were in better agreement with Beattie's than were those of Ramsey and Young.

CLEAR: In the overlapping areas Wilip's results were given more weight because they were in better agreement with Beattie's than with those of Ramsey and Young.

Each of these sentences labeled *ambiguous* or *incomplete* has two possible meanings; each revision has one unmistakable meaning. A writer is obligated to say exactly what he means. He should not expect a reader to stop, consider two or more possible meanings, and select the correct one. Even if a reader has sufficient specialized knowledge to interpret an ambiguous sentence, he resents having to interrupt his reading to do so. And sometimes it is difficult, or even impossible, to interpret an incomplete comparison, for example one like the following:

INCORRECT: The errors in the sampling technique are greater than Table 5.

CORRECT: The errors in the sampling technique are greater than those in Table 5.

CORRECT: The errors in the sampling technique are greater than Table 5 shows.

Omission of Standard of Comparison

Vagueness often results from failure to state a standard of comparison. When advertisers do this, they may be avoiding the standard because the only one that they can state without risking a suit from their competitors is unsatisfactory. Writers of functional prose should avoid this vagueness, and readers should view with suspicion products that are advertised, intentionally or unintentionally, by omission of a standard of comparison.

INCOMPLETE: The cocktails at the Knaves' Corner are better. (better than water? better than poison? or just better than no cocktails at all?)

INCOMPLETE: This system is more accurate. (more accurate than what?)

COMPLETE: This system is more accurate than Professor Delusive's.

COMPLETE: This system is more accurate than that of Professor Delusive.

COMPLETE: This system is more accurate than I expected (if the context makes clear how much accuracy was expected).

VAGUE: This drug is recommended because it is so safe.

IMPROVED: The Research Committee recommends this drug for marketing because experiments have proved that it has only one minor side effect, discussed on page 25.

IMPROVED: Dr. Jones recommends this drug to his patients because he considers it safer than any other on the market.

Omission of Necessary Restrictive Words

When objects of the same class are compared, some restrictive word such as *other* or *else* is necessary.

> INCORRECT: He is richer than anybody in the United States.
> CORRECT: He is richer than anybody else in the United States.
> INCORRECT: These filters are better than any filters.
> CORRECT: These filters are better than any other filters.

Confusion of Classes and Constructions

The terms of a comparison should be of the same class and in the same construction.[1]

> INCORRECT: The molecular weight compared favorably with Butol.
> CORRECT: The molecular weight compared favorably with that of Butol.
> INCORRECT: The temperature of Monkey A is the same as Monkey B.
> CORRECT: The temperature of Monkey A is the same as that of Monkey B.
> The temperature of Monkey A is the same as Monkey B's.
> Monkey A and Monkey B have the same temperature.
> INCORRECT: He attempted to separate the components rather than testing the combination.
> CORRECT: He attempted to separate the components rather than to test the combination.
> He attempted separating the components rather than testing the combination.

In a double comparison using both *as* and *than*, the terms of comparison should be completed after *as*.

> INCORRECT: This machine is as fast if not faster than ours.
> CORRECT: This machine is as fast as ours if not faster.
> CORRECT BUT AWKWARD: This machine is as fast as if not faster than ours.

Superlative Adjectives

When a superlative adjective appears twice and modifies singular and plural forms of a noun, the plural form should appear after the first use of the adjective, and the singular form may be omitted.

> INCORRECT: One of the greatest, if not the greatest difficulty, is the injection.
> CORRECT: One of the greatest difficulties, if not the greatest, is the injection.

There are several other ways of phrasing this sentence correctly, according to the emphasis the writer desires:

[1] See Parallel Construction, p. 251.

One of the greatest, if not the greatest, of difficulties is the injection.
One of the greatest difficulties, if not the greatest of all, is the injection.
One of the greatest difficulties, perhaps the greatest, is the injection.

Choice of Comparative or Superlative

The comparative degree is used for comparing two persons or things or ideas; the superlative degree is used for three or more.

COMPARATIVE: He is the more reliable of my two assistants.
    This typist is faster than the other.
    The second page has more errors than the first.
SUPERLATIVE: He is the most reliable supervisor in the company.
    This typist is the fastest I have ever seen.
    Page twenty has the most errors.

PARALLEL CONSTRUCTION

Sentence elements that are not parallel in thought should not be placed in parallel structure (page 251).

POOR: The patients received three injections on the first day, four on the second day, and on the third day they were discharged.
IMPROVED: The patients received three injections on the first day and four on the second day. They were discharged on the third day.
INCORRECT: Many accidents are caused by failure to use safety equipment, careless inspection of laboratories, and we need to warn our workers about these.
IMPROVED: Many accidents are caused by failure to use safety equipment and by careless inspection of laboratories. We should warn our workers of these dangers.
IMPROVED: We should warn our workers of the many accidents caused by failure to inspect laboratories carefully and by failure to use safety equipment.
INCORRECT: This drug will be rejected as there is no proof that it is safe, for it has not been tested on human beings for it does not have good marketing possibilities.
THE WRITER'S MEANING: Because this drug does not have good marketing possibilities, it has not been tested on human beings. It will be rejected for lack of proof of safety.

THE PLACING OF MODIFIERS

English word order is important. The sense of a sentence may depend on the position of the parts. If English were a more highly inflected language, the position of words might be less vital. In Anglo-Saxon, Latin, and German, for example, one can tell case by word endings, but in

English one tells it by position except for pronouns. In *The girl hit the boy*, *girl* is the actor, or the subject, and *boy* is the recipient of the action, or the object. In *The boy hit the girl*, *boy* is the subject and *girl* is the object. Switching the position of the words changes the meaning.

A good writer of English prose takes pains, therefore, to place his words correctly so that they convey his meaning precisely. Even when the context makes his meaning clear, a good writer does not misplace a modifier. A misplaced modifier may delay one reader, distract another, and confuse a third. It is courteous as well as accurate to place modifiers where they belong. A writer invites misunderstanding when he places a word incorrectly and expects a reader to determine his meaning.

Dangling Modifiers

Grammars call participial phrases, gerundial phrases, infinitival phrases, and elliptical clauses that do not refer unmistakably to the words they logically modify *dangling modifiers*. Confused, exasperated readers call them something worse, especially when the modifiers seem to be not merely dangling in a sentence but floating in outer space. Sometimes the writer of a dangling modifier unconsciously creates humor; sometimes he invites Freudian interpretation:

> Injected daily with this drug, the technicians were able to train the animals in three days instead of three weeks (dangling participle).
> Being slow and stupid, I cannot train Joe Gulch to operate this machine (dangling participle).
> After daydreaming and napping, Dr. Medical gave Joe Flutterbrain a thorough examination and many tests (dangling gerund phrase).
> To test effectively the monkeys must be injected with three grains of this drug (dangling infinitive phrase).
> While chasing around the cage, Dr. Jones observed the rats (dangling elliptical clause).
> Deliver the machine to the Purchasing Department as soon as properly greased (dangling elliptical clause).

A writer correcting these errors may choose from several methods:

1. Placing the dangling modifier next to the word it should modify:

> In three days instead of three weeks the technicians were able to train the animals injected with this drug.

2. Changing the subject of the sentence so that the introductory modifier will be followed immediately by the word it logically modifies and that word will be the subject of the sentence:

> After daydreaming and napping, Joe Flutterbrain was given a thorough examination and many tests by Dr. Medical.

The reviser may eliminate unnecessary or misleading words in some sentences:

> Being slow and stupid, Joe Gulch cannot be trained to operate this machine.
>
>   or
>
> Joe Gulch is too slow and stupid to learn to operate this machine.

3. Changing the dangling phrase to some other construction or to some other kind of phrase:

> If the tests are to be effective, the monkeys must be injected with three grains of this drug.
>
>   or
>
> For effective testing, the monkeys must be injected with three grains of this drug.

4. Completing the elliptical construction:

> Dr. Jones observed the rats while they were chasing around the cage.
>
>   and
>
> As soon as the machine is properly greased, deliver it to the Purchasing Department.

Dangling modifiers occur most frequently when a modifier begins a sentence. An introductory participle, gerund, or infinitive modifies the subject of the principal verb and should be followed by that subject, which must be the word it logically describes:

> INCORRECT: Finding many discrete wavelengths differing completely from the wavelength predicted by classical electrodynamics, the information was used to formulate quantum mechanics.
>
> CORRECT: Finding many discrete wavelengths differing completely from the wavelength predicted by classical electrodynamics, Hessenberg, Schrodinger, and others used the information to formulate quantum mechanics.

When a writer does not wish to follow the modifier with the subject, he should rephrase:

> INCORRECT: Instead of using a standard textbook, a pamphlet prepared in this laboratory may be substituted.
>
> CORRECT: A pamphlet prepared in this laboratory may be substituted for a standard textbook.
>
>   Instead of a standard textbook, a pamphlet prepared in this laboratory may be used.

Modifiers are also often misplaced before an *it* that is the subject of a main clause.

> INCORRECT: As chief of this department, it has been my pleasure to supervise research.
>
> CORRECT: As chief of this department, I have supervised research.

Many participial phrases at the ends of sentences modify the wrong nouns:

INCORRECT: The formulation was applied directly on the lesions starting on the third day of the infection.

CORRECT: On the third day of the infection and thereafter the formulation was applied directly on the lesions.

INCORRECT: These data indicate that MWD is affected only slightly using these control agents.

CORRECT: These data indicate that MWD is affected only slightly by these control agents.

These data indicate that MWD is affected only slightly when these control agents are used.

An exception to the rule for introductory gerunds, infinitives, and participles is that a phrase stating a general action rather than the action of a specific person or thing may stand before a word it does not describe:

Taking everything into consideration, the experiment was not too lengthy.

To sum up, the proposal is now ready for presentation.

Squinting Modifiers

Careless placing of a modifier between two parts of a sentence confuses readers, who cannot tell whether the modifier belongs with what comes before or with what comes after it. Writers should avoid placing between two parts of a sentence a modifier that may refer to either part. An adverbial modifier at the conjunction of a main clause and a dependent clause may be a squinting modifier:

SQUINTING MODIFIER: After the committee decided that the work must be completed by Monday, in spite of other commitments, it adjourned immediately.

A reader cannot tell whether the work must be completed by Monday in spite of other commitments or whether in spite of other commitments the committee adjourned. A comma will sometimes help, but English word order has a much stronger effect than punctuation; therefore a careful writer places the phrase where it belongs and does not depend on a comma.

CORRECT: The committee decided that in spite of other commitments the work must be completed by Monday. Then it adjourned.

or

After the committee had decided that the work must be completed by Monday, it adjourned immediately in spite of other commitments.

POOR: Although salaries were increased slowly the workers grew dissatisfied.

IMPROVED: Although salaries were slowly increased, the workers grew dissatisfied.

POOR: When the rats grew lethargic, gradually he increased the dosage.

IMPROVED: When the rats grew lethargic, he increased the dosage gradually.

Single Words and Phrases

Writers must place with special care words that can function as two parts of speech. The position of *almost, even, ever, hardly, just, mainly, merely, nearly, not,* and *only* should be checked carefully because they can modify many parts of a sentence. The meaning of the following sentence changes drastically as *just* is moved from one position to another:

> *Just* he thought that he would be promised a promotion.
> He *just* thought that he would be promised a promotion.
> He thought *just* that he would be promised a promotion.
> He thought that *just* he would be promised a promotion.
> He thought that he would be *just* promised a promotion.
> He thought that he would be promised *just* a promotion.

When it is his promotion that is in question, a writer can usually see the different meanings clearly. He should train himself to understand them in other sentences, such as

> Only I calculated the value of x in the equation.
> I only calculated the value of x in the equation.
> I calculated the only value of x in the equation.
> I calculated the value of only x in the equation.
> I calculated the value of x only in the equation.
> I calculated the value of x in the only equation.
>
> I nearly accepted his new theory.
> I accepted his nearly new theory.
> He would not consider even one experiment.
> He would not even consider one experiment.
> He fired almost all the members of his division.
> He almost fired all the members of his division.

A writer who can read these sentences accurately can usually correct his own once he is alert to the different meanings possible. He must remember that meaning may change with the shifting of a phrase:

> The technician placed the banana on the table beside the monkey.
> The technician placed the banana beside the monkey on the table.

Writers should check carefully the placement of phrases because it is easy to overlook even a ridiculous misplacing like *The manuscript was received in the mail from Dr. Simon* instead of *Dr. Simon's manuscript came in the mail* or *The manuscript from Dr. Simon was in the mail.*

> INCORRECT: In contrast to the rats, the writers reported that testosterone fails to increase this rate in mice.
>
> CORRECT: The writers reported that testosterone fails to increase this rate in mice although it increases the rate in rats.
>
> INCORRECT: Based on error the Accounting Department declared the estimate of taxes fraudulent.
>
> CORRECT: The Accounting Department declared the mistaken estimate of taxes fraudulent.
>
> The Accounting Department erred in declaring the estimate of taxes fraudulent.
>
> INCORRECT: The patient is progressing as well as can be expected under the treatment of Dr. John Doe.
>
> CORRECT: The patient, who is under the treatment of Dr. John Doe, is progressing as well as can be expected.
>
> INCORRECT: Long arguments often occurred about treatments during the conferences of specialists.
>
> CORRECT: During the conferences of specialists long arguments about treatments often occurred.

IS WHEN, IS WHERE, IS BECAUSE

Explanations and definitions should not be introduced by *is when* or *is where;* these phrases sound childish and illogical.

> INCORRECT: A broadband antenna is where certain specific characteristics of radiation pattern, polarization, or impedance are retained.
>
> CORRECT: A broadband antenna is one that retains specified characteristics of radiation pattern, polarization, or impedance.
>
> INCORRECT: Experimental teratology is when drugs and other chemical agents are applied to developing embryos.
>
> CORRECT: Experimental teratology is the application of drugs and other chemical agents to developing embryos.

Statements in constructions like "The reason . . . is because," are neater and briefer if they are expressed more directly.

> INCORRECT: The reason nuclear physicists tend to ignore the chemical bonding of the atoms they investigate is because the energies in nuclear reactions are larger than the energies in chemical bonding.
>
> CORRECT: The reason nuclear physicists tend to ignore the chemical bonding of the atoms they investigate is that the energies in nuclear reactions are larger than those in chemical bonding.
>
> CORRECT: Because the energies in nuclear reactions are larger than those in chemical bonding, nuclear physicists tend to ignore the chemical bonding of the atoms they investigate.

SHALL AND WILL, SHOULD AND WOULD

American usage of *shall* and *will* illustrates change in usage. In speech, distinctions between *shall* and *will*, *should* and *would* have disappeared (possibly because of the use of the contractions *I'll, you'll, he'll, we'll, they'll, I'd, you'd, he'd, we'd, they'd*). Whether to observe these distinctions in writing is a controversial issue that provokes handbook writers to present both views and then to emphasize their own view or even to yield in resignation and advise readers to skip the discussion if they are not interested in the controversy.

Skipping may suit college freshmen, but writers for government and industry must know what they are saying when they use these words. Writers of patents and contracts, of technical directions and safety regulations, of legal papers, and of directions for patients find the study of these verbs more important than some writers of recent handbooks do; therefore I shall describe the forms as they appear in formal style and advise writers for the professions how to choose the most suitable usage.

Until recently most handbooks instructed writers to use *shall* and *should* with *I* and *we*, and *will* and *would* with all other persons for the simple future tense. For the emphatic future tense—expressing the speaker's determination, threat, command, promise, or willingness—they instructed writers to reverse this practice.

Simple Future

I shall or should	We shall or should
You will or would	You will or would
He, she, it will or would	They will or would

Emphatic Future

I will or would	We will or would
You shall or should	You shall or should
He, she, it shall or should	They shall or should

Then "You will see the patient tomorrow" means that the speaker expects you to see the patient. "You shall see the patient tomorrow" means that

1. The speaker is determined that you see the patient, as in
   "You shall see the patient tomorrow even if I have to take you to him myself."
2. The speaker promises that you are to see the patient, as in
   "You shall see the patient tomorrow; I have arranged for you to be admitted."
3. The speaker commands you to see the patient, as in
   "You shall see the patient this week because I am going on vacation."

4. The speaker is willing that you see the patient, as in
   "You shall see the patient tomorrow if you wish."
5. The speaker is threatening that you are to see the patient, as in
   "You shall see the patient tomorrow if you do not send his refund today."

Some formal writers use in a question the form of *shall* or *will*, *should* or *would* expected in the answer.

> Shall I send this order now? (Answer: *You shall*—a command)
> Will you endorse my check? (Answer: *I will*—willingness)

Other writers consider this stilted, particularly in the second person:

> Shall you leave early today? (Answer: *I shall*—expectation)

But they do use *shall* (with the first and third persons) in requests for permission and commands.

> Shall I leave the book on your desk?
> Shall he leave the book on your desk?

These distinctions between *shall* and *will* are still used in formal writing. Some experts recommend them for all writing, a few handbooks label those who attempt to retain them as "purists," and other experts suggest more mildly that because *shall* and *should* in the first person sound pedantic to Americans, writers need not hesitate to use *will* and *would*. The choice affects the tone of writing. The traditional usage has a formal flavor. The newer forms—*will* for simple futurity in all persons and *shall* for emphatic future—seem modern and informal.

A period of change often places a burden upon the reader, and the shifting in the use of *shall* and *will* is no exception. A reader may have to discover how a particular writer is using them if he is to understand the writer properly. As this may be a time-wasting process, one cannot blame companies or divisions that order writers to use one method for the sake of clarity. Where company usage is not established, a writer should choose the forms that seem most appropriate to the taste of his readers. In business and government, which are conservative in language the better choice is formal usage. Advertising departments, however, are more likely to choose informal usage, which may appear also in business and personal letters and in memorandums. In speech the informal forms are usual; however addresses, presentations, and other dignified speeches are formal in style and may suitably employ the traditional usage. Above all, writers should be consistent, for a reader can make little sense of a paper that uses both. Consistency is a courtesy owed to the reader.

Some special uses of *shall* and *will* and of *should* and *would* are less controversial.

SHALL is used for all persons in laws, motions, resolutions, contracts, etc.

> LAW—The employer shall provide adequate safety equipment.
> MOTION—The fee for the Demosthenes Lecture shall be five hundred dollars.
> RESOLUTION—Resolved: That the Speech Division shall award a Euphues Prize for Elegant Verbosity annually as a tribute to Professor Abel Webster.
> CONTRACTS—The car shall be delivered on Monday, January 31, at 9 a.m.
> The car shall be tested at a speed of two hundred miles an hour for one hour.
> The machine shall operate under the conditions described in the following paragraph.
> The paper shall have 20% rag content.

SHOULD or WOULD is used to express a writer's doubt or uncertainty.

> He should be a good merchandise manager. (This expresses less confidence than the simple future does.)
> Would you recommend me for the position? (*Would* is more tentative than *will* in such a sentence.)

The sentence "This car should do two hundred miles an hour" expresses less certainty than "This car shall do two hundred miles an hour."

SHOULD used as an auxiliary verb to express obligation is weaker than *ought*. "You should recommend him for promotion" has less force than "You ought to recommend him for promotion."

In some sentences *should* is ambiguous; it may mean probability or obligation. A writer should rephrase such sentences.

> AMBIGUOUS: The typists should complete your manuscript before they leave.
> ONE MEANING: The typists are to complete your manuscript before they leave.
> ANOTHER MEANING: The typists will probably complete your manuscript before they leave.

SHOULD is used for all persons in subordinate clauses expressing condition.

> Notify your supervisor if you should care to go.
> If I should miss the train, do not wait for me.

Today most writers use the present tense in such clauses except when they wish to intensify the conditional element.

If the dyed fabric should look spotty, repeat the procedure.
If the dyed fabric looks spotty, repeat the procedure.

The first sentence does not suggest as strongly as the second that the dye will look spotty.

WOULD may be used in all persons for a wish, but writers are likely to use some less formal expression.

Would that the founders had lived to see this achievement!
If only the founders had lived to see this achievement!

WOULD is used in all persons for a habitual action.

Before this process was introduced, patients would complain of the chalky taste.
We would always have some explanation for our lateness.
You would complain of incorrect billing.

THE SUBJUNCTIVE MOOD

The subjunctive is used to express a wish, a supposition, a condition, or an improbability. It also appears in some clauses introduced by *that*. Usually these clauses introduce recommendations, resolutions, suggestions, and demands in a formal context.

In modern English the simple subjunctive form of a verb can be detected only in the third person singular and in the forms of the verb *to be*.

THIRD PERSON SINGULAR

INDICATIVE	SUBJUNCTIVE
the plant succeeds	the plant succeed
he retires	he retire
she withdraws	she withdraw

To Be

PRESENT SUBJUNCTIVE

(Seldom used today except in resolutions, motions, and other stereotyped expressions and in some *that* clauses)

I be	we be
you be	you be
he, she, *or* it be	they be

PAST SUBJUNCTIVE
(The form used most often today)

I were	we were
you were	you were
he, she, *or* it were	they were

WISH: I wish that I were able to solve the equation.

SUPPOSITION: This method would succeed if the chemical were pure.

CONDITION OR HYPOTHESIS: If the temperature were higher, the results would be the same.

IMPROBABILITY: If the estimate were as wrong as that, I would not send the proposal.

That clauses expressing recommendations, hopes, prayers, wishes, requests, or commands are expressed in the subjunctive:

The supervisor ordered that the machine be stopped

The supervisor ordered that the operator stop the machine.

I recommend that Robert Cratchit be given an annual increase in salary of $2,000.

I requested that the window cleaner report every Monday at 9 a.m.

Resolved: That the services of the Trumpery Publicity Agency be terminated by January 1, 1966.

This committee suggests that the investigation of the side effects of this sedative be continued.

It is necessary that every worker wear safety glasses during this entire experiment. (Some writers prefer the more direct statement: Every worker must wear safety glasses during the entire experiment.)

Writers should know that many ideas expressed by verbs in the subjunctive may also be expressed by the auxiliaries *may, might, should, would, let, must,* etc.

I wish that I could solve this equation.

If the chemical should be pure, the method would succeed.

If the estimate should be as wrong as that, I dare not send the proposal.

Let the company use the formula immediately.

Workers must wear safety glasses during the entire experiment.

Sometimes the auxiliaries give meanings slightly different from those of the subjunctive mood. This allows the writer an opportunity to select from fine shades of meaning the precise shade he wants.

TENSES

Present Tense

The present tense is used for permanent truths:

Many of the experimental techniques that have been applied to single-phase flow *are* applicable to two-phase flow.

H. N. McManus, Jr., wrote that many of the experimental techniques that have been applied to single-phase flow *are* applicable to two-phase flow.

Newton *is* the originator of that theory.

A verb in the present tense that expresses a timeless truth should not be changed to another tense because of a preceding or following verb.

INCORRECT: He taught us that the earth moved.
CORRECT: He taught us that the earth moves.
CORRECT: He explained that neurotic patients respond this way.

The use of the present tense for permanent truths presents a scientific decision to the experimenter, who may conclude that under the given circumstances a chemical *changes* or *changed* its structure. If he uses *changed*, he states only that it happened in his experiment. If he uses *changes*, he states that it always happens. It is important that a writer understand this difference in the meaning of the two tenses.

Present Perfect and Past Tenses

The past tense refers to past time, to completed action; the present perfect tense connects a past occurrence with the present time, as when (1) the action continues into the present or (2) the action has taken place just before events happening now.

CORRECT: I have worked harder today than ever before. (The day is not over.)
CORRECT: I worked harder yesterday than ever before.
CORRECT: I have worked hard today, and I am glad to be going home at last.

The present perfect tense should not be used for completed action which has no specific or implied relation to the present.

INCORRECT: I have completed that study ten years ago.
CORRECT: I completed that study ten years ago.
CORRECT: (for a student) I have studied physics in college and disliked it.
CORRECT: (for an alumnus) I studied physics in college and disliked it.

Tenses of Infinitives

The perfect infinitive is used for action completed before the time of the main verb; otherwise the present infinitive is used.

INCORRECT: We should have liked to have seen the factory before the bidding.
CORRECT: We should have liked to see the factory before the bidding.
CORRECT: We should like to have seen the factory before the bidding.

Tenses of Participles

A past participle indicates action that occurred before the action of the governing verb; a present participle indicates action occurring at the time of the action of the governing verb.

> PAST PARTICIPLE: Having attended meetings all day, we were ready for some sightseeing.
>
> PRESENT PARTICIPLE: Talking as we looked at the sights, we discussed the papers read at the meeting.

But if *after* or some other word indicates that the action is past, a present participle is used.

> INCORRECT: After having attended meetings all day, we were ready for some sightseeing.
>
> CORRECT: After attending meetings all day, we were ready for some sightseeing.

Shifts in Tense or Mood

A careful writer avoids unnecessary shifts in tense or mood. This does not mean that all main verbs in a paper must be in the same tense or mood; it means that actions occurring at the same time should be in the same tense—past actions in the past tense, future actions in the future tense, present actions in the present tense, etc.

> INCORRECT: When we examined the first products, we find crystals for x-ray analysis. We determined the structure.
>
> CORRECT: When we examined the first products, we found (both past events should be in the past tense—*examined, found*) crystals for x-ray analysis. We determined (past event in past tense) the structure.
>
> INCORRECT: Dr. Wrightwell read his paper so poorly that I hear only one word in three.
>
> CORRECT: Dr. Wrightwell read his paper so poorly that I heard (both past events are in the past tense) only one word in three.
>
> INCORRECT: Dr. Wrightwell read his paper so poorly that during his presentation I find it necessary to consult the copy that I made before the meeting.
>
> CORRECT: Dr. Wrightwell read his paper so poorly that during his presentation I found (both past events are in the past tense) it necessary to consult the copy that I had made before the meeting. (An event in the more distant past is in the past perfect tense.)
>
> CORRECT: The results of the third run are about the same. (Present tense is used for historical present.)
>
> INCORRECT: If the results should be positive and the reactions are poor, the patients will be examined.

CORRECT: If the results should be positive and the reactions (*should be* is understood; if one hypothesis is conditional, the other must be also) poor, the patients will be (future tense is used for future time) examined.

INCORRECT: First heat the mixture in the tank. Then you should add the contents of the flask.

CORRECT: First heat the mixture in the tank. Then add the contents of the flask.

CORRECT: First you should heat the mixture in the tank. Then you should add the contents of the flask.

INCORRECT: The enlargement of the Safety Committee was recommended. Then the Ad Hoc Committee suggested a new chairman.

CORRECT: The Ad Hoc Committee recommended the enlargement of the Safety Committee and suggested a new chairman.

ELLIPSIS

In formal writing, a necessary verb or auxiliary should not be omitted.

INCORRECT: The recommendations are useful and widely used.

CORRECT: The recommendations are useful and are widely used. (The first *are* is a main verb; the second *are* is an auxiliary.)
These useful recommendations are widely used.

INCORRECT: They never have and never will find the answer to that question.

CORRECT: They never have found the answer to that question, and they never will.

INCORRECT: The computer never has and never can be used for such work.

CORRECT: The computer never has been and never can be used for such work.
The computer never has been used for such work and never can be.

When two or more words require different prepositions, the prepositions should not be omitted.

INCORRECT: It is difficult to estimate whether the new tax laws will add or detract from the profits.

CORRECT: It is difficult to estimate whether the new tax laws will add to or detract from the profits.

INCORRECT: The chairman commented on the parliamentarian's knowledge, interest, and respect for the law.

CORRECT: The chairman commented on the parliamentarian's knowledge of, interest in, and respect for the law.

But when the preposition may serve for two or more words, it need not be repeated: *He works and plays with John; He was prevented and prohibited from working; He had no interest or confidence in the promotion plan.* Sometimes the preposition is repeated for euphony, clarity, or emphasis: *He spoke against, acted against, and fought against change.*

INCORRECT GRAMMAR IN PROFESSIONAL WRITING

Incorrect grammar sometimes interferes with clarity. Misplaced modifiers, incorrect comparisons, and wrong tenses, for example, may convey the wrong meaning to a reader. A writer who states, "This dye was reliable for all fabrics," when he should state, "This dye is reliable for all fabrics," makes a costly error because he does not understand that the present tense indicates permanent truth. Other mistakes in grammar and construction, like pronoun errors and incorrect parallelism, make writing fuzzy. Writers in the professions must be more exact than other writers. A writer of advertising may be purposely vague to avoid lawsuits or may purposely use illiterate English to flatter the uneducated. But those who are responsible for transmitting information in the professions must write clearly and appropriately.

Although clarity is the minimum expected of a writer in the professions, many scientists and technologists fight the editors and supervisors who change their English and who would train them to write better. I have known an engineer so muddleheaded as to pay for reprinting an entire article to correct an obvious typographical error in arithmetic but to balk at changing in a typed manuscript, "Little data are available." And a chemist who objected to erasures in his letters argued heatedly against changing the position of a misplaced *only*. "Only these three chemicals change the color of the drug," he wrote, and he insisted that it meant, "These three chemicals change only the color of the drug." He told the supervisor who wanted to correct this, "Leave it the way it is. My readers know enough about chemistry to know what I mean." But those readers are the first to ask why he did not know enough about English to say what he meant.

Other writers err by depending on their ears for correct English usage. Trained as business administrators, scientists, or technologists, they attempt what even a person trained in language and literature hesitates to do by ear. They fail to consider that the ear accepts and likes what it is used to. The ear may reject usages merely because they sound strange to it; therefore an ear accustomed to the weaknesses common in writings on science and technology is an untrustworthy guide. A professional man must learn to beware of the errors that his ear likes. If his ear accepts an error, that is the mistake he must search for when he revises. This does not mean that a writer must use what he does not like. There are innumerable ways of expressing a thought effectively, and a writer is free to choose any one that suits him. Nor does it mean that the ear is useless. For the more subtle harmonies and rhythms of language, a writer must use his ear. But he should not consider it an authority on grammar.

Chapter X

The Standard of Diction for the Professions

> Reading maketh a full man, conference a ready man, and writing an exact man.
>
> *Bacon*

AVOIDING COMMON ERRORS

In the prose of information the right word, like the right number, is of exceeding importance. Scientists, technologists, and business executives cannot afford to be satisfied with something close to what they mean. They must write exactly what they mean. Fuzziness, ambiguity, or misleading incorrectness may be dangerous. A doctor who writes, "Often these patients are depressed," when he means, "Many of these patients are depressed," may lead his reader into serious error.

One cause of many misunderstandings is the vague diction popular today in poor business writing. A director of medical TV programs wrote to the chairman of a program, "If any arrangements for this program have to be changed, contact me." When the three panelists scheduled for the program suddenly found it impossible to appear, the chairman reported this in a letter to the TV director, but the director, who had been two thousand miles away from his office, heard nothing until his plane landed at the airport three hours before the program.

"Why didn't you call or send a telegram?" he wailed. "The office could have reached me in California, and I would have come here a day earlier."

"But you told me to write," the chairman said.

To him *contact* meant *write;* to the director it meant *telephone* or *telegraph.* I have seen many other business executives face difficult and unnecessary emergencies because of such careless use of words.

Some business clichés are objectionable for another reason; they create an old-fashioned atmosphere just as inappropriate as paper cuffs fastened with rubber bands and a celluloid collar would be if worn by someone using the latest computer. A phrase like "your esteemed favor" suggests Bob Cratchit sitting on a high stool in Scrooge's office. One does not expect antiquated business phrases such as "in reply beg leave to state," "under separate cover," and "hoping to hear from you soon, we remain," to come from an electric typewriter.

One writer of a college textbook on technical reporting said that he was omitting discussion of old-fashioned business language because his students had never met it and did not need to be warned against it. But anyone familiar with modern business and industry could have told him that they would meet it soon. A supervisor would encourage them to use it, or young graduates would read it in correspondence and sprinkle it in their own letters to lend a "business tone." Some antiquated phrases are nearly indestructible because supervisors teach them to beginners who become supervisors and teach them to other beginners. Why? Largely because they are easy substitutes for thought. "Yours of the 14th inst. received and contents duly noted," flows from a writer without thought. To express some meaning about a particular inquiry or problem requires more effort. Often the user of business clichés is postponing as long as possible the labor of thinking—sometimes until the final sentence of his letter or report. All the time-worn phrases that precede his last sentence are just procrastination. Eliminating antiquated phraseology and business clichés may cost such a writer a little revision time and some effort at first, but later it will become automatic. And the result will be briefer and more effective writing.

Incorrect diction is a different fault, but it also distracts and interrupts and thus creates a poor impression. Frequent distractions of this sort may make a busy reader throw down a report before he has completed his reading. And a writer who uses incorrect diction appears careless, poorly educated, unreliable. His reader wonders whether he dare trust the scientific information or the professional judgment of a writer who makes elementary mistakes in the use of English words. To avoid such doubt, distraction, and distrust, good writers in the professions correct their diction carefully. And because usage is highly contagious, they guard against the language errors that they see and hear frequently.

A good writer does not confuse similar words like *accelerate* and *exhilarate; accept* and *except; affect* and *effect; adverse* and *averse; alternate* and *alternative; amount* and *number; common* and *mutual; continual* and *continuous; exploit* and *explore;* and *company, concern, firm, corporation*. Nearly every college handbook of composition contains definitions of words commonly confused. Theodore M. Bernstein's *The Careful Writer* [1] and *Watch Your Language* [2] contain dry, witty, and helpful comments on words and phrases frequently misused. Reading such lists and comments gives a writer a feeling for correctness and exactness in the use of words.

A writer who wishes to be correct must learn to be critical of the words he reads. Business executives, scientists, and engineers are often berated for careless use of words, the assumption of the critic being that their work should make them accurate in all ways. But they are children of their time, which offers them little encouragement, for they find many poor examples in their professional or other reading.

A signed article in a good newspaper, for example, notes that the home of a bride's family is "unprepossessing." A slum family? No, socialites who have an *unpretentious* home. The producer of a prize-winning documentary film is quoted as saying when the prize was withdrawn, "I'm very disappointed. I think it's unsolicitous of the Academy to publicly announce a nomination and later withdraw it." Unsolicitous? And the following misuse of *compunction* by a journalist is typical of the careless errors found in even the best newspapers: "An F.A.A. official said that the dike and all other aspects of La Guardia's operation met or exceeded Federal regulations and that pilots were under no compunction to land there if they believed the field was unsafe."

A publisher's advertising of a book on human behavior reads:

A Book of Fundamental Insight into the Forces Between Body and Psyche
which explains in simple non-technical verbiage
the meaning, purpose and promise of
PSYCHIATRY

Well, maybe it is verbiage, but who expected the publisher to admit it? And in an advertisement mailed by an institute that gives seminars on technical writing, *Principals of Clear Writing* is spelled that way twice. The advertisement states that a technical writing association has approved the advertisement "for distribution to its members as an outstanding example of one of the techniques for improving writing ability." The engineers and scientists to whom the advertisement was directed are able to distinguish between *principles* and *principals*. But the writer of the advertisement could not. A reputable publisher advertises as follows a book designed to improve business writing: "The book contains exercises to improve proficiency of grammar, spelling, and vocabulary

[1] Atheneum, New York, 1965.
[2] Channel Press, Manhasset, New York, 1958.

usage. Interspersed throughout the book are various checklists for inventory and self-evaluation on writing a letter, a report or a memorandum." Misusing *of* after *proficiency* and *on* after *self-evaluation* and the poor use of *inventory* suggest that the writer of the advertisement needs a few checklists.

Because a professional man finds such mistakes and weaknesses in his reading, even in the very material supposed to help him to write better, it is clear that he must plan to write more accurately and correctly than other writers, even apparently than some of those who would instruct him. To do so he must become alert to words, their uses and abuses.

Because usage changes, every writer faces the delicate question of whether to adopt a new usage. In advising writers in science, technology, and administration, I usually recommend a conservative choice. I have noticed that the men in those fields tend to resist changes in language, even at times to scorn them. Writers should therefore select conservative usage for such readers. A writer in an advertising division may well strive always to be the first to use the new, but other writers for business, government, and industry choose well when they prefer established forms. The scientist and the technologist, moreover, have an interest in maintaining established usage whenever it is more precise. They may advantageously cling to usage which their accuracy of expression requires, for thus they help to retain necessary forms that would otherwise disappear from use. When established usage is more helpful to them than the new is, they should stubbornly be "the last to cast the old aside."

The rest of this chapter discusses and illustrates the errors in diction to which readers in the professions are exposed most frequently. I hope that the discussion will help writers to avoid them and to acquire a feeling for precise and correct diction.

Comparison of Words

Some words do not permit comparison because they do not have degrees—*extinct, fatal, final, honest, impossible, inferior, libelous, matchless, moral, mortal, obvious, peerless, perfect, permanent, rare, safe* (meaning *not hazardous, not involving risk or loss*), *straight, unique* (meaning *being the only one of its kind*), *universal, vertical. A very unique discovery, a somewhat obvious approach, a very safe method, a rather peerless result, a very fatal illness, a quite impossible task*—all these phrases compare concepts that are incomparable, assign degrees to ideas that do not have degrees. If a man is lifeless, all that can be said about the absence of life is covered in *lifeless*. A writer may discuss the time and place of lifelessness, the reasons for stating that the man is lifeless, but it is illogical to discuss how dead he is. Words should not be used loosely in functional prose, and therefore the words listed above should not be compared.

Choice of Conjunction

Some writers use conjunctions so carelessly that their readers might easily assume that all conjunctions have the same meaning. Careless use of conjunctions confuses readers. They do not like to readjust ideas in midsentence or to reread in order to understand, and it is, therefore, discourteous to use an incorrect, an ambiguous, or even a temporarily ambiguous word.

The following published sentence misuses *yet* for *and: There is nothing in Westchester like our 3 models with wood panelling, carpeting, post and beam construction, yet everyone loves them.* Writers also confuse *however* with *and: Most stars are much larger than the earth; however a few are millions of times larger.*

Time and place are frequently interchanged by mistake. In the sentence *Where colleges do not schedule these conferences, meeting candidates takes two or three days instead of one,* the writer meant *when* or *if,* not *where.* And the sentence *In the instances where men neglect the methods of science and concentrate their thinking on the results of science, this also occurs* needs *when* or *if* in place of the wordy *in the instances where.* The writer of *The richest ore was found when the vein was deepest* meant *where,* not *when.* And the writer of *There are many examples when the computers would be more accurate than the methods now used* was not referring to time but to divisions of his company. Confusion of time and place is likely to occur in sentences containing unnecessary words like *in the instances, in cases,* and *in fields.*

Careless substitution of one meaning for another makes writing fuzzy, and fuzzy writing is confusing. After attempting to read a paragraph of it, a person is likely to shake his head and wonder what is wrong. He does not know that time and place or addition and contrast have been confused; indeed, only the best editors detect this error in a first or second reading. The average reader sees merely that the words look as though they should make sense, but they do not. A single ill-chosen conjunction may change meaning drastically, but many writers and readers do not know this. For example, a newspaper advertisement for six furnished rooms ended with "Adults or teachers preferred." A writer who has difficulty detecting misuses in the examples cited should study the following paragraphs and then examine carefully the conjunctions in his own writing.

Some conjunctions, *while* for example, should be used with particular care because, having two meanings, they are sometimes ambiguous. *While* means *as long as* and *during the time that;* but *while* also means *whereas* and *although*. In the sentence *While he wrote he paid no attention to anything else, while* means *as long as* or *during the time that*. In *His speeches are long and discursive while his reports are brief and well organized, while* means *whereas*. In *While he never seemed anxious about the deadline, he did press very hard to complete the experiments, while* means *although*. But what does *while* mean in *While the animals were quiet they did not seem sick?* Does it mean *as long as* or *although?* In sentences where *while* is ambiguous, a careful writer uses another conjunction. And this is true even though the ambiguity may be temporary, as in *While he did not like the defendant, his behavior was impeccably disinterested*. In the following sentence *while* is used incorrectly for *and: However, difficulties were encountered on a large scale because the oxime could not be filtered while centrifugation proved to be a long and tedious process.*

The conjunction *since* means (1) *in the period following the time stated (Since he was elected, he has spoken to me only once);* (2) *continuously from the time when* or *ever since (Since the accomplishment of atomic fission the world of physics has been changing);* and (3) *because* or *inasmuch as (Since the readings are inaccurate, the plant must repeat the runs)*. It is frequently used ambiguously by careless writers:

> Since the department was reorganized, the work has been more evenly
>   distributed;
> Since the FDA announced this ruling, the experiments have been re-
>   ported;
> Since storms have become severe the plant is closed four or five days
>   every winter;
> Since he learned that ambiguity may cause accidents, he has corrected
>   every safety publication carefully.

The writers of these sentences meant *ever since the department was reorganized, because the FDA announced this ruling, because storms have become severe, ever since he learned that ambiguity may cause accidents.*

The word *as* is an overworked conjunction that is often vague or completely confusing. It may mean *because, for, seeing that, since, in the manner that*. Sometimes by meaning too many of them, it means none of them: *It was easy to see that the patient was neither tired nor ill as he won the game of chess*. This sentence demands some other conjunction. The explanatory *as* clause introducing a sentence is less objectionable, but it is not always unambiguous, and it has been overworked. Truly objectionable is the substitution of *as* for a relative pronoun: *Writers have no opportunity to discuss publication dates as is offered to super-visors* should be written *Writers have no opportunity to discuss pub-lication dates such as is offered to supervisors* or *Writers do not have the opportunity to discuss publication dates that is offered to supervisors.*

The phrase *on the contrary* joins two statements of the same idea or point of view when one statement is positive and the other negative: *Keppler and Galileo are not altogether different; on the contrary both were greatly influenced by Plato and Pythagoras; He is not an unreliable worker; on the contrary, he is dependable. On the other hand* joins two statements of opposed or opposite points of view when both statements are positive or negative: *One theory viewed gravity as a body striving to reach the earth; on the other hand Keppler saw it as the earth attracting a body; He is not the best worker in the laboratory; on the other hand he is not the worst.* By confusing *on the contrary* and *on the other hand,* a writer is likely to confound.

The conjunction *but* is sometimes used illogically, as in the sentence *He is not a Cornell graduate but he attended Harvard.* The fact that he is not a graduate of Cornell does not contrast with the fact that he attended Harvard. However, *He is not a Cornell but a Harvard graduate* is correct. *But* should not be used redundantly with *however. He admired the beautiful simplicity of Aristotle's system, but it does not follow, however, that he disliked the complexity of other systems.* A contrast is stated adequately by *but* or *however.* In the illustrative sentence there is no need for either; a semicolon might be used between the two clauses. A *but* contrast within a clause introduced by *but* is an awkward con-struction. One *but* should be removed in each of the following sentences:

> He said that he would try to improve, but he did not improve but argued in the same way with his coworkers and his superintendent.
> The results were not conclusive, but they were interesting but not suggestive.

Fowler aptly describes this use of *but* as "wheels within wheels."

The conjunction *whether* may be followed by *or not* for emphasis or euphony but is more frequently used without the stated negative. Restatement of the alternatives should be avoided. It is not necessary and it is not emphatic. Thus *Whether or not the experiments do or do not succeed is the question* repeats ineffectively. Any one of the follow-ing sentences is better: *Whether or not the experiments succeed is the question; Whether the experiments succeed is the question; Will the ex-periments succeed? is the question. As to* preceding *whether* is unneces-sary. In *The question as to whether the experiment should be continued was discussed but was not voted upon* and in *They could not decide as to whether to call the meeting, as to* is unnecessary. *Whether* is sometimes confused with *if*. *Let me know whether you are coming* means let me know in either case; however *Let me know if you are coming* means that you need not let me know if you are not coming. *Therefore he could not decide if the new regulations were in effect* is poor because the writer meant *whether*. The sentence *Please notify us if this statement of your expenses is incorrect* means that notification is unnecessary unless the statement is incorrect. *Please let us know whether this statement of your expenses is incorrect* is a request for an answer in either case.

The conjunction *and so* means *as a result, therefore, consequently;* the conjunction *so that* means *in order that, for that purpose*. They are commonly confused, as in the following example: "Titles and side-headings are one of the most effective devices for stimulating reader interest and increasing reading ease. Newspaper and magazine publishers have long known this, so that today there is hardly a magazine or newspaper on the market that does not have an attractive format that invites the reader's interest. . . ." Here *so that* should be *and so*.

The conjunction *that* is sometimes omitted, as in the following sentences: *I told him he should do it; I hear they are revising the budget.* Writers should be careful to include *that* whenever the sense requires it and to place it correctly. The sentence *The reporter maintained during the conference that the public relations director had given him the figures* differs from *The reporter maintained that during the conference the public relations director had given him the figures*. If the conjunction *that* is not expressed, temporary misreading will occur: *The reporter said he had heard the information to be given at the press conference was incomplete*. A reader who understands that the reporter said he had heard the information to be given at the press conference is pulled up sharply by the *was incomplete* and has to reassemble the sentence in his mind or reread it. *The reporter said he had heard that the information to be given at the press conference was incomplete* is immediately clear.

If omission of *that* does not cause a misreading, may *that* be omitted? The conjunction *that* is expressed more frequently in formal writing than in informal writing and more frequently in writing than in informal speech. Conversational sentences are usually shorter and less intricate than written sentences and therefore require fewer guides. But even in formal writing some verbs are not usually followed by *that*, for example *believe, presume, suppose, think*. *That* is usually expressed after such verbs as *agree, assert, assume, calculate, conceive, learn, maintain, state,* and *suggest*. Many verbs are sometimes followed by *that*. The decision whether to express *that* after a verb may depend on the formal or informal quality of the writing, the sound of the sentence, and the writer's opinion of his readers' needs. An unsure writer should remember that omitting the conjunction *that* may be confusing. Unless his major aim is conversational informality, a writer in the professions who is unsure of his ear and judgment should express *that* after verbs that are sometimes followed by *that*. Careful observation of the usage of good contemporary writers will guide those who feel more sure of their perception.

But writers should take pains to avoid unnecessary repetitions of *that*. For example, the second *that* should be omitted from the following sentence: *They were told that although the convention would not recess until Monday that there was not time for new business*. And strings of interdependent *that* clauses, like strings of other interdependent clauses, should be avoided.

That is introduces a statement equivalent to the preceding statement, not one that corrects the preceding statement. In the following sentence the statements connected by *that is* are equivalents: *The entire research staff, that is administrators, scientists, engineers, laboratory technicians, laboratory assistants, secretaries, and typists, will move on Monday*. But *There are twenty-nine papers in the symposium; that is, three of them are abstracts* should be *There are twenty-six papers and three abstracts in the symposium* or *There are twenty-nine papers, three of them abstracts, in the symposium* or *There are twenty-nine papers in the symposium, but three of them are abstracts*.

Choice of Pronoun

The relative pronouns *who, whose, whom* are used for persons, personified objects, and sometimes for animals. *Which* is used for things, for lower animals, and for collective nouns (even when the collective nouns designate groups of people). The pronoun *that* may be used in place of *who, whom*, or *which*.

The pronoun *whose* may be used instead of an awkward *of which: The letter was sent to the department whose chairman had requested it*. When it is possible to avoid this substitution, it is better to do so, as the following sentences illustrate:

> He examined the reports whose bindings were damaged.
> He examined the reports with damaged bindings.
> He went to the library whose founder was his grandfather.
> He went to the library founded by his grandfather.

Awkward use of the relative pronoun *which* as an adjective should be avoided. *He did not present his vouchers on time, which negligence caused him trouble for weeks* might be rephrased in a number of ways: for example, *negligence that* (or *which*) *caused him trouble for weeks; Neglecting to present his vouchers on time caused him trouble for weeks; His negligence in failing to present his vouchers on time caused him trouble for weeks.*

The question of whether to use *that* only for restrictive clauses and *which* only for nonrestrictive clauses is much discussed. In such sentences as the following the distinction between restriction and nonrestriction depends on commas and on the context:

1. The formulas which are dangerous to birds are not to be used without authorization.
2. These two formulas, which are dangerous to birds, should be stored separately.

Fowler states, ". . . if writers would agree to regard *that* as the defining restrictive relative pronoun, and *which* as the non-defining [nonrestrictive], there would be much gain both in lucidity and in ease. Some there are who follow this principle now; but it would be idle to pretend that it is the practice either of most or of the best writers." [3] Although some writers of handbooks think that the practice today is to use *that* for restrictive clauses and *which* for nonrestrictive, Margaret Nicholson retains Fowler's remarks,[4] and I think her right. Some writers would use *that* to indicate restriction in Sentence 1 above, but others would use *which*. I doubt that handbook writers can change this, desirable though such a change may be.

The pronoun *one* should not be used for *I* or *me*. The sentence *My course in technical writing contained too much material for one to master in six hours* illustrates a poor use of *one*. The sentence might read: *for me to master, for the students to master,* or *material for six hours.* Using *one* instead of *I* or *we* for an expression of personal opinion does not increase impersonality or objectivity: *One thinks there was too much material for one to master.* In such a sentence *one* is awkward.

Choice of Preposition

A careful writer makes certain that his prepositions are idiomatic. Poor style results from cumbersome groups of prepositions; they should be replaced by simpler expressions. Writing that contains many such groups seems heavy and clumsy. The following sentences illustrate that

[3] H. W. Fowler, *A Dictionary of Modern English Usage,* 2 ed. (Oxford University Press, New York, 1965), p. 626; 1 ed. (1947), p. 635.
[4] Margaret Nicholson, *A Dictionary of American-English Usage* (The New American Library, New York, 1957), p. 577.

in regard to, by means of, and *in the matter of* are usually easy to omit or to replace:

> In regard to scientists, they are addicted to detective fiction. (Scientists are addicted to detective fiction.)
> By means of raising the temperature he solved the problem. (By raising the temperature he solved the problem.)
> In the matter of professional ethics it may be said that such action violates the code. (Such action violates the code of professional ethics.)

These groups of prepositions tend to attract other unnecessary words, and the total effect is fuzzy. When the unnecessary words are removed, the sentences become more clear-cut. A writer should not, however, omit necessary prepositions. Omitting necessary prepositions and conjunctions is characteristic of telegraphic style, and telegraphic style is neither clear nor readable (page 200).

The correct diction discussed in this chapter is the minimum expected of a writer in the professions. Good style requires not merely that a word be correct but that it be the right word in the right place. Choosing the right word from a multitude of possible words is the subject of Chapter XII. A writer who considers his diction correct but not so effective as it might be should consult that chapter for suggestions on how to make words work for him.

Chapter XI

Style: The Personality and Character of Writing

> In science the credit goes to the man who convinces
> the world, not to the man to whom the idea first occurs.
>
> *Sir William Osler*

Style is the personality and character of writing. Like the personality and character of a person, style makes a single impact on first acquaintance. When later analysis reveals that many qualities were combined in that first impression, they often prove difficult to trace, describe, and understand. The characteristics of style blend just as intricately and subtly as the characteristics of a person.

Style and the writer are so closely related that critics frequently describe style with the adjectives that are used for people. Style is weak, strong, muscular, flabby, graceful, clumsy, plain, ostentatious, cold, warm, coarse, elegant. The sports column is breezy, the book review is keen and witty, and the begging letter is too obsequious. The style of the politician we dislike is pompous and hypocritical; of the one we like, natural and honest. Shakespeare is profound, Milton is grand and lofty, and the King James Bible is earnest and sincere.

"The style is the man himself," said Georges Louis Leclerc de Buffon to the French Academy. And in the two hundred and fifty years since he spoke, hundreds of less penetrating thinkers than the members of the French Academy have repeated, "Style is the man." Many who quote these words apply them superficially: they expect a man with a sloppy appearance to express himself carelessly, an earnest looking writer to produce serious and ponderous works, and a prim looking person to write neatly and properly. When they read a book written by someone they know or when they meet the author of a book that they have read, they are shocked. The man with egg stains on his tie has written precisely and carefully, the doctor who is dour and unapproachable has written love letters in baby talk, and the dry-as-chalkdust schoolteacher has written ribald, bawdy stories in an earthy style.

Buffon was addressing a group of keen and subtle thinkers who did not expect human beings to be easy to understand. His statement is no less true because it does not necessarily apply to the outer man as perceived by an insensitive or casual observer. A man presents many images to the world and to himself; the true man may be a medley of all or some of these. The egg stain on a writer's tie may have escaped his notice because all his attention was concentrated on writing accurately. The stern and dignified doctor may have needed desperately the relaxation of playful affection. And the schoolteacher may have escaped the restrictions of her prim life through inner rebellion and revels, or she even may have been guiltily concealing a bawdy nature under a prim exterior. "The style is the man himself"—in all his complexity, elusiveness, and mystery.

One would expect these qualities of a man to be generally recognized in this Freud-ridden age. But so many people see only the obvious that a writer has difficulty overcoming an impression left by poor style. This may be true even though the style has been forced upon him by teachers or supervisors and is not his own. His annoyed readers (and who is not annoyed by poor style?) assign the defects of the style to the man. And when writing pleases readers by its good style, they assume that the writer has the virtues of his writing. Therefore a professional man who improves his style enhances his reputation.

The first step in achieving a good style is organizing effectively (Chapter V). Georges de Buffon states:

> This plan is not indeed the style, but it is the foundation; it supports the style, directs it, governs its movements, and subjects it to law; without it, the best writer will lose his way, and his pen will run on unguided and by hazard will make uncertain strokes and incongruous figures.[1]

An effective style for the professions is a clear style (Chapters IX and X) and a brief style (Chapter VIII). A well-organized, clear, and brief paper is adequate for many purposes and certainly better than much of the writing that circulates in industry and appears in learned journals. But such a style often leaves an intelligent writer vaguely dissatisfied and his readers apathetic or bored. Avoidance of error does not of itself constitute good writing; indeed, pedantically correct writing

---

[1] "Discourse on Style," trans. Rollo W. Brown, in *The Writer's Art* (Harvard University Press, Cambridge, 1932), p. 280.

may be dull and colorless. Many writers, supervisors, and instructors sense this and wonder what to do.

COMMON WEAKNESSES

The most helpful answer that I have found is to begin to improve style by eliminating the characteristics of weak and awkward style. Most writers find that as they remove these characteristics from their writing a good style emerges and develops. One of my most exciting teaching experiences is to free a person of superior intelligence from the clutter of weaknesses common in functional prose and to observe him acquire not merely the rudiments of style but an individual style that transforms his writing. A keen man with professional training can apply the principles of style so skillfully, so efficiently, and often so imaginatively that the results delight and surprise him and his readers.

The first time this happened I was speechless in astonishment— certainly a convincing indication of amazement in a woman. I had been teaching the kind of class I prefer, a democratic class ranging from a distinguished director of research to the newest B.Ch.E. The new employee and the director were average writers in my group of twelve, the first displaying such a spectrum of typical freshman errors and weaknesses and the second writing in such choppy, incoherent sentences that reading their reports was painful.

When I conferred with the neophyte at the end of the course, I found that he had finally made the progress that he should have made in his freshman writing course—hardly an accomplishment to dazzle an instructor. When the director, whose conference followed the young engineer's, began by giving me an article that he was writing for a journal, I was not optimistic. From the very first sentence, however, I was astonished, but not because the choppy sentences had disappeared. That much improvement I had expected of him. What surprised me was that his article was written better than any technical article I had ever read—written so well, in fact, that I soon forgot my amazement and became absorbed in the reading.

"All that I did was stop counting words and start applying the principles of good writing that you gave us," he explained. With intelligence, imagination, and good taste, he had applied these principles; and for the first time I saw how a superior mind trained in the sciences can effect an improvement in style, how it can root out errors and leap to mastery of the style that the scientist has always needed and wanted. The change had occurred with a velocity that startled me, even in this age of supersonic speed.

That day the thought of the director's wasted years of poor writing made me sad, but he was so happy with his success that I had to share his pleasure. We shared it again when his article, published without a single editorial change, brought him many enthusiastic letters from strangers who had not expected to enjoy an article in a journal of engineering and from friends and acquaintances who congratulated him on what they called "the marvelous change in his writing."

There was nothing marvelous in the basic principles he had applied so well. His flexibility in discarding bad habits of long standing, his superior intelligence, and his diligence were unusual. But the principles that improved his writing are those that any person with intelligence enough for a professional career can understand easily and apply effectively. The speed and quality of the improvement vary with each individual, but every professional man who sincerely wishes to improve can change his style for the better.

The first step—eliminating the bad habits that are impediments to the development of a good style—is simplified by the fact that nearly all writers in the professions have the same bad habits. The same few characteristics of poor style occur in the writing of scientists, engineers, managers, and other writers for business, industry, and learned journals. This repetition of errors makes it possible to correct them in a book of reasonable length. If there were more variety in the errors, I would have to present several volumes of instruction. But experience has taught me that writers in the professions seldom exhibit errors or weaknesses of style that are not the common errors that they have heard and read in their professional work.

These errors are frequent and pervasive. Many writers in the professions have come to speak—and even to think—in this same poor style. An improvement in writing often becomes, therefore, an improvement in thinking. Eliminating the unnecessary use of the passive voice, for example, leads to more decisive action. Thus the usual order of good thinking leading to good writing becomes good writing demanding good thinking. And good thinking well expressed leads to better decisions.

The Pervasive Passive

No undesirable feature of style is more common in the writing of professional men than the use of the passive voice where other speakers and writers would use the active voice. The active voice is clear and complete, and the order of the active voice is familiar to readers. The subject acts, the object receives the action, and the verb expresses the action clearly and directly:

1. He *struck* his wife.
2. The Tropical Belt Coal Company *made* a profit of ten million dollars.
3. God *helps* those who *help* themselves.
4. A stitch in time *saves* nine.

But in the passive voice the subject receives the action, the agent is omitted or is named in an awkward phrase beginning with *by*, and the verb needs the assistance of an auxiliary verb:

1. His wife *was struck.*
   His wife *was struck by* him.
2. A profit of ten million dollars *was made.*
   A profit of ten million dollars *was made by* the Tropical Belt Coal Company.
3. Those who *are helped by* themselves *are helped by* God.
4. Nine stitches *are saved by* a stitch in time.

Sometimes the passive voice serves a purpose. George's mother might say, "His wife was struck," to avoid admitting that George did it. A variation of Sentence 2 might be useful in a discussion of profits if the names of the companies were of no significance: "Profits of three million, seven million, and ten million dollars were made on the drug this year." But who would use the passive voice in all four sentences? Writers on science, technology, and business would and do:

1. His secretary was fired.
   His secretary was fired by him.
2. Mistakes were made in the stability tests.
   Mistakes were made in the stability tests by Reliable Testing Company.
3. The members of his team who are helped by their own ability and diligence are assisted in every way by this supervisor.
4. One hundred work hours a week are saved by this method.

Many writers in the professions would never use the active voice in these sentences or in any sentences like them. When these writers were students, their instructors taught them to use the passive voice, and later their supervisors required it. When the writers prepared articles for learned journals in science and technology, they found that the journals also used the passive voice. At conventions of professional societies and at business conferences, their colleagues talked in the passive voice. The passive voice became so familiar to these writers that the active voice sounded strange and wrong to them. It even alarmed them.

The prevalence of the passive voice in government and industry and in science and technology amazes those who are unfamiliar with it. They would find a recent experience of mine unnerving. A director of training asked me to confer with a foreign-born engineer who had learned English while working for two years in the United States. When I met the engineer, I apologized for my lateness.

"It is nothing," he replied courteously. "A cigarette was smoked and a book was read while waiting."

He was learning engineering English fast—not only the passive voice but the incorrect ellipsis that often accompanies it.

Later I asked another engineer and a chemist, "Can you improve the sentence 'A cigarette was smoked and a book was read while waiting'?"

"No error can be seen," decided the engineer.

"No improvement can be made," said the chemist, studied my expression, and added, "by me."

Fortunately a long acquaintance with the prevalent passive spared me the embarrassment of treating their answers as jokes. No jokes were being made by them consciously.

The passive voice weakens style because it is used, consciously and unconsciously, to evade responsibility. A popular passive construction is "It is thought that . . . ." Used anywhere but in science or technology, this indicates that a general opinion or truth follows. But when a writer on business, science, or technology uses it, he may mean "I think that . . . ," "we think that . . . ," "the Committee thinks that . . . ," or even "I hope that somebody reading this report thinks that . . . ." By close attention his reader may learn to interpret "it is thought that." The reader of a committee report may mentally substitute, "The committee thinks that." But after the reader has interpreted two paragraphs successfully this way, he comes to "it is thought that" followed by a common misconception, which is corrected in the next sentence. Does the writer mean that the committee held that misconception? Indeed, no. Now he is using "it is thought that" to introduce a general opinion that he wishes to correct.

A reader of minutes written in the evasive passive often finds himself sounding like a hoot owl as he screams, "Who? Who? Whooooo?" to statements like

> The cost of the TV program was estimated incorrectly.
> A letter to the FDA will be written.
> A report on these dyes will be submitted.
> It was said that the ruling will be ignored.
> A suggestion was made that marketing be postponed two months.
> It was reported that the new package had been well received.

In such writing all agents are anonymous, and many statements are ambiguous. Helpful and useful information is omitted. Nobody is responsible for anything.

For a whole year an apocryphal head of a college department evaded responsibility by writing sentences like the following:

> The new curriculum has been approved.
> The two suggested promotions from assistant to associate professor have not been approved.
> Budget allotments for travel have been reduced by twenty percent.
> An annual increase of $2,500 for the head of the department has been recommended.

Nobody knew that it was this worm who had approved and not approved, had reduced and recommended. But at the end of a year his department discovered the evader behind the passive voice, and in the unmistakable active voice the members requested his resignation.

When a writer using the passive voice names an agent, he has to employ a clumsy, wordy construction like, "The recommendation was made by the Safety Committee that testing be continued." The active voice is much neater and briefer: "The Safety Committee recommended that testing continue." The sentence "Papers were presented by John Jones and John Smith of our company" buries the credit due Jones and Smith. The sentence "John Jones and John Smith of our company presented papers" gives them due credit. If a writer wishes to emphasize the company, he may also do that in the active voice: "Two Polymer Company chemists, John Jones and John Smith, presented papers."

My favorite mixed-up sentence in the passive voice appears in reports of visits to factories and plants. The most inexperienced member of the visiting team writes the report. He begins with this gem, "On May 4, 1965, at the Polymer Plant Dr. A. J. Anderson was visited by the writer accompanied by Drs. Smith, Brown, and Jones." When I ask such a writer why he has used the passive voice and that monstrous phrase *the writer,* he is sure to reply, "It's more modest. You see, I was less important than the others and I didn't want to seem to be making myself important. I've always been told to use *the writer.*" It is difficult for him to see that *accompanied by* discourteously and immodestly subordinates his learned colleagues to himself, *the writer.* But if I ask him to put the sentence in the active voice, he writes, "On May 4, 1965, at the Polymer Plant Drs. Smith, Brown, and Jones and I visited Dr. A. J. Anderson," and he may even add, "to discuss the use of computers in our polymer research." He knows that common courtesy requires that *I* be last in the list, and if he does not use the passive and the unnatural and not-at-all modest *the writer,* he reports clearly and informatively, as well as courteously and modestly.

Passive verbs do have their proper place in style and are effective when used correctly. They may be used if (1) the actor is obvious, is unimportant, is not known, or is not to be mentioned; (2) the receiver of the action should be stressed, or the actor should appear in a subordinate position at the end of the construction; (3) the thought comes too rapidly in the active voice and needs a more deliberate presentation; (4) variety is needed in a passage expressed in the active voice; and (5) a weak substitute for the imperative is desired.

EXAMPLES

    (1) He was injured in action.
        Commencement will be held on May tenth this year.
        Awards will be presented at the annual dinner.
        The equipment was placed in Laboratory B, which has adequate space and proper lighting.
        The singer received an ovation.
    (2) His brother has been elected.
        A gold Cadillac was presented to the star by her producer.
        A bonus of a thousand dollars for every year of service was voted by the board.
        He was removed from office by a unanimous vote.
    (3) and (4) The active voice occurs far more often than the passive voice in exposition and narration, more than 90% of verbs being active according to one authority. The passive voice requires more words, blurs meaning, and uses the verb *to be,* which occurs in so many other constructions in English that it becomes monotonous. Inexperienced writers who employ the passive to avoid *I* or *we* create awkward sentences and shift voices without reason. They should use the active voice whenever possible and the passive voice only in those few constructions where the active voice is ineffective. Scientists and technologists must make special efforts to use the active voice because much of their writing requires the passive voice, and, being accustomed to it, they tend to use it where others would use the active. Poor scientific style can be improved by changing the passive to the active voice to gain brevity, clarity, and force.
        (The use of the passive voice in the final sentence of the preceding paragraph adds variety, changes the pace, and by contrast stresses the final sentence.)
    (5) The letter should be typed today.

(This polite command is different from *Type the letter today* and *Please type the letter today.*)

This stationery should not be used for my business letters. Use it for my social and personal correspondence.

(The imperative in the second sentence is more forceful than the disguised command in the first sentence. Two direct commands might seem peremptory.)

The inventory should be completed this afternoon.

(Addressed to an executive, this disguised command implies that he should order things so that the inventory will be completed. It does not suggest that he should complete it himself as the direct command does: *Complete the inventory this afternoon;* and it does not put him in the position of merely receiving commands to pass along as does *Have the inventory completed this afternoon.*)

Customers should not be addressed this way.

(This sentence implies that it is not correct or desirable or suitable to address customers this way. It seems to leave to the employee the decision to cooperate.)

An adroit use of the passive voice where it is suitable benefits style by permitting variations in meaning, stress, pace, and rhythm. Excessive use of the passive limits meaning, stress, pace, and rhythm. To write entirely in the passive would seem not just unwise but impossible; yet some misled scientists and engineers attempt it.

To write impersonally does not require frequent use of the passive voice; the active voice can be just as impersonal. Boring, Langfeld, and Weld, who use both *we* and *you* in *Foundations of Psychology*, also write impersonally when their subject matter dictates an objective point of view. The following paragraph is impersonal, but it uses the passive voice only in the last sentence:

Although these tests point to the possibility of detecting accident-prone individuals before they have had serious accidents, the past accident history of the individual is still the most reliable indicator we have of accident tendencies. For one thing the tests measure only some of the factors which make an individual accident-prone, and for this reason a person can be accident-prone even though his test performance is good. On the other hand, a person can very often compensate for his deficiencies and consequently can have a good safety record although his test scores are not at all satisfactory. At present, therefore, best results are obtained when the diagnosis is based both upon test scores and upon previous accident history.[2]

[2] Edwin Garrigues Boring, Herbert Sidney Langfeld, and Harry Porter Weld (John Wiley and Sons, New York, 1948), p. 485.

W. W. Kellogg begins an article with a short paragraph in the active voice:

> Conditions on Mars are quite different from those on earth—but perhaps not so different as to rule out the possibility that life exists there. Should this chance prove to be a fact, its many profound implications—religious, philosophical, scientific, and practical—must engage every thinking person's fancy.[3]

In the same issue of *International Science and Technology* R. G. Neswald begins an article with a lively, humorous paragraph that uses the active voice where many scientists and technologists would consider the passive necessary:

> In days of old, before space became so headily and incestuously intertwined with time that it tangled back on its own warped self, its various "continua" shot through with wormholes and chopped up into quanta, Nature was a pretty unsophisticated anthropomorphic simpleton. She abhorred vacua, favored simple symmetries, and, when pinched, punched, or otherwise perturbed, she reacted in kind with restoring forces, which (to a first approximation) were proportional to the magnitude of the original disturbances. The LeChatelier-Braun principle in chemical solutions, Lenz's law in electrical circuits, Hooke's law in mechanical systems reigned supreme.[4]

The Evasive I

The pervasive passive is sometimes due to the evasive *I*. First-person pronouns have long been absent from technical writing. They disappeared in the United States about 1920, when impersonal style began to dominate in science and technology. In the writing of many divisions of the government of the United States, and particularly in the writing of the Pentagon, *I* and *we* and any other indication that a human being is writing have for years been taboo. During the early twentieth century business and industry avoided pronouns in the first person by using business jargon like "Yours of the 10th inst. received and in reply beg to state . . ." and "Herewith are forwarded the reports under active consideration. Please be advised of general concurrence in desire to expedite matters." And since the 1940's business and industry, being more closely associated with the government and with science and technology, have been influenced by the impersonal, inflexible style of federal and technical writing.

An attempt to achieve objectivity by avoiding personal pronouns

[3] "Mars," *International Science and Technology* (February, 1964), p. 40.
[4] "Ultrasound in Industry," p. 29.

is a mistake, and the idea that using the third person instead of the first person achieves modesty is equally wrong. Discarding necessary common words like *I* and *we* merely leads to awkward writing marked by excessive use of the passive and by reliance on weak indirect constructions (page 130). Writers deprived of *I* and *we* turn to unnatural and objectionable substitutes like *the author, one, the present writer, this reporter, your correspondent,* and *the undersigned* or even to titles—*the vice president, the chairman:*

1. *The writer cannot accept these findings.*

   The man who wrote this sentence would seem just as modest if he wrote simply and naturally, "I cannot accept these findings."

2. *The national secretary of the society initiated the following improvements in the management of the central office.*

   Without his title, the national secretary of the society sounds more modest: "I initiated the following improvements in the management of the central office."

3. *When one observed that the floors were made too slippery by the new wax, one reported one's observations to the superintendent of maintenance.*

   The new employee who wrote this sentence would sound less pretentious and pompous if he wrote, "I reported to the superintendent of maintenance that the new wax made the floors too slippery for safety."

4. *The present man of letters is much indebted to the aforementioned authors.*

   The fact that the "aforementioned authors" and the self-titled "present man of letters" produce some occasional technical articles does not make them authors. The word *author* and the title *man of letters* are reserved for writers, authors, and scholars of distinction. A writer should not call himself a *man of letters* even if his admirers are kind enough to do so.

   The writer of Sentence 4 has misused these words and has dragged in the unnecessary *aforementioned* because he did not use *I* and write his sentence naturally as, "I am much indebted to these writers."

5. *The minutes will be sent to you every month by the undersigned.*

   The passive voice and the legal word *undersigned* are both unnecessary if *I* is used: "I will send you the minutes every month."

Some writers consider *we* less personal than *I*. In imitation of an editorial writer, who is expressing the opinions of a board, a writer may mistakenly use the plural *we*. The obvious result is confusion. In the first paragraph of the following letter such a writer uses *our* to mean himself and his correspondent and *us* to mean himself; in the second paragraph he uses *we* for his company and for his division of the company; and in the third and fourth paragraphs he uses *we* for all or none of these.

> Dear Professor Keppelbacker:
>
> Your letter with its references to our meeting at the Chicago convention brought back to us memories of a very pleasant evening—and a profitable one too.
>
> We have revised our formula as you suggested, and we are now testing the results. We will send you a copy of our report as soon as it is ready. In the meantime we are sending you the samples you requested.
>
> We hope to see you at the New Orleans meeting and would like to discuss having you consult with us at regular intervals. We can offer you a fee of four hundred dollars a day plus expenses.
>
> Please give our regards and the regards of our family to Mrs. Keppelbacker.

The substitution of *we* for *I* in this letter is awkward. The use of *I* for the writer, of *we* for the Research Division (*we of the Research Division*), and of *the company* or *our company* when the company is meant would at least be clear. Although the quoted letter probably caused no serious misunderstanding, the substitution of *we* for *I* can cause dangerous or embarrassing confusion. When a writer using company stationery states, "we will do," he obligates his company unless in the first sentence in which it appears he clearly defines the *we* to mean something else. The possible embarrassment is illustrated well by an experience of the Reverend John A. O'Brien when he proposed a conference on population growth. The last paragraph of a newspaper account states: "Although Father O'Brien used the phrase 'we propose' in connection with his proposals, a spokesman for Notre Dame said the professor was speaking for himself." The writer who uses *we* should be sure that he has authority to speak for others. And the only safe authorization is written.

Hope for the Future

Some laboratories have been experimenting with the use of the active voice in scientific and technological writing and with the use of personal pronouns where these are necessary and appropriate. The best argument for the active voice and personal pronouns that has come to my attention is the use of *I* and *we* and the active voice by the journals *International Science and Technology* and *Science*. The writers and editors of these journals employ the active voice and personal pronouns without any loss of objectivity.

All of us are susceptible to what we read and hear; some are more susceptible, some less. A scientist or technologist who decides to avoid unnecessary use of the passive voice and to use personal pronouns where they are apt should not expect the passive to disappear from and personal pronouns to sprout in his writing unaided. Exposed as he is to the passive and the impersonal, he must revise his papers carefully to achieve a style different from the one he reads. He should also, of course, read works that have good style (Chapter II).

Mountains of Modifiers

One of the characteristics that make the prose of information difficult and unpleasant to read is placing a string of modifiers before a noun. This is common and idiomatic in German. In that language one may write such a string as this without arousing comment: *the-meeting-at-two-o'clock-on-alternate-Thursdays-for-social-and-philanthropic-purposes-ladies-of-the-Church-of-St.-Peter-and-St.-Paul-cooking-and-sewing society*. In English a mountain of modifiers piled before a noun is unidiomatic and graceless. But that does not prevent technical writers from creating such mountains as the following: *the culturally disadvantaged child conference; specific diesel fuel system design variations; high level Armed Forces manuals speaker; environment electronic systems specification sponsor information; chemist and engineer advance placement information; satiated, 6 hour trained Strawberry Hill Farm rats; overall information exchange complex; a complicated kind of producer-to-middleman-to-consumer sequence; difficultly obtained objectives; biodegradable-detergent feedstocks; kerosene-range (C10–C16) normal paraffins; 1606-type earthquakes; raw materials and fuel cost differentials.* These strings of modifiers are objectionable for two reasons: (1) English idiom demands that some of the modifiers follow the noun and (2) too often nouns are used to modify nouns. Instead of *chemist and engineer advance placement information*, for example, why not *information for the advanced placement of chemists and engineers* or *advance information about the placement of chemists and engineers?*

These mountains of modifiers are lumpy, bumpy reading. The argument that they save a few words is specious. The words saved are prepositions, which a writer may as well use to improve the quality of his writing. Indeed, many writers who omit prepositions in these phrases with the excuse of seeking brevity are the same writers who insert unnecessary prepositions and other words in phrases like *head up, as to the nature of* (for *about*), *by means of* (for *by*), and *in order to* (for *to*). An occasional pile of modifiers, even of nouns modifying nouns, may do little harm to style; but few writers can use chains of modifiers only occasionally. Moreover so many terms in the sciences and technologies and pseudosciences contain chains of modifiers that writers forced to use these terms should avoid adding more. A writer who must use technical terms like *subject-action, verb-target of action; subject-linking verb-description of subject; liquid-liquid-liquid extraction; approach-avoidance conflicts and avoidance-avoidance conflicts; zero-sum, two-player games; 1500-Mev electron synchrotron;* and *Van de Graaff accelerator and electrostatic deflection system* should avoid other chains of modifiers. Such unidiomatic constructions make any prose sound like a poor translation from a foreign language. The foreign language might be called Insensitive-to-Style Science-Technology Pseudo-Science-Pseudo-Technology Anti-English. And if that does not hurt a writer's ear, he is in danger.

Besides being cumbersome, chains of modifiers without hyphens may be confusing. If a writer uses such poor style, one cannot tell whether *sulfur containing additives* means additives that contain sulfur or sulfur that contains additives. And what does *synthetic plant construction* mean? or *superior test monkeys?* or *economically more attractive pure quality chemicals?* or *productive time estimates?*

Telegraphic Style

The telegraphic style that I read in the publications of government and industry should be avoided even in telegrams. Omitting articles, some pronouns, and conjunctions saves money in telegrams. But it is difficult to determine what the writer of telegraphic style is saving. He is not saving money, for the confusion he causes is expensive. He is not saving time, for his readers have to waste time puzzling out his meaning. He is not saving typing or paper, for he often prefers long words to short. He may be trying to save face by attempting to conceal that he cannot write English, or he may be evading responsibility by clouding his meaning so that no one can tell who is responsible for anything or whether the writer understands what is happening.

Writers of minutes are addicted to telegraphic style, and because minutes are useful records of decisions and of responsibility for action, the smudged meanings of telegraphic style are particularly dangerous in such records. The following sentences are typical of the opaque expression of the writer of telegraphic minutes:

Drug 109 discussed re government approvals recommended further animal experiments. To be investigated.

Limited marketing Drug 111 Hospital Service suggestion. No action.

Suggested approved MD complete Drug 141 May pamphlet circulation. Pamphlet proofs pending action. Postponed March 6.

Even someone who attended the meeting has trouble understanding such reporting.

Sometimes a telegraphic writer does not even attempt to save words; he just moves them from one position to another. Here is a sample from a journal on writing: "This symposium was held for the purpose of exploring problems and the promise of 'More Effective Communication of Scientific and Engineering Information.'" The writer might begin his exploring by searching for the misplaced *the;* he meant "for exploring the problems and the promise of."

Telegraphic writers also scorn conjunctions and carelessly produce sentences like this, "For a molecular weight of 500 this would be 1.5 mg/ml for practical purposes we would like to have at least 15 mg in this case." The writer should have placed a *but* after *ml.* If his purpose was to save words, he might have omitted *in this case.*

A writer who is uncertain about wording minutes will find good advice in *Robert's Rules of Order,* including advice on the form of minutes, on recording discussion, on recording votes, on recording reports and resolutions, and on publishing minutes.[5]

A writer who is using telegraphic style in a misguided search for brevity can achieve it more effectively through other means (Chapter VIII). If by using a telegraphic style he is concealing carelessness or attempting to evade responsibility, he is a self-convicted nonwriter.

Words, Sentences, and Paragraphs

A writer who avoids the errors and weaknesses described in this chapter is ready to consider the more complex and more satisfying elements of style presented in the following chapters. Any order is suitable. A writer may follow his own interests and choose to begin with diction, for example, because words have always aroused his curiosity. He may be guided by his knowledge of his own weaknesses and study the style of paragraphs first because he has trouble developing paragraphs. He may be guided by his writing and start with sentences because he writes only short memorandums and has trouble with sentence structure. Or a browser may read here and there in these chapters to learn a little about

[5] Henry Martyn Robert, rev. ed. (Scott, Foresman and Company, Chicago, 1951).

sentences, study some words that he uses often, and find the answer to a paragraphing problem. Whether a writer burrows through the chapter like a determined mole or flits back and forth like a butterfly makes little difference in his improvement. It is just as easy to improve words, sentences, and paragraphs together as to work on one at a time. A wise writer will measure his progress not by the amount or order of the instruction he swallows but by the improvement in his writing.

Chapter XII

Style and Diction

> . . . and his word burned like a lamp.
>
> *Ecclesiasticus 48:1*

Choosing the right word is both an exasperating problem and an enticing pleasure. The fun and the difficulty coexist because English is rich in synonyms. It is so rich that some writers do not take time to view the supply fully.

WORDS—HOW TO CHOOSE THEM

If a writer wants to convey, for example, that a committee praised his report, he may choose from many synonyms for praise:

> acclaim, admire, advocate, applaud, appreciate, approve, ascribe perfection to, bow to, boost, butter up for, celebrate, cheer, clap, commend, compliment, defend, defer to, do homage to, endorse, entertain respect for, esteem, eulogize, express approbation of, extol, flatter, give credit to, give a favorable opinion of, hail, hail with satisfaction, have a good word for, have respect for, hold in high esteem, honor, look up to, overpraise, pat on the back for, pay deference, pay homage, pay respect, pay tribute, peal hosannas, praise to the skies, prize, puff, recommend, render a panegyric, render homage, render honor, render plaudits, respect, revere, salute, say a good word for, say it is OK, set great store by, shout applause for, slaver over, sound the praises of, speak encomiastically of, speak well of, speak highly of, stand up for, stick up for, support, think good of, think highly of, think much of, think well of, thunder plaudits, uphold, value highly, venerate, worship.

If none of these express his precise meaning or if he is discussing his own report and wishes to sound modest, he may deny the opposite of praise. He may say that the committee did not disapprove his report, did not cast a slur upon, cavil at, criticize, damn with faint praise, dislike, disparage, disregard, frown upon, fulminate against, make light of, over-look, pick to pieces, poke a hole in, push aside, rebuff, run down, scorn, shrug off, slight, speak ill of, sneer at, take exception to, turn up their noses at, undervalue, or view in a bad light.

Or he may say of the report that it accomplished what he wanted, answered his purpose, came off well, came off with flying colors, con-quered the committee, gained praise, had good fortune, hit the mark, scored a success, took effect, turned up trumps, triumphed, was go go go, was well received, went up like a missile, won over the committee, won the day (crown, cup, medal, palm, prize). He may also express this negatively by stating that the report did not come to nothing, fail, fall short of expectations in its reception, fare badly, flunk, mess things up, misfire, or miss the mark.

Writer's Influence

What influences his choice? Many characteristics of the speaker or writer—his training, knowledge, intelligence, taste, judgment, personality, circumstances—all influence his decision. If a speaker with a small vocabu-lary is conversing, he chooses from the few words that come to his mind, however lamely they may express his meaning. If a writer is revising, he may consult a dictionary, a book of synonyms and antonyms, or a thesaurus and choose from a large number of words. If he has sufficient taste to reject a cliché, he will avoid, "They praised it to the skies." Of his own work, he will not write, "They lauded the report," but may say, "It did not go badly." Writing the minutes of a meeting, he may record that the negotiators acclaimed the report that ended a long strike. Speaking at a memorial service, he may say of the reports of a deceased president, "The committee venerated his advice."

Reader's Influence

A writer adapts his language to his listener or reader. He may tell his professor, "The committee spoke well of the report." But when his young son asks how the report was received, he says, "It was go, go, go all the way." He writes to his brother that he hates to hear his colleagues slaver over the president's report. To his colleagues he says only that they are flattering the president. When his son brings home an *F* on his report card, the writer warns his wife, "Now, when you go to school, don't stick up for him." But he admonishes his assistant, "If you don't check those figures, we won't be able to defend this report." Speaking or writing to his professor, his brother, his colleagues, his wife, his son, and his assistant, he has adapted his language to the reader or listener. Thus the characteristics of the reader or listener—his training, knowledge, intelligence, taste, judgment, personality, circumstances, and connection with the writer—also influence the choice. Whether a writer is conveying information or sensations, influencing judgment, moving to action, arousing emotion, or evoking a mood, he must consider his reader when he chooses the words for his purpose.

Denotation

More keenly than other writers, a writer on professional subjects must strive for extreme precision in his choice. He is likely to consider denotation, the exact dictionary definition of a word, more important than connotation, the associations of a word, its overtones, its aura. The fact that words like *idiot, moron, neurosis,* and *sublimate* have acquired connotations in general writing does not prevent a psychologist from using them without these connotations in the technical writing he directs to fellow specialists. But when a psychologist communicates with others, the connotations may cause him difficulty; then it may be necessary for him to avoid confusion by explaining away the general connotation and emphasizing the definition or by substituting another word or phrase.

Medical doctors face a similar problem daily, because they communicate with their colleagues in technical terminology that might confuse or frighten patients and relatives. Successful communication with colleagues and laymen requires that doctors shift points of view frequently. One who neglects to shift may mislead his listeners, especially when a term has a different meaning for a layman. When an ophthalmologist says, "Good afternoon, Mr. Jones. I saw your wife this morning; she has a foreign body," he may startle Jones. Specialists become so used to the terminology of their fields that they forget what the terms mean to others. The first paper in chemical engineering that I edited was "Heat Transfer in Mixed Packed Beds." It took the chemical engineers in my office fifteen minutes to discover why I thought the title was funny.

Connotation

It is also easy to forget that a technical term has different connotations for readers. No matter how much the writer of informational prose is involved with careful selection of terms for precise meaning, he must not forget that there are many kinds of meaning and that one of the most important kinds is the atmosphere that a word conveys to readers. A dog, for example, may be a *bitch, canine, cur, hound, mongrel,* or *mutt.* The word *dog* may have pleasant associations, as in *a dog's life* and *watchdog,* or uncomplimentary connotations, as in *dog in the manger, to go to the dogs, to put on the dog.* And what *bitch* and *dog* mean at the American Kennel Club is not necessarily what they mean at a cocktail party when someone says that Jones has married a bitch or a dog. Just as the meaning and connotations of a word may change with the context, so they may change with the times. *Walking the dog*, for instance, assumed new connotations and new meaning for reporters walking President Johnson's dogs.

Many engineers and scientists would like each word to have a fixed meaning and no connotations except those that they establish. But this is not likely to come about. As soon as one reads or hears a word, the word has some overtones for him. Even the dictionary definition—"a domesticated, carnivorous mammal of many varieties"—has bookish or scientific flavor as compared with simple *d o g*. Sensitive awareness of the connotations of words is necessary for effective selection. Whether a writer wants colorful or colorless words, the problem is the same. He must understand connotations well enough to make a knowing selection. There is a marked difference between a *prize-winning poodle* and a *mop of lapdog* and between a *visionary egghead* and a *far-sighted thinker*, even if the difference is only in the eye of the writer. Listening and reading help a writer to develop the sensitivity necessary for distinguishing between words charged with associations and words that are more neutral and for selecting those appropriate to his writing.

Length

Many writers are confused by the advice that they should use only short words or by the statement that long words will make their work less readable. It is true that if a short word will function as well as a long one, a writer should generally choose the short one. But there is no point in replacing a polysyllabic word by three sentences of short words. Writers in the professions need not become counters of syllables. How long are the words? is not important. If readers understand the long words and do not understand the short ones, the long words are obviously the appropriate choice. Will readers understand the words? is the pertinent question. And variety in word length is desirable. Papers composed entirely of short words tend to read like primers, and papers composed entirely of long words look forbiddingly difficult.

Writers on professional subjects should not use clipped words or abbreviations like *d.t.'s, hypo, mike, VIP*. Some of them are slang; some, like *hypo*, are ambiguous *(hypochondria, hypodermic, hyposulfite)*; and all are inappropriate in formal style. Abbreviations like *Dr., Mr., Mrs., Jr., Sr., Ph.D., A.M., P.M.*, and initials commonly used for government agencies *(FBI, AEC)* and for long titles *(AFL-CIO, NATO, NBC)* are acceptable, as are all the standard abbreviations of a specialization. But clipping words or employing abbreviations not in general use does not shorten a paper for a reader.

Emphasis by Contrast

Writers should know one important principle about the length of words. A word that is markedly different—in tone, in quality, in length—from the surrounding words receives emphasis. I do not think that writers in the professions must use this device of emphasis, but I do think it important that they be aware of it to prevent it from operating against them.

EXAMPLES

> The proposed changes and modifications will increase the economy of operation, simplify semiannual budget planning, prevent competitors from bugging our meetings, and improve administrative efficiency. (The slang word *bugging* attracts too much attention in this sentence of routine business phrases.)
>
> He is a conscientious and painstaking assistant but a schmo about people. (The supervisor who wrote this satisfied his conscience by admitting the first two characteristics, but then he minimized them by *schmo*. The short slang word receives undue emphasis.)
>
> Proofread carefully your typing of formulas. Formulas that are inadvertently erroneous may ruin tons of chemicals. (The long and pompous *inadvertently erroneous* distracts attention from the main point. *Errors in formulas* would be more appropriate.)
>
> This catalogue exemplifies the administrative confusion, unnecessary expense, and injury to the reputation of the institution occasioned by the incorrect positioning of one device of punctuation. (The short specific phrase *one comma misplaced* instead of *the incorrect positioning of one device of punctuation* would contrast effectively.)

Fancy Words

Sometimes fancy words are confused with long words. Fancy words, short or long, are undesirable. They are used by writers who display language. Such writers *initiate* work rather than *begin* it; they *activate* a project rather than *start* it; they *proceed* to the administration building rather than *go* there; their work *comprises*, not *is*, research and development; and they earn *compensation*, not *pay* (Chapter X). These examples of fancy words are long, and the natural ones are short; this is often true, but there are some short fancy words, like *doff*, *dwell*, *prior*. The fancy word is the pretentious word, the one that is pseudo-elegant in its context, the pseudoscientific, pseudolearned word. Many misguided writers, conscious of their inadequate vocabularies, cultivate such unnatural language; and some professors in graduate schools and supervisors in industry and government deplore simple, natural language and train writers to use the fine writing of pedants, the clichés of business, the jargon of government, or even incongruous combinations of all three.

EXAMPLE

> Adumbrating that the complaints of the siblings of exceptional children would commence with concomitant discontinuance of overall parental manumission of affections, the speaker asseverated the diurnal requisite of minimizing the antipathy of the latter while potentiating the amelioration of the former by gratification at the advance and development of accomplishment.

A writer who uses words to fill a page or to impress his profundity upon readers instead of to convey meaning is in danger of writing sentences like "Unfortunately the kind of case that causes trouble in practice is that in which the nature of the use made of language is not of a transparently clear type." If a writer dots his work with *case, character, condition, degree, instance, line, nature,* and *type,* he should remove them when he revises. As pointed out in Chapter VIII, they result in a weak, diffuse style.

A writer who chooses fancy words instead of simple words may find that the fancy words are unnecessary, inaccurate, or incorrect. Even a professional writer's attempts to use elegant language often end in malapropisms. The *New York Times* writer of a signed special article from East Hampton, Long Island, blundered thus, "The houses of East Hampton generally dissuage visitations, but guests on today's tour will see . . . ."

Foreign Words and Phrases

Some writers err in considering it elegant or learned to decorate their writing with unnecessary foreign words and phrases. Foreign words are sometimes used because of the associations they add to meaning or because there is no good English equivalent. But the need for foreign words occurs less often in informational prose than in more atmospheric writing. And writers often misuse and readers often misunderstand foreign words. *Versus,* or *vs.,* is frequently misused for *and, or,* and *compared with.* And many professional people misread *i.e.* and *e.g.;* therefore when a writer uses these abbreviations to save time, they may waste it. Even *etc.* is misused; the items that precede *etc.* should make the category clear, but many writers place before *etc.,* two items that belong to more than one category. "Such candidates are found at Harvard, Dartmouth, etc." does not clearly identify the category.

Clichés

Stereotyped phrases, which are used in informational prose as commonly as fancy words, often cover an absence of thought. The user has borrowed not merely some worn-out words but an often-expressed thought. Perhaps the expression of the thought was striking and effective when it was fresh. The first lover who told a woman that her lips were like cherries and her cheeks like roses is a different thinker from the man who borrows the phrasing millions of users later. The first lover was imaginative and perceptive; the borrower is lazy and possibly unperceptive (the lipsticks and rouges of today provide more subtle shades). Some clichés are old—*acid test, believe it or not, better half, beyond the shadow of a doubt, bitter end, conspicuous by his absence, few and far between, field of endeavor, filthy lucre, first and foremost, in the last analysis, the irony of fate, it stands to reason, last but not least, on the ball, sneaking suspicion.* Some are newer (for a word may be overworked in a few years or even in a few months)—*drastic action, elder statesman, Iron Curtain, pending merger, senior citizen.*

Whether old or new, a hackneyed phrase betrays a user's willing acceptance of a vague approximation of his thought, if indeed he has one. Cliché writers use the phrase *the forseeable future* without a thought of how unforseeable the future is. Frank Sullivan's cliché expert, Dr. Arbuthnot, uses old and new worn-out phrases when he testifies, and his ideas are as hackneyed as his words. Given a question, he supplies the answer automatically, whatever the subject. In talking about atomic energy, for example, Arbuthnot uses "usher in the atomic age," "prove a boon to mankind," "spell the doom of civilization as we know it," "boggles the imagination." [1]

Some authorities find clichés less objectionable in conversation than in writing, but the value of keeping one's mouth shut when one has nothing new to say and no fresh way to say it should not be ignored. I find clichés particularly objectionable in political oratory, where they flourish. And the after-dinner speech stuffed with familiar phrases is also painful. Beginning with "unaccustomed as I am" and running through "which reminds me of a story," the after-dinner bore finally reaches "and so in conclusion" half an hour before he delivers the final cliché.

However, one can give new life to a worn-out phrase by twisting it wittily or comically. In a formal speech such turns of familiar phrases are best when they are unobtrusive, like John J. Meng's passing reference in a commencement address to the "leisure of the theory class." In

[1] "The Cliché Expert Testifies on the Atom," *The New Yorker* (November 17, 1945), p. 27.

extemporaneous talks the effect of such twists is heightened by the spontaneity; for example, a speaker at a dairy convention replied immediately to a question about methods of successful dairy farming, "Well, I like to start with a few well-chosen herds." A girl listening to her family argue at length in favor of a Sunday picnic remarked, "It takes you a long time to agree to agree." A banker who declined to risk his bank's money on the World's Fair observed, "None but the brave preserves the Fair." And when an office weeper was given a raise in salary, his coworker quipped, "There was method in his sadness." This device is effective in the title of a book or article and particularly useful if most of the suitable titles for the subject have been used. For example, in July of 1951 *Chemical and Engineering News* published the first of a series of articles by Robert L. Dean on writing (XXIX, 2729). Nearly every possible title for that subject had been used more than once, but Dean thought of a twist. He called his series *Watch Your Language.*

But I do not recommend that in striving for fresh phrasing writers of informational prose should choose eccentric expressions, like some common in advertising. A writer saying that his report was praised does not need to use freakish expressions like, "I ran it up the flagpole and they saluted" or "I smeared it on the cat and she licked it off." Such odd metaphors are quaintly ridiculous and even offensive outside the whimsical world of advertising. And writers of informational prose should not be misled by journalists who, striving for novelty, use ridiculous language. "They really tried to chic up the folksy sport of harness racing here last night," is an example of the poor taste that appears in the sports and social columns when writers strive too hard for novelty.

Euphemisms

Euphemisms, which soften unpleasant and offensive concepts and attempt to raise the lowly, are, like other lies, undesirable except when they are indisputably necessary. The word *die*, for example, is simple and dignified. It is far better than many of the substitutes for it: *to cash in one's chips, to pass away, to pass over, to pass to one's reward, to go beyond, to depart this world, to expire, to enter the valley of the shadow, to come to an untimely end, to perish, to be taken, to resign one's breath, to give up the ghost, to end one's days, to breathe one's last, to depart this life, to join the great majority, to kick the bucket.* The numerousness of such euphemisms illustrates that words designed to soften reality quickly lose their veiling power and are replaced rapidly. The poor become the *underprivileged, those in want*, the *deprived*, the *disadvantaged;* the aged are the *elderly*, the *mature*, the *old folks, those who have had their day*, the *senior citizens, our seniors*, the *patriarchs.* To those who are sensitive to language as well as to death and age, a euphemism often seems worse than what it is trying to soften and, besides, it soon becomes trite.

Vogue Words

A writer should not think that odd words or odd forms of words that are in vogue lend freshness. "Praisewise my report did all right" contains a faddish form that is just as trite as "praised to the skies." Overuse of a form like the *-wise* suffix is common in government and industry, and I object to it most strenuously there because it is weak from abuse by the time it arrives.

I first heard about the fad of *-wise* suffixes when I was abroad in 1951. "Wait until you get home and hear your students saying, 'Parkingwise I had trouble,'" teased a history professor who had just come from Washington. When I returned to the United States, I found my undergraduates talking of "improving *gradewise*," and in industry I read, "*Specificationwise* we wish to state . . ." and "*Psychologicallywise*, it is clear . . . ." Soon afterward the author of a satirical article expressed the feelings of many readers when he concluded that "wordwise" he was "fed-up-wise." Years later at a performance of *How to Succeed in Business Without Really Trying,* I was pleased that "How is he doing successwise?" drew a laugh from the entire audience. Nevertheless a few months ago when I removed *medianwise, budgetwise, batchwise, vatwise,* and *responsibilitywise* from a technical report and told the writer, "In addition to being ugly and unnecessary that *-wise* suffix has been overworked for at least fifteen years," he responded sheepishly, "I thought it was a new way to put it."

A writer in the professions should be sparing in his use of vogue words. He should be especially wary of those that have one scientific meaning and another popular meaning, like *allergy, exhibitionism, neurotic, sadism, subliminal.* Employing vogue words reveals, as the use of hackneyed phrases does, a failure to think, laziness, evasiveness, or a pathetic and belated attempt to seem up to date.

The vogue words *overall, type* as an adjective, and *hopefully* are overpopular in technical writing. *Hopefully* with the meaning *it is hoped that* is used to avoid stating who is hoping, but *hopefully* also means *in an optimistic manner* and *with agreeable expectations.* And so when a user of vogue words writes, "Hopefully management will meet with the union leaders again tonight," he means *it is hoped that,* and he is expressing some doubt that the meeting will occur. But some of his readers will think that the sentence means that management has agreeable expectations, that it expects a good result from the meeting. In German *hoffentlich* does not confuse readers, but *hopefully* used like *hoffentlich* does confuse readers of English. A careful writer avoids the careless use of *hopefully* in his own writing, and a careful reader is suspicious of it.

I once heard an administrator say to a project head, "But you wrote to me that you hoped that the results would be complete this month."

"No, I said I doubted that the results would be complete this month."

"Here's your memo. Look at your last sentence: 'Hopefully the results will be complete before December.' Now why did you write that if you didn't expect to be ready?"

"That's exactly why I wrote it. It means, 'It is only hoped that the results will be complete.' "

When I left they were still arguing. The project leader, who had tried to avoid trouble by using the evasive *hopefully*, was in trouble anyway. And the supervisor had learned to query every *hopefully*. He tells me that he has heard ten different meanings assigned to it by ten members of his division, and hopefully, or perhaps despairingly, he expects to hear more.

Type, another offender, should be used as an adjective only in technical expressions, like *A-type blood.* In other expressions the adjective *type* suggests the speech of gangsters, as it does in "marriage-type love" and "delicatessen-type sandwiches" or telegraphic style, as in *"an IBM-type employee."* Sometimes it is redundant: "a future-type bonus," "detergent type cleansers," "a wise type decision." I have even heard "an electric type typewriter."

Overall, which means *from one end to another,* is popular as a synonym for *total* and *general.* I recommend that writers of functional prose use it only for the first meaning and use other words, like *total* and *general,* for the other two meanings. *Overall* is likely to appear five or six times on one page of industrial writing and to have one meaning in the first sentence, another in the second, and sometimes no meaning at all. A mechanic wrote, for instance, that an engine needed "a general overall overhaul of all its parts." Hopefully it will be totally overhauled overallwise.

Vague Words

Closely related to the vogue is the vague. Words that convey too many meanings convey none at all. College girls use *nice* to describe their fiancés, their philosophy courses, their housemothers, and their new shades of nail polish. And a chemist may say that the apparatus for his experiment is fine, his supervisor is fine, his vacation was fine, and it will be fine to send out his letters tonight. Adjectives like *real, good, bad, horrible* convey little meaning when they are used loosely: *horrible cooking*, a *horrible movie*, a *horrible accident, horrible language*. A word that has fewer meanings says more, but if the search for a suitable word requires effort, there is a temptation to revivify a stock adjective by adding an intensifier—*very nice, real fine, definitely horrible, actually real*. Such overworked intensifiers not only lose their strength but become weakeners. Writers in industry and government must try harder than writers in other fields to avoid vague words and overworked intensifiers because they hear and read them often. Danger words are *actually, definitely, exceedingly, exceptionally, extremely, really*, and *very*. These are often used carelessly and thoughtlessly, as in the memorial resolutions that referred to an executive's "very fatal final illness."

Technical Language

Technical language is indispensable in conveying ideas to readers in the same specialization. It is the simplest, clearest, quickest road to precision. Much technical language has come into English in the past fifty years, and many writers use it where it is unnecessary and even confusing. A careful reviser replaces unnecessary technical language with nontechnical language when he can do so and keep the writing clear and brief.

One of the characteristics of poor writing in all the professions is a tendency to employ terms from other specializations. A chemical engineer, for example, should consider his readers and refrain from adding to the technical language of chemical engineering legal expressions like *aforementioned, hereinafter, versus*, and *abovementioned*. Business administrators should not use *in the order of magnitude of* for *about*; it means something else. The language of one specialization is enough—often too much. Readers can hope that the time will come when leaders in the professions will take an interest in removing some jargon from their own specializations and in improving technical language. There must be better ways of saying *liquid-liquid extraction, situational variables in interpersonal verbal interactions, maximization and minimization of linear functions subject to linear constraints, postdepositional and detrital origin*, and *cloud-track pictures obtained in uniform field spark breakdown experiments with timed square-wave impulse potentials at near atmospheric pressures*. Until the learned societies assume their aesthetic, and possibly their ethical, responsibility for improving language, the best that a writer can do is use the technical terms of his own specialization sparingly and avoid the needless use of technical language from other specializations.

General and Specific Words

Experienced writers on professional subjects have little difficulty with a problem in style that troubles other writers—the use of general and specific words. They choose the word that is appropriate to their meaning—not the too-general word which blurs meaning and not the overly specific word that is pedantic or fussy. But a beginner may be lazy about seeking a specific word that does not come quickly to his mind and substitute an ineffective general term. In the *Handbook of English in Engineering Usage* A. C. Howell warns writers not to say *contrivance* for *motor-generator, machine* for *apparatus, bottle* for *Erlenmeyer flask, a thing to measure angles with* for *protractor.*[2] And even experienced administrators, scientists, and technologists do not always realize that specific words can lend vividness and precision to their writing on subjects outside their profession. "A secretary who transcribes and types accurately, spells correctly, and writes good letters" is a clearer description than "a competent, efficient secretary." A request for "a report on the training division's use of visual aids, such as samples, pictures, slides, filmstrips, and teaching machines," will elicit a better report than will a request for "a report on what they're doing in training with some of these new teaching things that help you to see what you're learning." An executive who is inclined to use slovenly diction and to rely on meaningless general words like *thing* and *gadget* should take the time to replace vague words by specific terms. The incompetent spoken requests of many executives suggest that if they were surgeons they would say not, "Scalpel, Nurse," but "Will somebody give me that thing over there."

Abstract and Concrete Words

T. A. Rickard ably illustrates another weakness of technical writers—the unnecessary use of abstract language:

> The hankering for the abstract is exemplified by the vogue attained by "value" and "values" in mining reports. In a stope or in a mill the use of "value" in this way may cause no confusion even if it be an objectionable colloquialism, but in technical writing it should be taboo, as the very type of all that is nondescriptive and unscientific. "This mill is intended to catch the *values* in the ore" is a vague way of stating that the mill is designed to extract the gold or silver, the copper or the zinc—in short the valuable metals in the ore. In one mill the zinc, for example, may be not only valueless but a deleterious impurity; in another the copper may be insufficient in quantity to be extracted

[2] 2 ed. (John Wiley & Sons, New York, 1940), p. 26.

profitably, but sufficient to interfere with the saving of the gold by cyanidation. "Value" is the worth or desirability of a thing; it is an attribute, not a substance. A man who designs a mill "to catch the values" might as well build a railroad to pursue a quadratic equation.[3]

Just as specific words are often more effective and precise than general words, concrete words are more effective and vivid than abstract ones. Superfluous abstract words make writing fuzzy or meaningless. An appropriate use of concrete terms, even in writing on an abstract subject, enlivens and clarifies. George Holbrook uses concrete, specific diction and concrete, specific examples to develop his abstract thought in the following passage. He begins with an abstract idea, the importance of chemistry, enhances it with concrete illustrations, and concludes with another well-founded abstraction:

> Of all the sciences, none penetrates so deeply into the structure of the human environment as chemistry. Chemical processes and principles are basic to life in all its phases. They appear in such familiar activities as building a fire, raising crops, preparing food, relieving illness, and in producing virtually every commodity of the commerce which has marked civilization's ascent from the cave.
>
> For the better part of six thousand years of recorded history, however, men established their living conditions very much on the products of nature as they found them. They built with stone, wood or clay; they wove cloth from cotton, wool or silk; they made shoes, harnesses, and saddles from animal skins.
>
> Gradually, they began to make changes in the products of nature to satisfy their desire for a better way of life. They won metals such as copper and iron from natural ores, made concrete, paper, and gunpowder. In the course of the past half century or so, this innovating process has been most radically accelerated. The natural directions of chemical reaction have been replaced or augmented by a series of induced reactions which rearrange the limited raw materials of nature into endless patterns of usefulness. Now we build with metal alloys, glass, hundreds of plastics; weave nylon and other synthetic fibers; manufacture countless dyes and pharmaceuticals; make fuels, rubber, automobiles, airplanes, and spacecraft largely from synthetic materials.
>
> The process through which these opportunities have been seized and the benefits enlisted to the service of mankind is now recognized as chemical engineering, one of the newest of the professions.[4]

[3] *Technical Writing* (John Wiley and Sons, New York, 1931), p. 42.
[4] *Listen to Leaders in Engineering*, ed. Albert Love and James Saxon Childers (Tupper and Love, Atlanta; distributed by David McKay Company, Inc., New York, 1965), p. 63.

CLARIFICATION OF WORDS AND INFORMATION

Brief Interpretative Comments

Words that require interpretation, such as *appreciable, appreciably, considerable, considerably, relative, relatively,* may confuse readers. An appreciable difference to a microscopist may not be appreciable to an artist, a considerable amount in chromatography may be inconsiderable at a refinery, and a relatively mature student may be an immature employee. To convey such thoughts accurately, it is necessary to specify how large a difference, how great an amount, how mature a person. If one is writing on specialized subjects for nonspecialists, explanations of the significance of the amounts are essential. An effective technique to use for all readers is describing the amount meaningfully: *an unexpectedly large yield of two grams; a difference of 1.4, surprisingly small; two of the ten candidates—the usual proportion; even a new employee; three exceptions in the thousand instances, not enough to affect the conclusions; ten complaints from customers, and we usually investigate when there are as few as two.* Professor Reginald O. Kapp illustrates this well in a small book that every technical writer should study, *The Presentation of Technical Information:*

> You can point to the conclusion that is to be drawn from the information by the addition of words like "fortunately" or "unfortunately", "surprisingly" or "as is to be expected". Other, more specific, more thoroughly informative words can be even more helpful. I can imagine a situation in which it would be good to say, "and yet the points all lie on a straight line", while it would be even better to say, "and yet the points all lie, *deceptively,* on a straight line". Similarly it might be good to say, "the temperature reaches the high figure of 750°F", and better to say, "the temperature reaches the *dangerously* high figure of 750°F".[5]

No doubt some scientists and technologists think that these comments are not so impersonal and objective as they have been taught that their writing should be. But there is a difference between a comment based on an expert's thoughtful interpretation of evidence and a personal, subjective comment. Moreover, wishy-washy, evasive statements, however impersonally they are expressed, betray the timid, overcautious, self-protective attitude of the writer. A chairman of safety who writes to his committee, "Eight accidents seem due to faulty inspection; it has been suggested that there be an investigation," has weaseled out of his responsibility. A less equivocal statement is more objective: "The insur-

[5] The Macmillan Company, New York, 1957, p. 75.

ance investigators attributed eight accidents to faulty inspection. This large number clearly warrants an investigation by the Safety Committee." The comments *large number* and *clearly warrants* are not personal, subjective statements. They are the clarification of a responsible expert interpreting evidence for others. But to introduce a suggestion feebly with "it has been suggested" when an investigation is the normal procedure that a chairman of safety should demand is so misleading as to be dishonest. A reader seeing "it has been suggested" may justifiably conclude that the safety chairman is not backing an investigation. Thus this objectively worded statement is intentionally or unintentionally highly personal and subjective; it is obviously the work of a fence sitter who should not be trusted with any decision less objective than how many pencils are in the storeroom. Unfortunately some experts are deterred from conveying their knowledge and experience to readers because of a mistaken belief that all comments are personal and subjective. Others write timid statements with premeditated self-protection. "I'm not sticking my neck out," such writers will state unofficially, although scientific objectivity is their official excuse for depriving their readers of judgments that the writers are being paid to present, judgments that save time, money, and lives.

Longer Explanations

A brief comment leading the reader to a correct interpretation of numbers and other technical information will often spare both writer and reader lengthy, inconvenient explanations. But sometimes explanations are necessary, and they are necessary early. For example, the terminology of a technical subject presents problems to writers of popular articles, who must write clearly and simply for readers who are not experts. The best writers for the general public use nontechnical language whenever they can; and when they cannot, they define or explain as they first present the technical term or concept. They do not use a term three or four times and then explain it. By then the reader may have stopped reading.

Comparisons and Definitions

Good writers for the general public never forget the value of analogies with familiar concepts for explaining the unfamiliar (page 221). Glancing comparisons are also often helpful—a factory machine compared to an eggbeater, company benefits compared to an insurance policy, a book of laboratory instructions compared to a cookbook. When the comparisons are figures of speech (page 222), they both clarify and vivify the concepts. The important point in comparisons and analogies is that the familiar concepts should be familiar not merely to the writer but also to the reader.

Necessary definitions and other explanations should be expressed clearly. Some specialists write merry-go-round definitions that leave readers confused: "An appositive is a word in apposition"; "nonrepresentational—not representational"; "revocation, or the act of revoking." Specialists who are prone to fine writing (unnecessarily ornate writing or pretentious writing) define words by using more difficult words as though in emulation of Samuel Johnson's definition of *network:* "anything reticulated or decussated at equal distances with interstices between the intersections."

Achieving the desired emphasis. The comparisons and definitions necessary for a reader's understanding create problems in emphasis when the concepts clarified and the terms defined are not important. Then the amount of space devoted to explanation or the vividness of comparison may inappropriately emphasize a minor idea. What can a writer do to restore proper emphasis? Usually one of the following techniques works:

1. Eliminate a word or concept that is only partially relevant to a main idea. Close examination of words and concepts that require lengthy explanations often shows the words and concepts to be unnecessary. Removing them restores emphasis to main points and improves paragraph unity. In many paragraphs the topics become clearer and sharper when material that is not completely germane is removed. The thought or the word may have captured a writer's interest, but consideration may convince him that the reader is better off without it—and so is the writer's paragraph.

2. Many necessary definitions may be slipped inobtrusively into dependent clauses and phrases if a writer does not wish to stress them. Instead of using a paragraph or a sentence as he would for a definition he wishes to stress, a writer may place the definition in a phrase, a clause, or a parenthetical expression:

> The company, including the New York Office, the Trenton Plant, and all foreign subsidiaries, would be a desirable purchase only if ten million dollars were available for construction and repairs.
> The company, that is the New York Office, the Trenton Plant, and all foreign subsidiaries, . . .
> The company (the New York Office, the Trenton Plant, and all foreign subsidiaries). . . .

A book review in *Science* subordinates a term in an *or* phrase instead of giving it a sentence to itself:

. . . is an excellent selection of important articles in the general and not too well-defined area of anthropological linguistics, or linguistic anthropology as Hynes prefers to call it.[6]

In an article in the same issue of *Science* an appositive and its modifier convey information without overemphasizing it:

> It is remarkable that carbon monoxide, a known toxicant constituting 4.2 percent of tobacco smoke (1), has not been considered as an explanation of the diverse effects of tobacco smoke on the circulation.[7]

3. Sometimes definitions in a separate section—an introductory list or a list in an appendix—may be necessary. If a paper requires a number of definitions or explanations for words or concepts that are essential but not important and if a writer can find no way of introducing them unobtrusively into his paper without shifting emphasis away from his main thought, then he may have a separate section of definitions. The need for it seldom occurs, and a writer planning such a section should be convinced that it is necessary.

For example, if I were writing on standards of diction to undergraduates who have little knowledge of grammatical terms, I would consider appending an alphabetical list of definitions of grammatical terms. But because my readers have been educated in a profession, I assume that some will immediately understand a term like *appositive*, others can recall it, and some few who do not know and cannot recall it will use a dictionary. For a phrase like *fine writing*, however, I would provide a definition because the phrase might mislead those who do not recognize it as a technical term. My decision should be based on my judgment of whether readers need the definition, not on my wish to teach grammar, expand or shorten my book, or impress my readers.

Necessary and unnecessary definitions. In industry and government scientists, technologists, accountants, lawyers, and consultants of all kinds writing for management have problems very close to those of a writer of popular articles. The difference is mainly that they are writing for more experienced readers who are familiar with some terms. This means that a decision as to whether a technical term should be defined or a process explained becomes more difficult. Sometimes personal knowledge helps. A writer remembers from committee meetings that his readers are familiar with some terms, or he knows from past reports that the terms have been explained so often that his readers understand them.

[6] Oswald Werner, "Anthropology and Linguistics," CXLIX (July 9, 1965), 168.
[7] S. M. Ayres, Stanley Giannelli, Jr., and R. G. Armstrong, "Carboxyhemoglobin: Hemodynamic and Respiratory Responses to Small Concentrations," p. 193.

When he lacks this knowledge, his best decision is to explain. Technical reports in industry and government often contain unnecessary details (page 111), but they seldom offer too much explanation of technical matters for readers without technical training. Few readers in industry or government object to explanations and definitions. If a reader finds one unnecessary, he needs the next one; and anyway, he is inclined to skim the ones he does not need. If he gives them a thought, he feels superior because other readers apparently lack his knowledge.

A writer preparing his first financial report for a company consulted me about supplying the definitions of some terms. "I did it where I worked before this, but I am not sure whether this management needs the definitions," he explained. "Many of these terms do not appear in reports previously submitted to management here." I advised him to include whatever definitions and explanations seemed essential to him and to note the reactions. He reported that most of his readers did not react at all. But one division manager said, "I'm glad to see I know some of the financial terms that others don't know." And a vice president told him, "This is the first time I've been able to understand an annual report in this company. I always had to get someone to translate financial reports for me until yours came along."

The Problem of Condescension

Writers sometimes worry too much about seeming to condescend when they explain, and some of the worriers insist on apologizing for offering explanations or on detailing their reasons for explaining. This is too much. Expressions like *as you know, as you no doubt remember, as you may recall,* and *of course you are aware* irritate some readers.

One executive wanted to know, "Why do they write, 'as you no doubt recall,' and then spend a page and a half recalling it to me? Either they think I recall it, or they think I've forgotten it and need to be reminded. But they can't have it both ways."

"Do you usually recall it?" I asked.

"Usually it's something I never heard of, and for one report in five it's details I don't need to know in order to understand the report and will never need."

A writer in industry and government should courageously include the explanations necessary to his reader at the point where the reader needs them. He should phrase them in the briefest manner consistent with clarity and refrain from apologizing. About those unnecessary details there is only one word of advice: omit.

FIGURES OF SPEECH

By using figures of speech John Donne presents the abstract subject of brotherhood in memorable concrete terms (page 228). Many writers in the professions who are interested in other qualities of language never give much thought to figurative language. They think it the province of poets and never notice how often the best writers in the professions find it useful. By omitting consideration of figures of speech, books on business writing and technical writing encourage writers on business, science, and technology to ignore the techniques of using figures, and so uninstructed writers use poor figures of speech for inappropriate material, omit figures where they would be of value, and even misread them in the works of others.

Everyone uses some figures of speech—*break the ice, cold shoulder, family tree, red tape, skeleton in the closet*. Every writer should know enough about them to avoid common errors, to use them effectively, and to read them correctly. Figurative language properly employed can clarify, strengthen, and vitalize at the same time that it lends a welcome touch of imagination. To help writers in the professions to understand this neglected subject I shall discuss in detail the principal figures of speech as well as the advantages and problems of using them in the prose of information.

Analogy

One of the most useful figures of speech for writers in the professions is analogy: extended treatment of similarities (often of properties, relations, behavior, or function) in things unlike in kind, form, or appearance, for example the heart and a pump.

Whole paragraphs and even whole short works may be developed by analogy (pages 48, 264). Writers of informational prose often find it effective to compare difficult technical concepts new to a reader with simpler concepts familiar to him. This puts the reader in a proper frame of mind to understand the technical concept because the familiar by mitigating fear of the unfamiliar puts readers at ease. Such a comparison may clarify better than a definition and may even extend the meaning of a term beyond its definition and enlarge a reader's understanding of the definition. An analogy of three or four sentences is not difficult to write, but a long analogy requires skill in organization and expression. The development of an analogy is presented and illustrated in Chapter XIV.

An analogy explains and clarifies; it does not prove. It may be used to enforce or enhance proof, but in itself analogy is not evidence. Although comparision of similar subjects may be useful, things alike in some respects are not necessarily alike in others. In the absence of other proof, they may be thought to be alike, but the analogy, although it leads to this supposition, does not prove anything about the points that are not compared.

Simile and Metaphor

Similes and metaphors, which present a similarity in objects otherwise unlike, are used frequently in technical prose, but not always effectively. One editorial in *Science*, "The Research and Development Pork Barrel," has a metaphor in its title and a sprinkling of figurative language throughout: "on the road to becoming new Appalachias," "a Middle West 'brain drain,'" "face-to-face with a most serious kind of over-concentration," "road to manpower chaos," "whatever midwestern site appears to be most in the running after initial screenings," "the region exerts its maximum potential pressure." [8] Similes and metaphors are particularly useful for making abstract general ideas concrete and specific.

In Robert Oppenheimer's talk to the Princeton Graduate Alumni, "The Scientist in Society," appropriate figures of speech abound:

> There is something inherently comforting about a panel of experts. One knows that the partial and inadequate and slanted and personal views that he expresses will be corrected by the less partial, less personal views of everyone else on the panel; it is not unlike the experience of the professor who always is glad that he has to meet his class again because he can correct the mistakes that he made the last time. . . .
>
> This is a vast terrain—one full of strange precipices, chasms and terrors. . . . [9]
>
> I know that it is a very happy occasion at the Institute [of Advanced Learning] when some piece of work turns up which is of interest to both the mathematicians and the physicists. It is a very rare occasion and we tend to ring bells when a small bit of cement can be found between their interests. . . .[10]
>
> The experience of science—to stub your toe hard and then notice that it was really a rock on which you stubbed it—this experience is something that is hard to communicate by popularization, by education, or by talk. It is almost as hard to tell a man what it is like to find out something new about the world as it is to describe a mystical experience to a chap who has never had any hint of such an experience.[11]

[8] CXLIX (July 2, 1965), 11.
[9] J. Robert Oppenheimer, *The Open Mind* (Simon and Schuster, New York, 1955), p. 119.
[10] P. 123.
[11] P. 126.

Similes state a comparison—*a backbone like jelly, no more sense of value than a magpie, a report as interesting as a mud flat and just about as clear.* Some writers think that only *like* or *as* may express the comparison, but other words may be used. Metaphors imply a comparison instead of expressing it—*rubberneck, his coltish manners, expecting stocks to zoom.*

A simile or metaphor should be appropriate to the context in which it appears. If a comparison in a formal text is expressed in slang, if a comparison in a sober work is too extravagant for the meaning, or if a comparison in a paper of workaday prose is too decorative, a writer should discard it. *The Government refused to play ball on this issue* is unsuitable for a formal report to stockholders. *Research and Development rocketed into space with this new tranquilizer* has a metaphor inappropriate to the meaning. *After the fire the company resurrected itself like a phoenix* contains a figure too far-fetched and decorative for a financial report.

Trite comparisons should also be deleted; removing them usually strengthens a sentence. A writer should avoid clichés like *at one fell swoop, beggars description, bolt from the blue, the Buckeye State, busy as a bee, chalk up sales, cheap as dirt, clear as crystal, fall by the wayside, ironclad agreement, memory like a sieve, method in his madness, spice of life, sweat of his brow.*

Many comparisons are dead or dying—*the head of a pin, the tail light of a car, the foot of a bed, the heart of the matter, toe the mark, point a finger of scorn, show guts, shoulder a suggestion aside, elbow one's way to promotion, knuckle under to authority, scratch for ideas, a thin* (or *thick*)-*skinned person.* If a comparison is dead, the literal meaning does not come to life and confuse readers: *He stepped on the foot of the ladder. He engraved the Declaration of Independence on the head of a pin. The hurricane lashed a branch of a tree against the tail light.* Here *foot, head,* and *tail* mean nothing but *bottom, top* and *rear.* And this is true even though *lashed* suggests a literal meaning for *tail.* Therefore a writer need not avoid a dead metaphor; it is not trite, and a substitute might be awkward. But other metaphors still have some evocative qualities, not strong enough to make the figure effective but strong enough to make it ridiculous in certain contexts: *He could see the long arm of coincidence in her broken leg; Because of all the red tape, they could not bandage his finger. Showing guts* says nothing more than *showing courage* yet has vigor enough to prevent a sensitive old lady from using it. And the literal meaning may revive awkwardly: "In the middle of the operation the surgeon showed guts." Between the dead and the dying metaphors is the metaphor that seems dead but revives in some contexts. *Rubberneck,* for example, would seem to be a dead metaphor, but it shows life in *bouncing rubberneck.*

This literal meaning seems so obtrusive to a reader that he cannot understand why the writer did not see it and remove the figure. But many writers in the professions seem unconscious of the need for care in the use of figurative language or unaware that they are using figures. I have read many poor examples like, "As president of the American Goiter Society, he said that he intends to 'stick his neck out' at the April meeting and stump for less conservative use of thyroid." When a figure revives its literal meaning in a sentence concerning the ill, the disabled, or the dead, the result may be so unpleasant as to open a writer to a charge of poor taste.

Synecdoche and Metonymy

Synecdoche and metonymy are not so common in prose as are metaphor and simile, but they do occur. *Synecdoche* is a substitution of the name of a part for the whole or of the name of a whole for a part, as in *factory hands, hungry mouths, America's winning the cup, using his head, a strike against a plant.* Somewhat similar is *metonymy,* the substitution of an attribute or an association for the word meant, as in *playing to the gallery* (for *the audience in the gallery*), *sweets* (for *candies and desserts*), *Blue Points* (for *oysters dredged near the village of Blue Point*). A company may use the name of a town or city for the plant located there—*Baton Rouge, Yonkers* (for *the divisions at these locations*). Synecdoche and metonymy are useful when one has to repeat a word often; they are especially useful in avoiding the repetition of long names or titles. The only requirement is that the substitute be clear. Metonymy sometimes seems informal. When it does, the writer of a formal paper should use the original term or a pronoun rather than confuse the tone of his writing.

Irony

Irony, expressing a thought by stating its opposite, is more common in persuasion than in exposition. It is not unusual in conversation and in speeches, for example *my great success* (a project that failed), *his usual short, pithy remarks* (two hours of rambling discussion), *my mink* (an inexpensive cloth coat). Irony may be as brief as these examples or as long as a whole work, like Jonathan Swift's *A Modest Proposal.* It is the opposite of the cliché in that it presents the unexpected juxtaposition, the imaginative contrast of the incongruous. But it is easily misunderstood, even by sympathetic readers if they are insensitive to irony. To stress the inhumanity of the English, Swift presented a mock proposal that the Irish avoid starvation under absentee landlords by eating Irish infants; but some English readers, hardened in their hearts toward the Irish, reproached him for having gone too far—for a clergyman. And some book reviewers missed the obvious irony of Hannah Arendt's *New Yorker* series on Eichmann. Irony is not for the literal-minded reader, nor the insensitive, nor the unsubtle.

Irony is often confused with sarcasm, particularly by those who dislike ridicule, whether it is intended to correct or to hurt. Irony may be sarcastic, and sarcasm may be ironic; but each may exist without the other. Sarcasm is intended to hurt or injure a person or a group; irony is designed to correct follies and evils or to express, wryly perhaps, the oddness of the world. When a supervisor says to a good writer, "Another poor report, I suppose," his words are ironic though not witty. But when he says the same thing to a poor writer, the words are sarcastic and still not witty. When a woman speaks of another's "charming pink-candy hair," the expression is sarcastic if the pink-haired one will be injured by it but otherwise the "charming" is ironic. After unsuccessful labor negotiations, disgruntled representatives may report with sarcastic irony. The company representative states, "Showing its usual concern that our company should not lose money, the union proposed increases of one dollar an hour"; the union representative reports, "With its usual concern for the welfare of the workers, the company proposed wage cuts of ten cents an hour."

Overstatement and Understatement

Akin to irony are overstatement and understatement. Overstatement, or hyperbole, is extravagant exaggeration used for emphasis or for comic effect: *He acts as though an error in typing will blow up the plant; I expect to be worrying about that point in my grave; He has worked here a million years at least; This report has more fancy words than the unabridged dictionary.* Understatement, deliberate restraint or playing down, is most effective when a subject is overpowering, as in John Hersey's controlled, almost pent-up presentation of the shocking material in *Hiroshima.* When it is difficult for words to match the strength of the subject matter, a writer may well consider using understatement. And sometimes minimizing one's angry convictions is humorous. Samuel Johnson defined a Tory as "one who adheres to the ancient constitution of the state, and the apostolical hierarchy of the Church of England, opposed to a Whig," and then coolly expressed his scorn in an understated definition of a Whig as "the name of a faction." Understatement may take the form of litotes, negation of the opposite of what is meant: *The danger is not insignificant; His bonus was by no means a small one; Her bikini was no Mother Hubbard.*

Personification

Personification, endowing something not human, for example objects or abstract qualities, with human attributes, is not unusual in prose. It may sound old-fashioned or strained or fancy, as in "The subtle villain Envy tricked him into that wrong decision." A personification such as *Liberty added her voice* is not likely to be used today except in Fourth-of-July oratory, where old-fashioned devices flourish. But *alma mater* means only *college;* it has no more life than any dead metaphor. Contemporary prose also uses personification: *And 10 Downing Street looked melancholy; The computer had a nervous breakdown; The evidence did not have even a speaking acquaintance with the conclusions.* Personifications lend emphasis and vividness because of man's ability to understand best his own reactions and experiences: *Machines grow old and have to be retired.*

Puns and Other Plays on Words

A pun is the use of a word (or of two words that sound alike) in more than one sense at once. Today puns in prose are used mainly for humor, but puns have been used for wit. In the second paragraph of *Victory* Conrad writes,

> The Tropical Belt Coal Company went into liquidation. The world of finance is a mysterious world in which, incredible as the fact may appear, evaporation precedes liquidation. First the capital evaporates, and then the company goes into liquidation. These are very unnatural physics. . . .

Called the lowest form of wit, puns often convey the highest meaning. Poets use puns as vehicles for their profoundest insights, as the Bible does. That punster Mercutio conveys more than obvious meaning throughout *Romeo and Juliet* by his plays on words, not the least of all by his pun after he has received his mortal wound, "Ask for me to-morrow, and you shall find me a grave man." In the work of a witty writer puns may be effective even in a serious context, and in speeches they may be welcome light touches. The humorous pun should not be strained because when one of the meanings does not quite fit or when the use of the pun lacks point, listeners flinch. But listeners who wince and groan at every pun lack both originality and perception.

Paradox and Oxymoron

A paradox is a seemingly self-contradictory or absurd statement that, properly understood, is reasonable, a statement opposed to common sense but true in a larger sense. "His bankruptcy in 1930 was so profitable that it was the foundation of his success in the company he started in 1932." Sometimes a paradox is based on a pun. A patient explained his visits to a psychiatrist as necessary "because his office is the only place where I can lie down and relax undisturbed."

Paradox is closely related to oxymoron, the juxtaposition of words that are apparently contradictory. A writer discussing the population explosion may call it the death from too many births. The Christian martyrs were said to die to live eternally. A worker who performed poorly on the first few days in a new job and thereafter performed well said that he failed only to succeed.

Allusion

Allusion is a brief oblique reference to a person, place, quotation, or event that a reader may be expected to recognize. An allusion is indirect; a reference is direct. Writing, as they usually do, for educated readers, men in the professions may use many allusions. But writing should not seem studded with references, for readers will consider the writer pretentious. A successful allusion avoids the hackneyed. Even the best literature does not stand up well under incessant quotation, as witness "to be or not to be." A reference to "Pavlov's dog" to explain habit is equally trite; so are allusions to Waterloo and to St. Patrick driving the snakes out of Ireland, quotations like "a plague on both your houses," and proverbs that are too familiar, like "a stitch in time." A successful allusion is woven neatly into the writing and introduced without fanfare. Robert Oppenheimer uses two allusions effectively in the following passage:

> These two mutually interdependent ideals, the minimization of coercion and the minimization of secrecy, are, of course, in the nature of things, not absolute; any attempt to erect them as absolute will induce in us that vertigo which warns us that we are near the limits of intelligible definition. But they are very deep in our ethical as well as in our political traditions, and are recorded in earnest, eloquent simplicity in the words of those who founded this nation. They are in fact inseparable from the idea of the dignity of man to which our country, in its beginning, was dedicated, and which has proved the monitor of our vigor and of our health.[12]

[12] Oppenheimer, p. 50.

A successful allusion is accurate. A writer who is unwilling to take time to verify his allusion and to make it an integral part of his text should discard the reference.

Allusions in the family to family jokes—the company joke at a dinner for a retiring officer, the college joke at a commencement, the engineering joke at a convention of engineers—succeed because an audience feels comfortable when it recognizes a family joke; an audience in Columbus, Ohio, for example, is pleased by a speaker's allusion to the latest Ohio State football victory. But the mention should be a passing one; attempts to build a successful family allusion into a successful paragraph usually fail. And a speaker who is using an allusion lightly to please his audience or to bring himself into harmony with his audience should choose a pleasant allusion; families are not delighted by references to their mistakes or their black sheep. But an allusion, like a pun, is not restricted to the aptly pleasing or entertaining; it is more likely to be serious.

Some allusions are echoes of phrases, characters, titles of literature. Titles may spring from the writing of another; John Donne's words, for example, have been suggestive:

> No man is an island, entire of itself; every man is a piece of the continent, a part of the main: if a clod be washed away by the sea, Europe is the less, as well as if a promontory were, as well as if a one of thy friends or of thine own were; any man's death diminishes me, because I am involved in mankind. And therefore never send to know for whom the bell tolls; it tolls for thee.

The titles *No Man Is an Island* and *For Whom the Bell Tolls* are much richer in meaning when one knows their origin. And this is the advantage of an allusion; it clarifies, enlarges, and heightens meaning and feeling; and it does this with economy. If an allusion is the best kind, readers will not feel cheated if they do not recognize it and will feel pleasantly enriched if they do. This requires that when an allusion is woven into a sentence, the meaning should be clear for those who do not recognize the allusion—less rich, less full, less vivid, perhaps, but still clear.

Selection of Figures

Skillful use of figurative language can clarify and enliven thoughts at the same time that it entertains and pleases readers. A figure of speech is an effective way to emphasize a main point. It may be persuasive and mnemonic, for its vividness makes it powerful; therefore an imaginative writer who can provide fresh, appropriate figures of speech can convey his ideas precisely and forcefully. But trite figures of speech advertise that they are worn out. It is better to state that she is pretty than that she is pretty as a picture. And expressions like Mother Nature and Father Time and their progeny should be shunned.

It is dangerous to shift so rapidly from one figure of speech to another that they blend in the reader's mind. One figure may be incompatible with the other in tone or meaning, for example, *Whenever he feels dog tired he behaves like a bull in a china shop, multiplying blunders like rabbits,* or again, *The blushing bride was green with envy.* Mixed figures may be delightful when reprinted in *The New Yorker,* but they are an embarrassment in a serious work. Writers should avoid mixed figures like the following: *Faced with concrete criticism, he buries his head like an ostrich and hopes that the egg he laid will go away; The company newspaper flooded us with dead news that was dry as dust; These high school dropouts will land with a thud in the face of present employment conditions.*

An inappropriate figure of speech—one that does not suit the tone of the writing, one that overemphasizes a minor point, one that confuses rather than clarifies—is an obtrusive error because of the vividness of figurative language. If a writer feels unsure of a figure, he is wise to omit it. And a writer should not so crowd his work with figures that it becomes tiresome and therefore ineffective, as this published sentence does: "This is where your proposals will either hit pay dirt and lead to a contract or strike out." Figurative language should be used with taste and judgment. A writer may develop these through reading and through studying effective examples.

THE SOUND AND RHYTHM OF PROSE

Rhetorical figures—climax, anticlimax, antithesis—concern structure and arrangement. They are discussed and illustrated in Chapter XIII. Some rhetorical constructions and sound patterns are seldom used or are avoided in informational prose—alliteration, onomatopoeia, and rhyme. A careful writer avoids ineffective repetition of a word used in two senses: *A timer timed out; They could not understand his stand on the budget; They took no stock in the stockbroker's advice; As soon as we meet him, let us make sure that he meets our qualifications; The letter entered the case because it did not satisfy the letter of the law.* Such awkward uses are easy to correct: *They could not understand his position on the budget; They did not trust the stockbroker's advice.* And repetition of an unimportant word results in poor emphasis: *He said that the regulations said that a doctor should be present.* Accidental rhyme or alliteration is undesirable: *His attitude would be less cold if the plan involved more gold; He will iron out the cation problem; Neither his calculation nor the secretary's negotiation improved the situation; In space flight the spacecraft speeds sufficiently to supply necessary centrifugal force; With the weight of this warhead why would we wish for wider spread weapons?* Sentences like these may appear in first drafts; a reviser improves them by a judicious use of pronouns and synonyms, by omitting, and by recasting.

The sound and rhythm of prose should not attract unfavorable or unwanted attention. Disturbing sounds distract a reader from the sense; therefore harsh combinations of sounds should be avoided. Because English has a large number of consonants, a writer must strive consciously for euphony. Reading aloud helps him to avoid ugly sounds like these: "In this display all textbooks exceeding the approximate size are without prejudice disqualified, but registration and admission fees are returnable by the administration on continuation or retention of registration for succeeding equivalent exhibits." Jogging rhythms are also unattractive and distracting in prose. The rhythms of parallel construction are acceptable, but contemporary writers prefer even these to be subtly modified to avoid regularity. The drumbeats of a list of words with similar rhythm should be avoided. The following example unhappily combines rhyme with monotonous rhythms, as many jogging lists do: *Introductions, presentations, graduations, celebrations, grand occasions demand special services.*

Writers sometimes use harsh sounds, rhymes, and regular rhythms for special effects in prose, but such effects are more common in fiction, essays, and other literary prose than in reports, memorandums, and other informational prose. Advertisers use these devices to capture and hold attention because they consider them catchy. But constant dinning makes such phrases irritating. A phrase like *from womb to tomb* captures so much attention the first time one sees it that it does not bear much repetition. Professional men are more likely to use special effects in speeches than in writing. If a catchy phrase is not injudiciously repeated, it may be a success in a speech or an interview.

AVOIDING CONFUSION IN MEANING

Technical and Nontechnical

When a word has a technical meaning in a specialization and a different meaning in general use, it should not be used with first one meaning and then the other. It is better to use it with the technical meaning in writing about the specialization and with the general meaning in other writing. *Cohesion*, for example, has, besides its general meaning, one special meaning in physics and another in botany. The physicist should use *cohesion* not in its general sense, not with the meaning that it conveys in botany, but with the special meaning it has in physics. In an unusual paper a physicist might use *cohesion* with the meaning it conveys in botany; he must indicate that he is doing so. He should also carefully revise such a paper to be sure that a reader is not likely at any point to assign *cohesion* one of its other meanings. In some specializations this problem arises more often than in others. Economics, for example, has a terminology based largely on assigning special meanings to words in the general vocabulary—*bond, distribution, stock, market, run, panic, depression, recession* (how did the economists miss *obsession?*), *production, consumption.* Chemistry on the other hand has taken few words from the general vocabulary to give them special meanings.

Whenever a writer uses a technical term for readers who do not have technical training in the field, he must define it. Whenever a technical term is also a word in the general vocabulary, he must be certain that his readers continue to think of the word in its technical sense throughout their reading of his work even though this requires that they be reminded of the special sense. A writer complicates his task unnecessarily if, having established a special definition for a word, he then employs the word in its general sense. No reader should be expected to follow such switches in meaning.

Many Meanings

A word that has two or more dissimilar meanings may cause difficulties.

> Formal—The report is not quite ready.
>> His recommendations are quite acceptable.
> Informal—She is quite pretty.
>> He is quite successful.

Quite, which means *totally* or *entirely*, also means, in informal English, *rather*. When writing is not distinguishably formal or informal but lies on the border, a writer should be certain that his use of a word like *quite* cannot be misunderstood. If there is any question in his mind, he should replace *quite* by a word that is not ambiguous. Failure to consider the meaning a reader may assign to a word causes misunderstandings. The word *girl*, for example, means a female child, a young unmarried woman, a female servant, a secretary, a daughter, a sweetheart, and a woman of any age. An executive who wrote to a housing chairman that he was bringing his wife and his girl to a meeting was dismayed to find a crib in his room (his daughter, who was not with him, was an infant) and no accommodations for his secretary.

Changing Meanings

Changing meanings also cause difficulties. The word *lady* has changed its meaning almost as often as men say that women change their minds. In some professional societies, like the engineering societies, older members will not change the old-fashioned title Ladies' Program although *lady* has been denigrated by terms like *scrublady* and *lady of the evening*. This provides some problems for convention chairmen, one of whom wrote to the wife of a member, "I know that the women in your group will enjoy the Ladies' Program." Changing times—in this example the disappearance of the lady of leisure and an increase in the number of career women— create problems by changing the meanings of words. But changing times may eventually solve the problems; the title *Ladies' Program* will disappear when the husbands of engineers enjoy the program for guests while their wives listen to papers on engineering.

Disinterested and *uninterested* also indicate the difficulties due to changing meanings. Handbooks of English used to state flatly that *disinterested* meant *impartial, unselfish, without selfish interest* and that *uninterested* meant *indifferent* or *not interested*. Some handbooks still differentiate between the two. But writers have ignored the difference so stubbornly that *disinterested* has come to mean *lacking in interest*. I have noticed it used for that meaning more frequently than *uninterested*. If a writer of minutes states, "The committee was disinterested in voting on the proposal," some readers will assume that the committee was impartial and some that it was not interested. Unless the context guides readers to a clear understanding of words with changing meanings, a writer should avoid such words. *Not interested, uninterested,* or *impartial* would not have been ambiguous in the minutes.

Clinging to outmoded language is just as foolish as adopting the latest fad in language, but there are those who do both and speak a language all their own: "Hopefully the girls will find the Ladies' Program successful moneywise even if they are disinterested in the choice of activities."

FINDING THE RIGHT WORD

A writer in the professions is interested in the qualities of diction and the techniques of using language mainly because he hopes to learn to express his meaning precisely and accurately. He may think that this separates him from other writers, but it does not. Accuracy is the foundation of all good prose style. To avoid blurred expression a writer selects from synonyms the exact shade of meaning that he wants. In spite of the number of synonyms in English, there is usually just one that expresses the sense precisely, one pat to the meaning; all the rest are makeshifts.

General dictionaries list some words of similar meaning. But a writer searching for an elusive word may not find it in such a brief list. He should turn to *Roget's International Thesaurus* (the Third Edition, 1962) or to a dictionary of synonyms and antonyms. Roget lists not just synonyms that are the same part of speech but also other parts of speech that have similar meanings. Thus a person who looks up a noun will find handy not only nouns with similar meanings, but verbs, adjectives, adverbs, phrases, and sometimes interjections. I consider these lists particularly helpful because many writers habitually use nouns where verbs would be more effective. The inclusion of all parts of speech in one listing offers freedom to a writer; he does not have to use an adjective simply because the word that came to his mind and the synonyms in his dictionary are adjectives.

A thesaurus is helpful too because it refers by number to other sections that list words of somewhat similar meaning. When a writer is searching, the word that comes to his mind is sometimes not near enough in meaning to enable him to find the word he wants among the close synonyms a dictionary provides. But the thesaurus with its longer listing and its many references to related words is likely to supply his word, or it will enable him to express his ideas by denying the opposite, for it lists antonyms. So much to choose from may be too much for a beginner, but it is just what other writers need when the word they want will not come to mind.

The right word presents an idea to a reader with such startling precision that he rejoices in grasping the thought as though a screen between his mind and the writer's had been removed. The reader of carefully selected words need not struggle through a haze of inexact words and a clutter of useless modifiers; he does not have to translate the idea from jargon to understand it; he does not experience the sensation of almost but not quite perceiving the idea. He grasps it as surely as though it were his own thought; only he has, too, the gratification of knowing that he is understanding another person's thought with ease. But he must never be deluded into thinking that the writing was easy. A reader's easy perception of an exact shade of subtle meaning comes from a writer's untiring search for the right words.

Chapter XIII

Style and Sentences

> Pregnant in matter, in expression brief,
> Let every sentence stand with bold relief.
>
> *Joseph Story*

No other advice has been pressed upon modern writers so relentlessly as, "Write short sentences." Because papers on management, science, and technology are not always easy reading, the advocates of short sentences attack most vigorously those who write on these subjects. One adviser comments on a forty-three-word sentence in an article on engineering: "If this sentence is read aloud the reader will be out of breath by the time he reaches the end." A speaker at a technological convention summarizes: "We have been hearing much from the readability experts about the need to write simply. They say, 'Use short words and sentences.'"

But when the scientist or technologist, true to his training, examines standard handbooks on writing, he finds that they do not favor any particular sentence length. One widely used handbook of writing states, "There is no special virtue in either long sentences or short ones, but there is a virtue in making the length of any one sentence appropriate to what is being said and in varying the lengths of sentences in a sequence." [1] "The most common and offensive kind of repetition of sentence length, however, is the use of a sequence of short, choppy sentences," explains another handbook. [2] And an expert writes, "Your style will emerge once you can manage some length of sentence, some intricacy of subordination and parallel, and some play of long and short, of

[1] Porter G. Perrin, *Writer's Guide and Index to English,* 4 ed. revised by Karl W. Dykema and Wilma R. Ebbitt (Scott, Foresman and Company, Fair Lawn, N. J., 1965), p. 308.

[2] Hulon Willis, *Structure, Style, and Usage* (Holt, Rinehart, and Winston, New York, 1964), p. 126.

amplitude and brevity." [3] Another states plainly, "A skillful writer maintains at least some variety in the length of his sentences." [4]

Panaceas are misleading. Offering the short sentence as a cure-all demonstrates the dangers of half knowledge. When a short-sentence addict complains that reading a sentence of forty-three words aloud leaves him out of breath, he has reached an extreme of pneumatic testing. The idea that a sentence must be read in one breath was buried long ago in a family plot next to the idea that a comma always represents a short pause for breath (or is it a pause for a short breath?); a semicolon, a longer pause; and a period, a full stop. Lincoln's *Gettysburg Address* was written to be read aloud. Could even a trained singer read its eighty-two word sentence in one breath? Picture a breathless husband and wife at the breakfast table panting to each other the fifty- to seventy-word sentences in their morning newspaper. And what of the Elizabethans, who wrote even longer sentences? Were they longer-winded?

The final irony of the sentence choppers is that they often urge scientists and technologists to read the classics to improve their style. But they do not account for the exceedingly long sentences in the classics—even in the least likely modern fiction. In one Hemingway story a textbook writer found sentences averaging eight and one-half words in length and in another Hemingway story in the same volume, forty-nine. [5] Businessmen, scientists, and engineers, ignorant as babes of the rhetorical principles involved, may well conclude that *no* particular sentence length is correct or that *any* length is correct.

THE READER AND SENTENCE LENGTH

Short and *readable* are relative terms. An intelligent person's concept of sentence length changes with age, education, and reading experience. A sentence that looks long to a fourth-grade child may look short to a college junior. A man whose only reading is a few letters and newspaper headlines will find long a sentence that looks short to a reader of current literature. It seems reasonable, therefore, to adjust sentence lengths to readers. Appropriately a story for children has sentences averaging fifteen words, and newspapers and magazines directed to those of little education also use short sentences; but *The New York Times,* learned

---

[3] Sheridan Baker, *The Practical Stylist* (Thomas Y. Crowell Company, New York, 1962), p. 42.

[4] Hans P. Guth, *Concise English Handbook* (Wadsworth Publishing Company, California, 1961), p. 125.

[5] Porter G. Perrin, *An Index to English* (Scott, Foresman and Company, New York, 1939), p. 545.

journals, and technical reports just as appropriately have longer sentences. In general it is safe to say that sentences in material for educated adult readers may average between twenty and thirty-five words. A higher or lower average indicates that a writer should inspect his sentences critically, but it does not necessarily mean that anything is wrong. Sufficient variety in type, construction, and length is more important than the average number of words.

To a certain extent writers on science and engineering naturally adjust sentence lengths to readers as material permits. An engineer at a meeting wrote relatively short sentences in his letters to his children about the local zoo. His letter to his wife, telling her about the trip, explaining some banking arrangements, and relating the news of the wives at the convention, had longer sentences. The sentences in his discussion of a paper presented were similar in length to those in his letter to his wife. When the discussion, taken from tape, was sent to him for editing, he put several related thoughts into one sentence and compressed the whole into slightly longer sentences. He made this adjustment of sentence to reader naturally without any consideration of rhetorical principles.

THE INFLUENCE OF THE DEMAND FOR PRIMERS

Those who prescribe the short sentence for all writing ills would have a writer go against this natural adjustment of sentence lengths to his reader and his subject matter. Some of the most demanding of these prescribers cannot read with ease above the high school level. They find the short sentence easy, just as the school child does, and they mistake their needs for universal needs. If a professional man must write for them, he must adapt not just his style but also his material. Elimination of difficult and subtle material and simplification of sentences and of vocabulary can place his writing at the level of these poor readers. Very likely he can give them only a page of simple summary of a fifty-page report, for that is probably all that they can master.

Those few readers who insist that complex scientific and technological material be brought to the level of a dull high school student would probably demand the article in comic-book form if they dared. They need special writers and cartoonists to simplify adult material for immature readers. Such readers cannot grasp complex ideas, fine distinctions in meaning, adult thinking. Even if professional men were to write with consummate skill, such readers would still complain. It is not the style that makes it difficult for them to grasp the ideas; it is the ideas themselves that are too difficult for them.

A writer in the professions who tries to suit the whims of readers or of "experts" who demand primer style will soon find himself in the position of the professors in *Gulliver's Travels* who engaged in compressing polysyllables into single syllables or who strove to abolish words altogether. Swift presents comically the inevitable result:

> However, many of the most learned and wise adhere to the new scheme of expressing themselves by things; which hath only this inconvenience attending it, that if a man's business be very great, and of various kinds, he must be obliged in proportion to carry a greater bundle of things upon his back, unless he can afford one or two strong servants to attend him. I have often beheld two of those sages almost sinking under the weight of their packs, like pedlars among us; who, when they met in the streets, would lay down their loads, open their sacks, and hold conversation for an hour together; then put up their implements, help each other to resume their burthens, and take their leave.

A writer burdened with instructions that will gradually eliminate language is in danger of sinking under his difficulties, as Swift with the foresight of genius predicted. Short sentences and short words spread ideas so thin that it may take twice as long to express an idea. Subtle distinctions disappear, and only the most obvious ideas and the most elementary vocabulary and style remain; in effect, writer and reader might just as well communicate with objects. That might satisfy the executive who no doubt thought his expression brilliantly economical when he advertised for a secretary able to write "short basic English." He, of course, would object to Swift's long sentences as wasteful.

OTHER INFLUENCES ON SENTENCE LENGTH

A writer who wishes to use sentences of various lengths instead of attempting to express every idea in a brief sentence should examine the influences on sentence length. The reader has already been considered. The subject matter, type of writing, and demands of variety and emphasis are also important.

The demands of subject matter vary. A plea for better salaries does not require sentences as long as those in an article on ultrasonics. A discussion of a new name for a division of a company may well have shorter sentences than are required for a technical exposition of a project.

The nature of the presentation also influences the sentence length. A good speaker will tell an anecdote in relatively short sentences and use longer ones in his argument. The description of apparatus in a technical article may be expressed in long sentences that group related details. Informal speaking has the shortest sentences; formal writing, the longest: an explanation to a fellow worker during a coffee break calls for much shorter sentences than those in a published article.

A writer's natural style also influences length. Some men think in terms of groups of related details; others naturally separate small divisions of thought. There is nothing wrong with either style provided that it is not allowed to become monotonous. A writer with a natural tendency to aggregate should practice the short terse sentence, which he may use most effectively for emphasis by contrasting it with his longer sentences. A writer who naturally places every division of a thought into a separate sentence should try showing relationships by reducing some unimportant short sentences to words, phrases, or dependent clauses.

USES OF THE LONG SENTENCE

The long sentence is suited to grouping a number of related details clearly, neatly, and economically. A journalist illustrates this when he answers in his first sentence the most important of the six questions who? what? where? when? why? and how? Causes and reasons, lists, results, characteristics, minor details may all be expressed tersely, clearly, and effectively in long sentences.

To illustrate the advantages of grouping related details, the following four sentences have been compressed into one. In order that the illustration be fair, the four sentences chosen are those of a competent writer on chemical engineering and the changes made are only those necessary for the alteration in sentence structure.

> The seventeen materials used for study were examined by several methods other than the compression-permeability method, in order to obtain as much information as possible concerning their physical properties. The materials in dry form were examined under the electron microscope, and the photomicrographs of Figures 4 to 7 were taken to establish size and shape of ultimate particles. Nitrogen-adsorption measurements were also made, and specific surface values were calculated for each material, employing the Brunauer-Emmett-Teller method. Air-permeability measurements were made on the dry materials in most cases, using the Fisher subsieve sizer, and the corresponding specific surface was calculated for each by use of the method and slip-flow correction presented by Arnell, and by Carman and Arnell, employing a slip factor Z 3.5.

To obtain as much information as possible about the seventeen materials used for study, they were examined by several methods other than the compression-permeability method: (1) examining the materials in dry form under the electron microscope and taking photomicrographs (Figures 4 to 7) to establish the size and shape of ultimate particles, (2) measuring the adsorption of nitrogen and calculating specific surface values for each material by the Brunauer-Emmett-Teller method, (3) measuring the air permeability of most of the dry materials by the Fisher subsieve sizer and calculating the specific surface by the method and slip-flow correction of Arnell and of Carman and Arnell employing a slip factor Z 3.5.

The difference in effect and the compression result solely from the changes in sentence structure.

Because of its usefulness in bringing a number of related thoughts together, the long sentence is often effective for a summary conclusion. Whenever he is expressing several conclusions in one summary sentence, a writer should try to place them in parallel construction and to arrange them in logical, chronological, or climactic order. A long summary sentence may be emphasized by contrast with several short sentences. Then the sentence stands out by the bulk of its length, the weight of the important ideas, the careful construction, and the contrast with surrounding sentences. It is a strong ending.

CHOPPING SENTENCES

A sentence which was used as an example in an article advocating short sentences provides a striking illustration of the economy of the long sentence:

Although it is possible for the refiner to control the selectivity deterioration by continually discarding a fraction of the catalyst in the unit and replacing it with fresh material of good selectivity, this expedient increases operating costs because of the additional catalyst consumption.

The comment of the article follows:

If this sentence is read aloud the reader will be out of breath by the time he reaches the end. This is a fine example of trying to do too much in one sentence. The author has three thoughts here and each one should have its own sentence.

The refiner has a way to keep the selectivity up. He can keep adding fresh catalyst and throwing away part of the old. But this costs him money because he uses more catalyst.

Once more, fewer words, with no sacrifice of meaning spell a gain in simplicity.

No sacrifice of meaning? On two scores objection must be raised—to changes in meaning and to using three sentences to do the work of one.

The original sentence stated, "this expedient increases operating costs"; the revision reads, "this costs him [the refiner] money." There is a decided difference in meaning. The chemical engineer who wrote the original quite properly did not go into the problem in economics of who would pay the increased operating costs—refiner, middleman, consumer. The revision changes the meaning by stating that the expedient costs the refiner money. If such carelessness were shown in revising a legal paper, the change in meaning would be serious.

The original speaks of "fresh material of good selectivity"; the simplification drops the modification "of good selectivity." Saving three words by discarding them would invalidate a whole experiment if the use of replacement material of average or poor selectivity were to give a different result.

Reducing length by discarding necessary words is not to be recommended. By failing to convey accurately the exact thought of the original long sentence, these three short sentences illustrate the disadvantages of simplifying too much. Oversimplification not only loses distinctions in thought but soon makes writers insensitive to fairly obvious differences in meaning. There is no point whatsoever in simplifying at the expense of meaning.

The reviser states that the original sentence has three thoughts requiring three sentences, but the thoughts in the original sentence are so closely related that separating them makes them harder rather than easier to read. Only one sentence is needed:

The refiner may maintain selectivity by continually replacing part of the catalyst with fresh material of good selectivity, but he thus increases production costs.

The original sentence has forty-three words; the revision in three short sentences has thirty-three; the revision in one sentence has twenty-four. The longer revised sentence is more economical than the three short ones. It has fewer words even though it includes the modifications in meaning omitted in the three short sentences.

A writer should never be urged to use short sentences where longer sentences present ideas to his readers more effectively and economically. A writer for a professional journal has intelligent adult readers. For his fellow engineers and for the intelligent reader not in the engineering profession, a well-constructed long sentence is clearer than a jumble of short sentences. Inexperienced writers have as much trouble constructing a series of good short sentences as one good long sentence; therefore they gain nothing by using the short sentence where it is inappropriate. By selecting the most effective sentence length, a writer makes his own task and the task of his reader easier.

USES OF THE SHORT SENTENCE

Short sentences have their uses too. A crisp, clear sentence is a good opening, a polished short sentence gives an effect of wit and sparkle, and a terse concluding sentence may be used for sharp emphasis. A short sentence may also be used for effective contrast after a series of long sentences if an important idea appears in the short sentence. An editorial began

> In almost every talk we give, and in many conversations we have with our members on the problems of publishing an engineering magazine, the question is invariably asked, "Why don't you sell more advertising?"

It might have started with the short question—

> "Why don't you sell more advertising?"

A book review began

> As the authors tell in the preface, this book is not a manual of engineering drawing. Rather it is a summary of the revolution that took place when the General Electric Company decided to simplify its drafting practices.

This is an attempt to use a short opening sentence. But a really short one would be more effective—

> Here is a revolution in drafting practices.

Once a writer has his rough draft of a letter or an article, he will often find in the first or second paragraph a terse sentence that with a little polishing will make a good short opening. Few writers automatically begin a first draft with an epigrammatic sentence, but many writers bury among the first ten sentences one that may be reduced in words and sharpened in expression to provide sparkle.

An effect of force and wit is sometimes achieved by a brisk closing sentence. Brevity is rapierlike in the last sentence of many anecdotes. A chemist discoursing on the eccentricities of his first boss may end this way, "And so sometimes before he left a conference the boss would turn to us and say, 'I suppose you fellows all think I'm crazy,' and you know we did think that he was insane." Ending with a terser statement increases the effect: "And so sometimes before he left a conference, the boss would turn to us and say, 'I suppose you fellows all think I'm crazy.' We did." This two-word closing gains effectiveness from contrast with the longer preceding sentence. The shorter the contrasting sentence, the greater the emphasis.

THE HAPPY MEDIUM

Sentences of medium length are frequent in the writing of professional men. The material expressed in sentences of intermediate length receives less emphasis than the material expressed in sentences of contrasting lengths. And sentences of medium length are likely to become monotonous. Therefore when he is revising, a writer should add interest to sentences of similar length by varying beginnings, constructions, and rhetorical types. And by removing unnecessary words, he may shorten some sentences of medium length. He should construct his sentences of medium length effectively; being most of the sentences in his paper, they may determine the general style and tone.

VARIETY, THE FOUNDATION OF SENTENCE STYLE

Variety in sentence length is much more important than average length. Too much worrying about reducing the average length may lead to short sentences of similar extent and construction and thus result in monotony. Any continued repetition of sentence length is dull, but a passage of short sentences is unbearably monotonous when there is little variety in structure and rhythm. Dull paragraphs of sentences formed in one mold are as depressing as the vista presented by a typical cheap housing development—hundreds of houses all the same size, all with the same architectural plan—deadening duplication. The short-sentence enthusiasts forget that although one short sentence may have punch, a paper of short sentences leaves one punch drunk.

Knowing the uses of sentences of all lengths helps a writer achieve pleasing variety in length. And infinite variety contributes to interesting sentence style just as it does to attractiveness in women. Other variations in sentence structure that contribute interest to style are variety in sentence beginnings, in grammatical structure (simple, complex, compound, compound-complex), in rhetorical structure (loose, periodic, balanced), in the elements (words, phrases, clauses), and in sentence rhythms. A tendency to use one kind of beginning, one grammatical structure, or even one order may escape a writer's notice but drone his readers into drowsy inattention.

I do not believe that it is necessary to check everything that one writes for all these kinds of variety, but I have noticed that the monotony found in one sample of a writer's work also deadens other examples of his writing. I recommend therefore that a writer check the variety of his sentences in two or three typical examples of his writing. His findings will enable him to improve his other writing by removing the weaknesses found in his sample.

Anyone with very little time for revision should devote this time to varying his most important sentences—the first and last in his paper and the first and last in each paragraph. These sentences ought to contain important ideas. They deserve a reviser's labor because they attract a reader's attention.

VARIETY IN BEGINNINGS

Much writing for business, government, science, and technology has monotonous sentence beginnings. In published engineering papers, for example, I found a strong need for variety in sentence beginnings. Too many engineering writers begin sentences similar in length with subjects or with conjunctions like *however* and *hence* followed by subjects. There are many ways of beginning any sentence, as the following illustrations show. The original sentence in each case is taken from a published article.

ORIGINAL ORDER

This gadget, marketed under the name of Glamorglow, was first offered to industry in the fall of 1950 after a period of development and laboratory tests.

VARIED BEGINNINGS

Marketed under the name of Glamorglow, it was first offered to industry in the fall of 1950 after a period of development and laboratory tests.

In the fall of 1950 after a period of development and laboratory tests, this gadget, marketed under the name of Glamorglow, was first offered to industry.

After the gadget had been developed and had been tested in the laboratory, it was offered to industry under the name of Glamorglow in the fall of 1950.

First offered to industry in the fall of 1950 after a period of development and laboratory tests, this gadget was marketed under the name of Glamorglow.

ORIGINAL ORDER

Accurate prediction of either bubble-cap or perforated-plate behavior is complicated by the large number of variables which must be considered.

VARIED BEGINNINGS

Because of the large number of variables which must be considered, accurate prediction of either bubble-cap or perforated-plate behavior is complicated.

The large number of variables which must be considered complicates accurate prediction of either bubble-cap or perforated-plate behavior.

Because a large number of variables must be considered, accurate prediction of either 'bubble-cap or perforated-plate behavior is complicated.

A writer may vary his sentence beginnings by placing first an adverb, an adjective, a participle, a prepositional phrase, a participial phrase, or even the simple conjunctions too often spurned by writers on science and technology—*and, but, or, nor, yet.* A little effort can avoid the deadly droning that occurs when every sentence begins with its subject:

There were six designs chosen to receive Aluminum Company of America's 1963 Student Design Merit Awards. All were conceived by industrial design students. Each winning design was selected by the school's design faculty as the outstanding student project employing aluminum.

Three of the award-winning designs are described below: . . . .

VARIETY IN GRAMMATICAL TYPES

A writer should use all grammatical types of sentences as he needs them. Any long work should have examples of the following types.

SIMPLE: Engineers wishing instruction in statistics may wish to consider the two courses offered next month: (1) a course in the fundamentals for beginners and (2) a course in the latest developments for engineers with a mastery of the fundamentals.

A simple sentence is not, as some writers think, necessarily a short or uncomplicated sentence. It is merely a sentence with one main clause and no dependent clauses. Such a sentence may have complicated appositives and phrases and may be just as long as any other type. Its simplicity is only a simplicity in clauses. It may, of course, be short and simple, like these three examples: (1) Go. (2) He increased the pressure. (3) It is hot.

COMPLEX: When he tried to register for the advanced course, he found that it conflicted with the meetings of his division.

Because he had taken two elementary courses, he did not register for the first course.

A complex sentence contains one main clause and one or more subordinate clauses. In spite of its name, it may look like a simple, easy sentence: "If he comes, give him the report."

COMPOUND: The first course concerns the fundamentals of statistics, and the second course concerns new developments in statistics.

The students in the first course found it too fast, and the students in the second class found it too slow, but the instructor progressed at the same speed and covered the same amount of material in each course.

A compound sentence contains two or more main clauses and no subordinate clauses. The two or more main actions are coordinate:

The attention of the class faltered, and the instructor worried.

This is quite different from the unequal emphasis of a complex sentence:

When the attention of the class faltered, the instructor worried.

COMPOUND-COMPLEX SENTENCE: Although the students in the first class found it too fast and the students in the second class found it too slow, the instructor progressed at the same speed, and he covered the same amount of material in each.

In March, when our director, the head of training, said that he would take the course, we believed him, and we continued to believe him—right up to registration day in June.

A compound-complex sentence contains two or more main clauses and at least one subordinate clause. It is usually long or at least of medium length. Its length and complexity permit some juggling of ideas. A number of main clauses, a number of subordinate clauses, and of course other minor constructions for ideas less important than those of the subordinate clauses give a writer the opportunity to try various arrangements.

Sometimes writers overwork one grammatical sentence structure, particularly the simple or compound. Excessive use of simple or compound sentences equates every thought with every other and shows only the most elementary thought relationships, as a child does. Such style needs the subordinate constructions for minor ideas that are provided by complex and compound-complex sentences; by compound subjects, predicates, and objects; and by participles, appositives, phrases, and other modifiers (page 247).

Example 1: This executive trains new employees of his division and he directs research and he supervises writing.

Example 1 with Compound Predicate: This executive trains new employees of his division, directs research, and supervises writing.

Example 2: Harold Jones is the director of research and he supervises writing and he recommended this course.

Example 2 with Appositives: Harold Jones, the director of research and supervisor of writing, recommended this course.

Example 3: The schedule of the secretarial pool was crowded and no one could type his report immediately.

Example 3 with Phrases: Because of a crowded schedule for the secretarial pool, no one could type his report immediately.

Example 4: He is a well-trained assistant and he is conscientious and he always shows tact.

Example 4 with Adjectives: He is a tactful, well-trained, conscientious assistant.

Example 5: This company is one of the largest publishers of instruction manuals in the world, and it has a schedule of hourly work, and that schedule should be helpful to us.

Example 5 as a Complex Sentence: This company, which is one of the largest publishers of instruction manuals in the world, has a schedule of hourly work that should be helpful to us.

Example 5 as a Complex Sentence: Because this company is one of the largest publishers of instruction manuals in the world, its schedule of hourly work should be helpful to us.

Example 6: He fired his secretary and he felt guilty and so he gave her a good recommendation.

Example 6 as a Compound-Complex Sentence: He fired his secretary, but because he felt guilty he gave her a good recommendation.

Example 6 illustrates the looseness of the compound sentence and its stringy effect. Subordination provides the necessary tightening and indication of thought relationships.

VARIETY IN RHETORICAL STRUCTURE

Writers of English may use three rhetorical structures for the sentence—(1) the loose sentence, which moves from subject to verb to object or predicate nominative and permits the addition of minor ideas almost in the order they occur to the writer; (2) the periodic sentence, which suspends grammatical structure until the last word or nearly the last word; and (3) the balanced sentence, which contains clauses similar in length and in movement that are expressed in parallel constructions. The loose sentence has a more natural, conversational word order: *The applicant was interested in coffee breaks, holidays, fringe benefits, job security, and quick advancement.* The periodic sentence has a more unusual order, sometimes almost bookish, but useful for emphasis and suspense: *Coffee breaks, holidays, fringe benefits, job security, and quick advancement—only these interested the applicant.* The loose sentence may have a suspense of its own—that of climax:

> The instructor began in a leisurely manner with the simple principles, moved faster over more complicated advanced material, and at the end left us confused as he rushed through the most difficult points.

Although the reader of this loose sentence may stop many times before the end, the arrangement of material in the order of increasing interest is designed to keep him reading. Periodic order demands that he read to the end for a complete thought:

> Beginning in a leisurely manner with the simple principles, moving faster over the more complicated advanced material, and at the end rushing through the most difficult points, the instructor left us confused.
>
> The instructor, beginning in a leisurely manner with the simple principles, moving faster over the more complicated advanced material, and at the end rushing through the most difficult points, left us confused.

The balanced sentence (page 253) is useful for comparisons, which are frequent in technical writing.

The writing on business, government, science, and technology that I have read uses the loose sentence almost exclusively. It might with good effect include a periodic or a balanced sentence occasionally to provide variety and to emphasize a main point.

VARIETY IN SENTENCE ELEMENTS

A writer should always bear in mind the many ways of subordinating ideas. Careful choice provides variety, enables him to express subtle relationships, and makes possible a desired rhythm. A description, restrictive or nonrestrictive, may be expressed in different kinds of dependent constructions with varied effects:

(1) A CLAUSE: Caesar King, *who is the best customer of our perfume department.* . . .

(2) AN APPOSITIVE: Caesar King, *the best customer of our perfume department.* . . .

(3) AN ADJECTIVE PHRASE: Cleopatra, *sweet with musk.* . . .

(4) A PRESENT PARTICIPLE: Cleopatra, *wearing Naughty Nile.* . . .

(5) A PAST PARTICIPLE: Caesar King, *scented with Roman Pleasure for Manly Men.* . . .

(6) PHRASE CONTAINING A GERUND: *After selling the perfume to them,* the clerk felt he needed deodorizing.

(7) AN ABSOLUTE CONSTRUCTION: He watched her approaching on the gaudy barge, *his hopes of resisting her growing fainter as she drew nearer.*
Her journey completed, she smiled slightly.

The clause (1) is more leisurely and less taut than the appositive (2). The appositive verges on the telegraphic. The adjective phrase (3) is neatly attached to the noun it modifies. Such close positioning tightens a sentence like

My secretary, who is always careful and accurate about details, found the error.

This becomes

My secretary, always careful and accurate about details, found the error.

Participles (4 and 5), having much more flexibility, may replace strings of verbs or short clauses for a smoother, more sophisticated effect. Gerunds and absolute phrases also permit subtle expression:

VERBS: We finally *talked* with Dr. Jones, *asked* him many questions, and *realized* that frequent conferences with him would be necessary.

CLAUSES: *We talked with Dr. Jones, and we asked him many questions; then we realized that frequent conferences with him would be necessary.*

PARTICIPLES: *Talking* with Dr. Jones and *asking* him many questions, we realized that frequent conferences with him would be necessary.

GERUNDS: After *talking* with Dr. Jones and *asking* him many questions, we realized that frequent conferences with him would be necessary.

ABSOLUTE CONSTRUCTION: *Our conferences completed,* we reported that the problem was still unsolved.
Its morale lowered, its plans confused, its relationships with other divisions tangled in ill feeling, the research division needs immediate reorganizing, *Smith being the man to do it.*

ABLATIVE ABSOLUTE: *Smith being the man to do it.*

These varied effects tempt writers. Experimenting with them is interesting and profitable if a writer is not a rank beginner addicted to dangling participles and misplaced modifiers. When a writer uses subtle constructions effectively, he will experience a pleasant satisfaction. Even a professional writer pats himself on the back for a discerning use of an ablative absolute.

SENTENCE EMPHASIS

CONTRAST

As the discussion of subordination illustrates, sentence variety and sentence emphasis are Siamese twins. Revision to achieve variety aids emphasis, and many of the techniques of emphasis provide variety, none more than the principle of contrast: Any sentence markedly different from the preceding sentences receives stress—a short sentence after several long ones; a periodic sentence after loose sentences; a simple sentence after a series of complex, compound, or compound-complex sentences. To make contrast effective, a writer must be sure that the sentence that is different contains a major thought. If the contrasting sentence states an unimportant point, that point receives stress regardless of the writer's intentions.

Like other principles of emphasis, contrast functions relentlessly, and the writer ignorant of the principle may find it his master rather than his tool. All writing has emphasis, whether the author knows it or not; and if the stress is on the wrong idea, the results may be just as disastrous as the results of ignorance of logic. That they are likely to be far worse makes it essential for a writer to understand and use the principles of emphasis correctly.

It is unfortunate that many textbooks and instructors consider emphasis advanced optional study, just icing on the cake. A teacher who leaves a writer unaware of the principles leaves him at their mercy. Many writers in the professions spurn emphasis as an advanced technique, "all right for fiction and poetry and such literary works," but not necessary in the prose of information. One might just as well spurn the laws of gravity. Gravity does not cease to function because someone refuses to acknowledge it. To keep falling on one's face through defiance of gravity is idiotic. Sometimes one falls far and hard.

I met a supervisor who was meticulous about correct grammar and diction, particularly in the writing of his subordinates. Emphasis he considered a decoration suitable for the work of those who had nothing better to do with their time. Every time he sent a memorandum, he stated furiously that his colleagues could not read. Everyone, he complained, always got the wrong idea from his writing. If he wrote about the side effects of a drug, they remembered only some trifling remark about the label. If he wrote about vacation schedules, readers thought he was writing about coffee breaks. And every time that he directed an assistant to do something important, the assistant performed two less important tasks. Why, even vice presidents could not read: they never seemed to get the meat out of his memorandums.

This supervisor had a dull, turgid style that tempted readers to skim as much as possible. Such styles being common in industry and government, this alone would not have caused misunderstanding. But the supervisor defied the laws of emphasis. At the end of a memorandum written in long prosy sentences, he would append an afterthought expressed briefly and colloquially, sometimes as a question or exclamation. These brief postscripts, besides being in the position of principal emphasis, contrasted sharply in language, length, and structure with the rest of his writing. Naturally the principle of contrast operated, and his readers noted and remembered the afterthoughts.

POSITION

Sentences containing important thoughts sometimes lack emphasis because instead of being in an important position—the beginning or the end—the main idea is buried in the middle. Placing important words in the emphatic positions is natural to English idiom. An undergraduate says, "If I don't pass that English test today, I'll die," not "If I don't pass that English test, I'll die today." His father says, "Tonight I want you home by ten o'clock," thus stressing both *tonight* and *ten o'clock*. An engineer says, "Another incorrect pressure chart from that technician, and I'll fire him," with the stress on *fire*. But when they write, they neglect the idiomatic stress of English. "In my opinion," writes the undergraduate, emphasizing his opinion as though he were an expert on the subject, "Chaucer is serious when he describes the prioress and in many other instances too." He could not have found less important words to stress than those at the beginning and end of his sentence. A chemist writes, "In accordance with your urgent request, I am replying as soon as possible," and not only throws away the positions of stress in his sentence but opens his letter with an unnecessary sentence.

An improvement in emphasis may reduce wordiness. Placing important words first and last leads to more compact expression in the following sentences:

> Prior to the start of this experiment
> Before this experiment

> When one proceeds to this further step of written communication
> When one writes

> In experiments with water the air bubbles were gotten rid of by
>   thoroughly boiling the liquid.
> The water was boiled thoroughly to eliminate air bubbles.

To make doubly sure no leak occurs, a bead of adhesive is run around the edges of the filter on both sides.

To avoid leaks, the filter is edged on both sides with a bead of adhesive.

It is not desirable to leave filters in a system after the resistance has increased to the point where there is a substantial decrease in the flow of air.

Filters should be removed from a system if the resistance causes a substantial decrease in the flow of air.

A more rigorous derivation would be extremely complicated and would not be justified in view of uncertainties existing with respect to basic information necessary for practical use of the result.

A complicated, more rigorous derivation is not justified when the basic information for practical use of the result is uncertain.

On the basis of the foregoing discussion it is apparent that
This discussion shows

PARALLEL CONSTRUCTION

A major device for sentence emphasis is parallel construction. Equal thoughts demand expression in the same grammatical form. Repetition of structure within a sentence is a most effective device for making the long sentence easy to read, and repetition of structure in two or more sentences connects them. An understanding of parallelism is therefore essential for emphasis and coherence.

To illustrate the various kinds of parallelism, I have deliberately chosen mundane material of no literary pretensions. I have chosen three units in parallel construction because three is a most satisfying rhythmical number.

Single Words in Parallel Construction

NOUNS: The location, size, and price of the factory are satisfactory.
ADJECTIVES: The factory is convenient, large, and inexpensive.

Any single words—verbs, adverbs, participles, gerunds, etc.—may be used in a series in parallel construction. The important point is to maintain the parallelism. It is easy to permit a construction to slip out of parallel construction with untidy, ineffective results like

The factory is large and convenient, and it doesn't cost very much either.

Phrases in Parallel Construction

PREPOSITIONAL PHRASES: They will be interested in the convenience of the factory, in its size, and in its price.

INFINITIVE PHRASES: To find a factory with a convenient location, to make sure that the size is right, and to arrange a low price, send Jack.

Subordinate Clauses in Parallel Construction

SUBSTANTIVE CLAUSES: Jack made clear in his telegram that the factory was conveniently located, that it was large enough, and that the price was satisfactory.

CONCESSIVE CLAUSES: Although the factory was large enough, although it had a convenient location, and although the price was low, Jack was too shrewd to show much interest.

CAUSAL CLAUSES: Because the factory was large enough, because it had a convenient location, and because the price was low, Jack bought it.

Parallelism in Main Clauses and in Sentences

MAIN CLAUSES: The factory is located conveniently two miles from the city on a main road, it is divided into five areas suitable for our research activities, and it is priced five thousand dollars below our budgeted cost.

SENTENCES: Located conveniently on a main road two miles from the city, the factory can be reached easily by train or car. Divided into five areas suitable in size and arrangement for our research activities, it has adequate truck entrances to the areas and more parking space than we need. Priced five thousand dollars below our budgeted cost, it is ten thousand dollars less than any other suitable property in the selected area and requires fewer structural changes and repairs than any other site we have considered.

Repeating Introductory Words

When a writer repeats the introductory words of a parallel construction, he emphasizes each thought; when he uses the introductory words only once, he emphasizes as a unit the ideas in parallel construction.

A. The Development Committee recommends that a committee be appointed by the president to consider new systems because the present system duplicates work, because it creates unnecessary delays in the work of several divisions, and because it fails to use effectively the machines bought last month.

B. The Development Committee recommends that a committee be appointed by the president to consider new systems because the present system duplicates work, creates unnecessary delays in the work of several divisions, and fails to use effectively the machines bought last month.

Most writers would choose Sentence *B*. But Sentence *A* is useful if the paper discusses each weakness of the old system. For stronger emphasis on each weakness to prepare for the discussion of each, a writer may indent or indent and number.

    C. The Development Committee recommends that a committee be appointed by the president to consider new systems for these three reasons:
       1. The present system duplicates work.
       2. It creates unnecessary delays in the work of several divisions.
       3. It fails to use effectively the machines bought last month.

But Sentence *C* is inappropriate if the paper does not discuss these weaknesses and instead turns to the advantages of new systems, the composition of the committee, or some other topic.

Parallel Construction for Lists

Lists, such as those in Sentence *C*, should be parallel in construction, and the ideas should be equal or nearly equal divisions of a subject. The following sentence illustrates the disadvantages of constructions that are not parallel.

    D. The present system has the following five disadvantages:
       1. It causes delay in the distribution of incoming mail.
       2. Too expensive.
       3. That it has been disapproved by two illustrators in advertising.
       4. It fails to use effectively the machines bought last month.
       5. No inspection of efficiency of workers.

Additional discussion of consistency in lists appears in Chapter VI.

Balanced Constructions

Two sentences in balanced, or parallel, construction connect so closely that conjunctions and other connectives may be few. When a pattern of words, phrases, or clauses is repeated for equal ideas in two sentences, the sentences are balanced. If the parallel ideas contrast, the device, called *antithesis*, increases emphasis. The classic example of antithesis is Pope's "To err is human, to forgive divine."

    Example that needs balance: Chemical literature is doubling every eight years in volume. Every ten to twelve years there is twice as much biomedical material published.
    Example of balance: Chemical literature is doubling in volume every eight years. Biomedical literature is doubling every ten to twelve years.
    Example that needs balance: It is acknowledged at the outset that detailed requirements for all possible isotope laboratories will not be described by this standard. Rather the general requirements which

are applicable to the categories of radioisotope laboratories as further defined in the next paragraph will be identified.

Example with unnecessary words and unnecessary passives removed and balance supplied: This standard does not describe the requirements for all isotope laboratories. It describes the general requirements for the radioisotope laboratories defined in the next paragraph.

Similar details about several subjects are suitable for parallel construction—job descriptions, comparisons of bookkeeping entries, comparisons of drugs or chemicals. When the ideas are presented in parallel construction, a reader can compare the details easily. But when the information is jumbled into a variety of structures, it is troublesome to compare details. If information suited to tabular arrangement must be presented in sentences, it should be expressed in parallel construction.

EXAMPLE: Secretaries Grade A have typing speeds of 75 words a minute and shorthand speeds of 135 words a minute, they are able to write good letters and to assume responsibility, and their salaries range from $125 to $150 weekly. Secretaries Grade B have typing speeds of 60 words a minute and shorthand speeds of 120 words a minute, they are able to write adequate letters and to supervise file clerks and typists, and their salaries range from $95 to $130 weekly. Secretaries Grade C have typing speeds of 45 words a minute and shorthand speeds of 100 words a minute, they are able to file and proofread, and their salaries range from $75 to $100 weekly.

Eugene M. Emme in his "Introduction to the History of Rocket Technology" in *Technology and Culture* presents writers and papers in balanced construction:

Dr. Wernher von Braun, one whose career has been invested in rocketry, kindly wrote on "The Redstone, Jupiter, and Juno." Official government historians, Drs. Robert L. Perry and Wyndham D. Miles, filled gaps on "The Atlas, Titan, and Thor" and "The Polaris," respectively. And lastly, Dr. G. A. Tokaty has provided a historical summary on Soviet rocket technology hitherto unpublished in the United States.[6]

Two of G. Edward Pendray's sentences in "Pioneer Rocket Development in the United States" in the same issue indicate the slightly varied balance that is characteristic of modern prose:

In 1909 he began to speculate about using liquid hydrogen and liquid oxygen as rocket propellants. In that year he also hit on the scheme

[6] IV (Fall, 1963), 382.

of using step-rockets—or rockets consisting of multiple stages on which he later obtained a patent.[7]

In the prose that treats material less pedestrian than routine comparisons of drugs, chemicals, and jobs, balance is usually more subtle, the members being varied sufficiently in lengths or beginnings to provide the advantages of balance without monotony.

CLIMAX

Arrangement of three or more units in climactic order is another device of emphasis. The crescendo of louder and louder beats ending in a big bang is agreeable. A haphazard arrangement is disagreeable, and a number of louder and louder beats succeeded by a soft one (anticlimax) is an unpleasant surprise unless it is amusing.

> CLIMACTIC: Miss Jones has been a competent file clerk, a good typist, and an excellent secretary.
>
> HAPHAZARD: Miss Jones has been an excellent secretary, a competent file clerk, and a good typist.
>
> ANTICLIMACTIC INEFFECTIVE: Miss Jones has been a competent file clerk, a pleasant receptionist, a very good secretary, an excellent assistant manager, and a good typist.
>
> ANTICLIMACTIC FOR HUMOR: Grandchildren are anticipated with eagerness, greeted with loving pride, spoiled with boundless enthusiasm, and then avoided with desperate lies and tricks.

SENTENCE RHYTHM

The relationship among parallelism, climax, and sentence rhythm is close, for parallel construction provides sentence rhythm, and a series of three climactic parallel constructions is common and may be the most satisfying of English rhythms. Three parallel sentence elements provide a number of rhythms, such as the following:

1. Three parallel elements with the third expanded
    a. Man, tools, and extinct animals
    b. Number, sex, and average age
    c. Profits of thousands, of tens of thousands, and of tens of millions of dollars

Example *c* illustrates a popular form of this arrangement; each member increases in length thus: —— ——— ————
Example *b* illustrates the long first member, short second, and longer third: ——— —— ————

[7] P. 386.

Example *a* has roughly equal first and second members (the second has a slightly longer vowel) and an expanded third member: — — ——— —

> 2. Three parallel elements with the third the shortest
>   This reorganization will increase the efficiency of the Shipping Department, speed by at least twelve hours all shipping east of the Mississippi, and save money.

The stress on *save money* is increased by the contrast with the length of the second member.

> 3. Three parallel members of equal length
>   *a.* Red, white, and blue
>   *b.* Patients, nurses, doctors
>   *c.* Knowledge, training, and practice
>   *d.* By land, by sea, by air

When the parallel elements are long and number more than three, the final member is usually the longest:

> When a doctor breaks an appointment, try to make another with his secretary. When a doctor refuses to see you, inquire tactfully about his reason. When a doctor limits the length of an interview, stop your talk at exactly the time he set or earlier. When a doctor sees you promptly, try to estimate whether he is meticulous about appointments and would like a brisk talk or whether he is relaxed and has time for a leisurely conversation.

The rhythm of two balanced sentence elements is also common in English. Balance is effective when the elements contrast; antithesis is a good device for emphasis as well as for rhythm.

> The inspector said that we were late submitting samples when he was late in examining them, and he implied that we were not testing accurately when he was not recording accurately.
> The chairman of a meeting should be patient but not docile, strict but not discourteous, informed but not informative, fluent but not longwinded.
> A good business letter, like a chat, should be personal and informal, but it should not be slangy or discursive.
> He was a good leader in the presence of followers and a good follower in the presence of leaders.
> He was a good assistant and a good man for work, but he was a poor executive and a poor source of ideas.

Careful attention to rhythm and to euphony is most important when one is writing speeches and letters. These should follow closely the rhythms of a writer's normal speech. To test his work, a writer of speeches should read his work aloud and mark any sections that are difficult to say. Actors sometimes find such passages in plays and complain that certain groups of words do not fit in the mouth. When a writer finds groups of words that do not fit in the mouth or roll from the tongue, he should rephrase until they do. The only good test is reading aloud. When a secretary reads a letter aloud from her notes, an executive can repeat any phrases that she stumbles over. If he finds them difficult to say, he should replace them. Sometimes it is not the secretary's shorthand that is at fault but the rhythm or euphony of the passage. It is essential that the person who is to deliver a speech read it aloud beforehand. The speech patterns of a writer may be stumbling blocks for a speaker, as writers for presidents of the United States have sadly discovered. The criterion must always be the ease with which the speaker can utter the words. Reading aloud sometimes helps letter writers who have been criticized for bookish or unfriendly styles. Unless they are extraordinarily pompous speakers, saying the words helps them to rephrase passages to achieve conversational rhythms; the use of such rhythms is the basis of the success of good letter writers and speakers.

REVISION THAT CHEERS

A writer who is not in the habit of revising may at this point be surprised by the time and effort involved in correcting and improving sentences. The only comfort for him is the fact that intelligent attention to the suggestions given will bring satisfying results and that some parts of the work will be fun. Beginners often learn by writing each sentence ten different ways; successful authors spend as much as an hour on the revision of one sentence. If a writer in the professions will take his best report and try writing the sentences as many different ways as possible, he will be pleasantly surprised not only by the improvement in his writing but by the enjoyment he finds in revising. Revision is dull only when a writer works without any idea of what to look for and how to improve. As soon as he understands a few basic principles, he works with a purpose, and the encouragement he gains from his progress keeps him going even when a sentence proves especially recalcitrant. In fact, at that point he will dig in, determined to lick the sentence if it takes all night.

Chapter XIV

Style and Paragraphs

> The whole is greater than its part.
>
> *Euclid*

I have noticed during walking tours that some guides choose the flattest, dullest road to a destination. At first when I walk with one of them, I look ahead at the straight expanse and think that the journey will be easy. But I soon weary of the sameness, for even skimming by in a car I would find the flat monotony endless. The scenery is all the same, and the telegraph poles come at exactly the same distances. At regular intervals we pause, and so even the stops become routine. Occasionally we meet a rough patch of road, but my guide moves on at the same pace as though there were no difficulties. The temptation to give up the journey is strong, and if I do finally trudge to the end, I am so tired and bored and at the same time so restless that I wonder how such a short walk could have seemed so long and boring.

I have had guides who were different. They chose roads of infinite variety with spectacular scenery and no lack of entertainment on the way. Most of the time the road wandered away from our destination, and I had no idea in which direction it lay. We jumped over small streams and waded through wide ones because there were few bridges and those few in poor repair. And in the hills my guide expected me to leap from crag to crag as though I were a mountain goat. After a while I dragged myself along without viewing the scenery, and when the road stopped and my guide took off across fields and up difficult cliffs, I barely kept him in sight. For his part he did not seem to care whether I followed or not as he wandered from the path to view a new sight. I had little hope of reaching our destination, but three or four detours later we did arrive. I was too tired and too irritated because of all the unnecessary aimless wandering to notice that my guide did not even say good-bye but hurried off on some other trip, where I certainly would not follow him.

The guide I like chooses a fairly direct road with some variety. I enjoy a small climb through a forest, a lovely descent to a valley, the beautiful vistas and the encouraging views that include some glimpse of our goal, which is nearer each time. We walk happily and quickly together along the straight easy stretches, and he slows to my pace when the path is a little rough and gives me a hand when we climb. He encourages me by telling me how far we have come or how little more we have to go. The bridges are all in good repair, and my guide is concerned that I should cross each safely. Before I have time to be tired, we arrive at our destination. When my guide says good-bye, I realize that the exercise has been so refreshing that I am satisfied but not tired. I am ready to go farther with him and hope to have such a good guide the next time I take a walking tour, but I know that he will be hard to find.

Sometimes reading functional prose is like the first walk. The opening paragraph suggests a quick and easy journey, but every paragraph is like the first. Even if I skim, the reading seems infinitely monotonous. After a while only the paragraph indentions tell me that I am progressing, and the progress is always to another paragraph like the last one. Even when the material is more difficult, the writer explains no more or less than he did for easy material. After a while I do not care whether I complete the reading or not, and when I do reach the last paragraph, which of course is exactly like all the others, I am exasperated by having read so much to get so little.

But sometimes I have had a different experience. The paragraphs were varied and entertaining, but so many of them wandered from the subject that I began to doubt that the writer would ever cover his topic, if he had one. There were no transitions or only poor and confusing ones, and the writer jumped incoherently from subject to subject. Twice he seemed to be back where he had started. Too tired to be entertained or amused by his digressions, I had difficulty continuing. And when he reached his conclusion, I knew it only because I turned the page and found no more.

The writer I like has paragraphs varied in length, development, and organization. He lets me know where he is going, moves quickly through simple material, and explains and illustrates more difficult points. His paragraphs are carefully connected, and when there is a marked change in thought, there are enough indications to help me follow the shift. He does not repeat unnecessarily or digress; instead he covers his subject thoroughly and briefly. While I am still interested, he completes his work in a satisfactory final paragraph and leaves me wishing that there were more writers like him.

Whether a writer is a poor guide or an excellent one depends on his interest in presenting his ideas to his readers courteously and effectively. And such presentation requires a knowledge of the principles of paragraphing. Some writers do not think of helping their readers, and some little know how to help. Some would rather not help; they want readers to find the subject too difficult for them and to be impressed by the writer's profundity. The first group need only learn the principles and start applying them to be good guides. But the other groups will have to learn the principles and realize that readers are not favorably impressed by poor writing. Like walkers, readers blame a poor guide for his bad judgment and his failure to help them.

LENGTH

Logic and the Paragraph

A paragraph, like a stage of a journey, is a logical division of the whole. Also like part of a journey, it may be a complete work in itself. As a unit of a larger work, a paragraph marks divisions of thought, thus enabling readers to perceive more easily the structure of the whole and to observe the progress of their reading. A good paragraph signals a shift in thought and a step toward comprehension of the whole.

Logic is a principal influence on paragraph length. Some subjects have natural divisions that it would be foolish to ignore. A discussion of three characteristics of a polymer may occupy one paragraph or three. A generalization and an example may be developed in one paragraph or two. Three causes and an effect may be paragraphed in a number of ways: (1) in one paragraph; (2) in two paragraphs, one for the causes and one for the effect; (3) in four paragraphs, one for each cause and one for the effect; (4) in more than four paragraphs—some for explanation of the effect, for methods used to modify the effect, and for new methods suggested for trial, and in addition any number of paragraphs for the causes. The long paragraph on coke-oven gas on page 270, for example, might have been divided into three paragraphs, the second one beginning with *Of the material* and the third beginning with *Coke-oven gas.*

Obviously, even though a subject has inherent divisions, a writer still has some choice. If he exercises this choice intelligently, he will not break a weighty subject into slivers that are difficult for a reader to perceive as a whole, nor will he build mountainous paragraphs that deter a reader. Rather he will use paragraphing as a device to stress the inherent divisions of a subject effectively for his readers. For example, the following long paragraph of Alice S. Rossi is necessary to show the unity of four ideas, and it is skillfully broken by indention and numbering:

If we want more women scientists, there are several big tasks ahead:

1) We must educate boys and girls for all their major adult roles—as parents, spouses, workers, and creatures of leisure. This means giving more stress in education, at home and at school, to the future occupational roles of girls. Women will not stop viewing work as a stopgap until meaningful work is taken for granted in the lives of women as it is in the lives of men.

2) We must stop restricting and lowering the occupational goals of girls on the pretext of counseling them to be "realistic." If women have difficulty in handling the triple roles of member of a profession, wife, and mother, their difficulties should be recognized as a social problem to be dealt with by social engineering rather than be left to each individual woman to solve as best she can. Conflicts and difficulties are not necessarily a social evil to be avoided; they can be a spur to creative social change.

3) We must apply our technological skill to a rationalization of home maintenance (*15*). The domestic responsibilities of employed women and their husbands would be considerably lightened if there were house-care service firms, for example, with teams of trained male and female workers making the rounds of client households, accomplishing in a few hours per home and with more thoroughness what the single domestic servant does poorly in two days of work at a barely living wage.

4) We must encourage men to be more articulate about themselves as males and about women. Three out of five married women doctors and engineers have husbands in their own or related fields. The views of young and able women concerning marriage and careers could be changed far more effectively by the men who have found marriage to professional women a satisfying experience than by exhortations of professional women, or of manpower specialists and family-living instructors whose own wives are homemakers.[1]

Format and Paragraph Length

Without the indentions, this paragraph would have looked formidable in the narrow columns of *Science*. A careful writer does not ignore the fact that his paragraph length should suit the format. Paragraphs that are good lengths in handwritten manuscript may be too long in the narrow columns of a newspaper, too short in typescript, and too fragmentary in a printed book. Writers of informational prose can learn adaptation of paragraph length from journalists. In the narrow columns of a newspaper, where paragraphs of many sentences would appear cumbersome, a reporter uses very short paragraphs, many one-sentence paragraphs. When columns are wider, as on an editorial page, newspaper paragraphs are longer.

[1] "Women in Science: Why So Few?" *Science*, CXLVIII (May 28, 1965), 1201.

Many writers of informational prose never visualize their paragraphs as they look to a reader; consequently they write forbidding paragraphs three and four typewritten pages long. When these are published in narrow-column periodicals, they seem interminable. And some writers in business and industry who are used to writing short paragraphs in letters do not realize that the brief paragraphs suitable to a letter look very different in type. A careful writer anticipates the final appearance of his writing and plans his paragraphs to be neither scrappy nor ponderous, even though planning may require counting the words of a particular format to estimate how paragraphs will look.

The Reader and Paragraph Length

Paragraphs written for poor readers should be shorter than those directed to competent readers. To a poor reader short paragraphs indicate that he will not be asked to grasp too much at one time, that the subject has been divided into tiny segments for easy understanding. A competent reader may consider such short paragraphs baby food and feel that he wants to use his teeth on ideas that are not predigested. But he does not mean that he wants paragraphs of three pages or more, like those in some scholarly articles. A reader who rejects baby food does not necessarily want to bite into a whole joint. The average reader of literature on science, business, and technology wants normal portions, and he recognizes that some pieces will be larger than others because of the structure of the whole.

Most readers of literature on professional subjects expect paragraphs of one hundred to three hundred words. When his readers are not well educated, a writer may plan shorter paragraphs. If it is impossible to shorten a long paragraph, he may break it by numbering internal divisions, by using several methods of development (page 274), by dialogue, or by an adroit placement of a topic sentence near the middle of a paragraph. Unbroken paragraphs longer than three hundred words should be infrequent, even in papers directed to experienced readers. Long paragraphs that slowly drag their lengths along like freight trains are a burden and a discourtesy to readers.

Variety and Emphasis

Contrast in paragraph length may be used to good effect. After a number of short paragraphs, a long one receives strong stress; after a number of long paragraphs, a short one receives stress; after a succession of paragraphs of medium length, a long or a short one receives stress. By placing an important idea in the paragraph that differs, a writer can highlight that idea and subordinate unimportant ideas.

Ignorance of this principle accounts for some failures to communicate effectively. If a writer of a memorandum of four paragraphs, each of one hundred to two hundred words, places a minor thought in a twenty-word paragraph, he will find that readers note and remember the unimportant information of the twenty-word paragraph. While revising, a writer should be certain that any paragraph markedly different in length from the preceding paragraphs contains material suitable for major stress. And a writer wondering how to emphasize a division of his subject might consider placing it in a paragraph distinctly longer or shorter than the surrounding paragraphs. Skillful use of contrasting paragraph lengths provides economical and effective stress and variety. And it is not difficult or onerous to write paragraphs of contrasting lengths.

Many writers do not vary paragraph length sufficiently. If their monotonous paragraphs are long, the style is likely to seem slow moving, heavy, difficult, and even turgid. A reader may consider the writing too deep. If monotonous paragraphs are short, the style will seem choppy, rapid, light, or even childish. A reader may think the work superficial. But even long paragraphs mingled with short ones become monotonous. A writer's paragraph lengths should not be only elephants and mice. There were also animals of intermediate size in the ark.

Achieving effective paragraph length is part of the art of writing. For each work a careful writer weighs the relative importance of the demands of the subject, format, readers' preferences, need for variety, considerations of emphasis, and effect on style. Many writers usually judge subconsciously. Those who have never thought about the length of their paragraphs may have to weigh and choose consciously for a time, but after they have done this for a while, they too will plan effective paragraph length without much conscious effort.

UNITY

Whether it is long or short, a paragraph develops one main idea. The central idea may be stated in one sentence—the topic sentence. This may appear anywhere in the paragraph. Often it opens or closes a paragraph, but sometimes the topic sentence is so obvious that it is not expressed.

If everything in a paragraph concerns the topic sentence, the paragraph has unity. Readers expect unity in a paragraph. Bits and pieces of other ideas confuse them and weaken or even destroy the central idea. A writer who is inclined to digress should test the unity of his paragraphs when he revises. Anything that does not enforce the topic sentence should be removed entirely or placed elsewhere. This clarifies and sharpens the main point of a paragraph and is thus a major step toward a clear, clean-cut style.

METHODS OF DEVELOPMENT

Paragraphs are usually more than mere statements of central ideas; they are developments of central ideas. Each paragraph offers variations on a theme. Good writers do not just state an idea and then jump to some other subject, because that would confuse readers, who expect ideas to be developed. There are many methods of developing paragraphs, and writers often use several methods in one paragraph to display facets of a topic effectively or to vary a long paragraph. Some of the common methods of paragraph development follow.

Analogy is frequently used to explain ideas, particularly to acquaint readers with unfamiliar concepts by comparison with familiar ones; analogy is helpful, for example, in explaining technical matters to a layman. Much depends on the choice of the familiar concept, which is usually a simple one with which readers are well acquainted; it should be original, appropriate, and consistent. Sometimes a comparison with a concrete subject vividly clarifies an abstract subject. An analogy may also impress upon the memory of a reader something that has just been explained. Analogy has the appeal of the picturesque and the imaginative; it may please readers by its cleverness, help writers to simplify, and provide a change from more mundane reasoning. Analogies may be poetic or almost poetic.

Loren Eiseley in an effective analogy describes a naturalist looking backward:

> The door to the past is a strange door. It swings open and things pass through it, but they pass in one direction only. No man can return across that threshold, though he can look down still and see the green light waver in the water weeds.[2]

This says much that would be difficult or impossible to state clearly without the analogy, as does the following paragraph by Marjorie Hope Nicolson:

> For three hundred years men have vainly tried to put together the pieces of a broken circle. Some have been poets, some philosophers, some artists. They have shared a common desire for a unity that once existed, and have sought a "return to medievalism," when life seemed integrated about a strong center, whether of the Church or of a

[2] *The Immense Journey* (Random House, New York, 1957), p. 54.

monarch. Except for an occasional individual who has found peace in old religion, their efforts have proved fruitless. Poets and artists have deliberately revived old styles, but these attempts have been equally abortive. Modern critics have kidnapped to our times poets like Donne, in whom they find a "unified sensibility" of feeling and thinking. Philosophical poets—Pope, Wordsworth, Tennyson—have tried to express a world view, as did Lucretius for the ancients, Dante for the Middle Ages, Milton for the seventeenth-century Protestant. But all the king's horses and all the king's men cannot put Humpty-Dumpty together again. Mere fitting together of pieces may remake the picture in a jigsaw puzzle; it will not remake an egg. Nor can we reconstruct the old Circle of Perfection, broken by modern science and philosophy. Donne spoke truly when he said: "Nothing more endless, nothing sooner broke." [3]

John R. Platt presents a clarifying analogy to describe strong inference:

> It is like climbing a tree. At the first fork, we choose—or, in this case, "nature" or the experimental outcome chooses—to go to the right branch or the left; at the next fork, to go left or right; and so on. There are similar branch points in a "conditional computer program," where the next move depends on the results of the last calculation. And there is a "conditional inductive tree" or "logical tree" of this kind written out in detail in many first-year chemistry books, in the table of steps for qualitative analysis of an unknown sample, where the student is led through a real problem of consecutive inference. Add reagent A; if you get a red precipitate, it is subgroup alpha and you filter and add reagent B; if not, you add the other reagent, B'; and so on.[4]

Later this writer uses analogy for one of its principal advantages—its contribution to the coherence of a whole section. In the paragraph that follows the section just quoted, he echoes the analogy with "to proceed to the next fork," and in the next paragraph he writes, "Strong inference, and the logical tree it generates . . . ." He concludes this part of his discussion with another appropriate analogy:

> The difference between the average scientist's informal methods and the methods of the strong-inference users is somewhat like the difference between a gasoline engine that fires occasionally and one that fires in steady sequence. If our motorboat engines were as erratic as our deliberate intellectual efforts, most of us would not get home for supper.[5]

[3] *The Breaking of the Circle* (Columbia University Press, New York, 1960), p. 123.
[4] "Strong Inference," *Science*, CXLVI (October 16, 1964), 347.
[5] P. 348.

When I consider how effective these analogies are, I regret that men in science and technology use analogy so little. Of all the methods of paragraph development discussed in this chapter, analogy was the most difficult for me to find illustrated in writings on science and engineering. Yet no other method of paragraph development is more effective for making the reader feel at ease, clarifying a concept, and vivifying ideas to make them memorable. I think it was the frustration of my search that made me begin this chapter with an analogy—or maybe it was just a desire to balance the scales. In any case, I hope that more writers in the professions will use that efficient and effective method of presenting and developing ideas—analogy.

Analysis, or classification, occurs frequently in writings on science and technology. In explaining a method or process, a writer may divide his subject into such topics as materials, apparatus, steps, and results. Part of a paragraph, one paragraph, or several paragraphs may analyze each subject. Robert L. Sproull ends a paragraph with

> Of all the types of accelerators we discuss only two, the cyclotron and the synchrotron. References that describe the betatron, linear accelerator, synchrocyclotron, and other accelerators are listed at the end of the chapter.[6]

Cause and effect or *question and answer*—which should come first? This is a question that troubles some writers. It is usually easier for a reader if the paragraph begins with whichever is more familiar to him. It may begin with a question to arouse interest, with background if a reader requires preliminary material to understand the query, or with material leading to a question. A paragraph may state a cause or causes, an effect or effects, or both causes and effects.

The following illustrative paragraph lists first a cause and the general effect and then specific effects:

> If the 50,000 control devices in the oil refineries of the U. S. should go "on strike," we would be faced with social disaster. The refineries would become lifeless industrial monuments. If we undertook to replace them with old-fashioned, manually operated refineries to supply our present motor-fuel needs, we would have to build four or five times as much plant, cracking and some other modern chemical processes would have to be eliminated, yields of motor fuel from crude petroleum would drop to a quarter of those at present, costs would skyrocket, and quality would plummet. Automobile engines would have to be radically redesigned to function with inferior fuel. And because of

[6] *Modern Physics* (John Wiley and Sons, New York, 1963), p. 18.

lower motor-fuel yields, we would need to produce crude petroleum several times as rapidly as we produce it now. Technology in refining would be set back to the early 1920s.[7]

C. P. Snow develops a convincing paragraph by stating the result and then two causes:

> I said earlier that this cultural divide is not just an English phenomenon: it exists all over the western world. But it probably seems at its sharpest in England, for two reasons. One is our fanatical belief in educational specialisation, which is much more deeply ingrained in us than in any country in the world, west or east. The other is our tendency to let our social forms crystallise. This tendency appears to get stronger, not weaker, the more we iron out economic inequalities: and this is specially true in education. It means that once anything like a cultural divide gets established, all the social forces operate to make it not less rigid, but more so.[8]

A popular paragraph development presents first the cause or causes and then the result or results. Boring, Langfeld, and Weld use such a development and vivify it with two examples that are easy to remember:

> The commonest trouble into which language can get your thinking arises from the same word's having several different meanings. The meaning shifts as thought progresses from one sense in the premise to another in the conclusion. Said one newly naturalized immigrant: "Of course I'll vote Democratic. This country's a democracy, isn't it? They told me so when I was studying to be a citizen." And then there is the old joke from the Victorian era: "A piece of bread is better than nothing; nothing is better than Heaven; therefore a piece of bread is better than Heaven." [9]

Presenting a result in a question, Jerome Wiesner completes a paragraph with an unacceptable cause:

> What then is the problem? Why do so few engineers proceed for a doctorate? We reject any notion that they are limited in academic potential. Our studies suggest that as many as 20 percent of the baccalaureate recipients have both ability and inclination to complete a doctorate.[10]

[7] Eugene Ayres, "An Automatic Chemical Plant," *Automatic Control* (Simon and Schuster, New York, 1955), p. 41.
[8] *The Two Cultures* (Cambridge University Press, New York, 1959), p. 18.
[9] Edward Garrigues Boring, Herbert Sidney Langfeld, and Harry Porter Weld, *Foundations of Psychology* (John Wiley and Sons, New York, 1948), p. 207.
[10] *Where Science and Politics Meet* (McGraw-Hill Book Company, New York, 1965), p. 113.

Comparison and contrast should be chosen for comparable subjects. The most satisfactory comparisons treat concepts that seem much alike but on close examination show differences, or they treat concepts that seem obviously different but also have important similarities. Although a long comparison—a long memorandum, a report, a chapter of a book— does not lend itself to a treatment of first one concept and then the other, followed by a comparison of the two (Chapter V), a single paragraph may be organized in this way. It is less likely than is a long work to fall apart where a writer shifts to a second concept, and a reader is less likely to forget the details of the first concept before he reaches the comparative details of the second. In a paragraph one might discuss first Pension Plan A and then Pension Plan B, or one might compare the details of A with those of B point by point. When a comparison is to be presented point by point, a writer should choose an appropriate order for the points—chronological, climactic, spatial, etc. (Chapter V); if he treats first one concept and then the other, the treatments should be parallel. A tight plan is important in comparison and contrast, for helter-skelter presentation confuses a reader and makes it difficult for him to know where he has been and where he is going next or even to see the similarities and differences on which the paragraph development depends.

To analyze variations on the ammonia process, I. M. LeBaron offers a general comparison:

> Continuing investigations have developed a number of ammonia processes. The principal ones, identified by the men or group of men developing them, are the Badische Anilin und Soda Fabrik, Nitrogen Engineering, Claude, Casale, Fauser, and Mont Cenis processes. These processes are fundamentally the same in that nitrogen and hydrogen react at elevated temperatures and pressures in the presence of a catalyst. They vary in arrangement, construction of equipment, and the pressures and temperatures used. A number of processes have been developed for producing the synthesis-gas mixture which depend primarily on the source of the gas, whether it be coke, natural gas, coke-oven gas, or by-product hydrogen.[11]

In two paragraphs D. S. Greenberg contrasts attitudes of consultants toward fees:

> This business-like approach to consulting appears to be something of a rarity. Much more common is the scientist who is called upon by

[11] "Fifty Years of Chemical Engineering in the Plant Food Industry," *Chemical Engineering in Industry*, ed. W. T. Dixon and A. W. Fisher, Jr. (American Institute of Chemical Engineers, New York, 1958), p. 52.

an industrial firm to provide counsel on a given problem or to agree to make himself available if problems arise within his professional area. In many of these cases, the offer of a consultantship is money from heaven, and whatever the company offers, the scientist happily accepts —and sometimes with a naiveté that must arouse the wonder of the business world. For example, a young physical scientist was invited to serve as a consultant to the research division of a large industrial firm. The fee, he was told, would be $125 a day. He explained that he would prefer to start at $100, and, if the company found his services satisfactory, the amount could be raised.

While many scientists are altogether pleased with the going rates of up to a few hundred dollars a day, or several thousand dollars a year for long-term consulting, there are others who feel that industry has been paying incredibly cheap rates for what it's been getting. As one scientist views it: "A multimillion dollar company calls in a top-flight physicist, and for a few hundred dollars he gives them the benefit of twenty years of training and experience. He feels happy about getting $200 for an afternoon of conversation, but what he doesn't realize is that his advice can be worth millions of dollars to the company.[12]

And in the same issue of *Science* the authors of "Poliovirus Type 1: Neutralization by Papain-Digested Antibodies" demonstrate the efficiency of a compact contrast:

Three basic differences must be considered in comparing the biological qualities of antibody fragments I and II with intact $7S$ antibody. Fragments I and II have a molecular weight of about 50,000; they are monovalent, possessing only one combining site and they do not fix complement. The $7S$ rabbit antibodies have a molecular weight of 160,000; they are divalent and are able to fix complement.[13]

Definition of a formal kind places the term to be defined in a class and then distinguishes it from the other members of the class, but in literary definition, other methods may supplement this procedure or even substitute for it. Almost any method of paragraph development may be used to amplify a definition. Literary definitions may include examples, derivation of the word or words, description of the appearance, names of the parts, comparison and contrast, an explanation of what the term is not, an explanation of how it works, an explanation of how it was made. Even causes and effects, history, the name of the inventor or discoverer, or the location of the object or term being defined may augment the definition. From these a writer selects the topics most helpful to his readers. Deductive order is often chosen, and other methods are

[12] "News and Comment," *Science*, CXLV (September 25, 1964), 1417.
[13] Arnold Vogt, Rudolf Kopp, Gunter Maass, and Leo Reich, p. 1447.

used to develop the formal definition that stands first. But definitions may begin with word derivation, examples, description, or any other details.

A descriptive definition appears in *Modern Physics:*

> The *cyclotron* is an accelerator for protons or heavier particles. It is illustrated schematically in Fig. 1-6. An evacuated box (the tank) is situated between the cylindrical pole pieces of a large magnet. Inside the vacuum tank there are two electrodes, called "D's" because of their shape. These are hollow, open, copper boxes each with a cylindrical side and semicircular ends. Near the center of the chamber is an ion source. If protons are to be accelerated, the source is an electric arc in a hydrogen gas atmosphere. If doubly charged helium ions (alpha-particles) are to be accelerated, the gas is helium. In any case, gas is admitted in a fine stream at the arc and is pumped rapidly away by the pumps evacuating the tank.[14]

Ernest O. Ohsol discusses many of the topics of literary definition when he writes about coke-oven gas—analysis of contents, value and some history of value, variation in yield, properties, uses, and some history of uses:

> Coke-oven gas can be defined as containing those by-product materials with boiling points below room temperature. Ammonia may therefore be included in this discussion. Coke-oven gas has been and still is the most valuable by-product from the production of coke from coal; however, its value has been decreasing along with that of the other by-products as the years have gone by. In 1937, for example, gas was 19 per cent of the total value of the products from the coke oven and in 1950 11 per cent. Presently in many plants where the gas can no longer be sold to city gas companies the value has decreased to 5 per cent. Even at 5 per cent it is well above that of any of the other by-product components. Of the materials made in the high-temperature coking of coal, the first five in weight percentage are either gases or coke. For example, 2,000 lb. of coal yields 1,400 lb. of coke; 132 lb. of methane; 43 lb. of carbon monoxide; 30 lb. of hydrogen; 20 lb. of ethylene; 11.7 lb. of benzene, a liquid product; 6.7 lb. of hydrogen sulfide; 6.2 lb. of naphthalene, a solid; and 5.2 lb. of ammonia, a gas. Also of some interest in a consideration of the gas would be the propylene yield at 3.4 lb., butylenes at 2.8 lb., and HCN at 1.7 lb. There is, of course, some variation in these numbers with different coals and different coking operations. The properties of coke-oven gas are as follows: heating value, 550 B.t.u./cu. ft.; specific gravity, 0.38; volume composition, 57 per cent hydrogen, 28 per cent methane, 7 per cent carbon monoxide, and some nitrogen, illuminants, and carbon dioxide. Coke-oven gas was a very important product for addi-

[14] Sproull, p. 18.

tion to manufactured gas for city use; however, as natural gas came north, it displaced manufactured gas. For some time coke-oven gas was added to natural gas by city gas utilities, but this practice has been partially abandoned with the continued stripping of higher hydrocarbons from the natural gas in the south. The primary use of coke-oven gas today is for fuel purposes inside the plant itself. This is still not true in Europe: the lack of hydrogen and methane in Europe has made coke-oven gas a valuable raw material for the production of ammonia, methanol, and the like.[15]

Charles W. Palmer defines a written procedure by stating its functions:

> The written procedure is a document designed to:
> 1. Direct employees to perform specific operations.
> 2. Help employees understand the significance of operations.
> 3. Serve as a reference of how and why things are done.
> 4. Provide for supervisory review and control.
> 5. Expedite job completion by allowing several employees to work on a single job.
> 6. Help assure compatibility between employees and their jobs.[16]

Details and particulars should be carefully selected, for they can add life and vigor to writing, or they can bore and discourage readers. Nothing is more useful in developing a generalization than specific details. Nothing is less useful than unnecessary details.

If details are essential but repetitious, climactic order may hold a reader's interest. Sometimes details are combined effectively with a generalization. Details and particulars may be arranged in many different plans—simple to complex, known to unknown, chronological, spatial, or (if they accompany a generalization) inductive or deductive (Chapter V). Any series of paragraphs or any long paragraphs of details signal a reviser to explore the possibility of relegating the details to appendices or of discarding some items. It is often necessary to discard unessential particulars to secure proper emphasis on main points; paragraphs of details should never be permitted to overwhelm the main points. The question is how many details must the reader have to understand the main point? not how many details would the writer like to include?

Details of examples both clarify and vivify the examples in the following passage from Tobias Dantzig's *Number: The Language of Science:*

> But, also, wherever a counting technique, worthy of the name, exists at all, *finger counting* has been found to either precede it or

---

[15] "Coke By-Products and Gas," *Chemical Engineering in Industry*, p. 297.
[16] "The Written Procedure—Welcome Relief for the Engineer," *STWP Review*, XII (April, 1965), 11.

accompany it. And in his fingers man possesses a device which permits him to pass imperceptibly from cardinal to ordinal number. Should he want to indicate that a certain collection contains four objects, he will raise or turn down four fingers *simultaneously;* should he want to count the same collection he will raise or turn down these fingers *in succession.* In the first case he is using his fingers as a cardinal model, in the second as an ordinal system. Unmistakable traces of this origin of counting are found in practically every primitive language. In most of these tongues the number "five" is expressed by "hand," the number "ten" by "two hands," or sometimes by "man." Furthermore, in many primitive languages the number words up to four are identical with the names given to the four fingers.[17]

And Kenneth M. Wilson begins his editorial "Of Time and the Doctorate" with an idealized description. Descriptive details, like other particulars, require careful organization. Wilson uses a generalization followed by chronological order:

The idealized picture of a new Ph.D. in science is of a student who had his course well charted in advance and who was aided by assistantships and fellowships to earn the doctorate in approximately 4 years. As a matter of fact, only about one student in ten gets through that quickly. The typical one finished college without expecting to go on for the doctorate and without clear plans for any graduate work. In the B.A.– Ph.D. interval he spent 9 months in military service, worked a couple of years, usually as a college teacher or in other professional work, was enrolled in graduate school for more than 3 years on a full-time basis and for another year and a half part time, and finally got the doctorate nearly 8 years after the B.A.[18]

Examples and illustrations can advance the thought of a topic sentence vividly, dramatically, and convincingly. Paragraphs of examples and illustrations are useful for clarifying generalizations and for adding meaning and force to abstract statements. They are helpful in teaching; a student who forgets a general point may recall a specific example and thus regain the generalization.

The textbook *Foundations of Psychology,* used as a source earlier in this chapter, is, as every good textbook is, a mine of paragraphs developed by examples and illustrations. Discussing the need for control in experiments, the authors illustrate as follows:

On the other hand, hunch comes into this business too. No one can keep all the conditions constant, and the experimenter has to guess

[17] Doubleday and Company, Garden City, N. Y., 1956, p. 10. Reprinted by permission of the Macmillan Company.
[18] *Science,* CXLVIII (May 21, 1965), 1045.

which conditions are the most important. Suppose you discovered on a Tuesday that a certain percentage of automobile drivers cannot tell a red traffic light from a green, except by knowing that the red is on top. (You could do it by interchanging the red and green in one signal, provided you prevented accidents in some other way.) Well, that was Tuesday. Would you have to repeat the experiment on Wednesday and all the other days? No, you assume that the day of the week makes no difference, that eyes see the same on Tuesdays and on Wednesdays. Nor does the phase of the moon matter, nor the last name of the driver. It is by hunch that you leave these matters out of control. You hope they make no difference. Sometimes, when a long-accepted generalization turns out later to be wrong, it is because some such essential condition was not controlled when the original generalization was formed. For instance, most people would expect sex to make no difference in observing traffic lights, but it does. Very few women are color-blind.[19]

Reiteration requires that one repeat a topic in different words, but it is essential that the idea repeated be important enough to justify the repetition. To develop a long paragraph by reiteration requires special skill. For example, some variety may be achieved by viewing the subject from different angles. Although in art the repetition of good patterns is enjoyable, the repetition of poor patterns and excessive repetition are painful. If each sentence does not add force or vividness to the idea being repeated, then reiteration seems careless rather than purposeful and becomes irritating. But used effectively, reiteration can stress an idea and impress it firmly upon the reader. It is a particularly helpful technique in speeches.

Reiteration as used by Gordon D. Friedlander of *Spectrum* follows:

> Operation and maintenance expenses for the project have been estimated on the basis of labor requirements for completely automatic operation and maintenance experience as reported for other hydro projects. The operation and maintenance expenses for the thermal plant are based on Con Edison's experience with existing modern plants.[20]

The following example of effectively varied reiteration from Robert Oppenheimer is, not surprisingly, from a paper prepared originally as a speech:

> For one thing, we have changed the face of the earth; we have changed the way men live. We may not change the condition of man's life, but we have changed all modes in which the condition occurs. I

[19] Boring, Langfeld, and Weld, p. 14.
[20] "Pumped Storage—an Answer to Peaking Power," I (October, 1964), 71.

do not by this mean to say that from the existence of science, from the discovery, knowledge, technique and power of science the particularities of the present time follow. But we all know that if life today is very different from what it was two hundred years ago, if we meet our human and political problems in a quite new form, that has much to do with the fact that we know how to do a great many things, and that there are people who are eager to do them, not typically scientists, but people who are glad to use the knowledge and with it the control which science has made available.[21]

Combined methods of development are so numerous that there is no practical way to illustrate the possibilities. Because most paragraphs exhibit more than one method, a good paragraph plan is essential. Paragraphs, being small essays in themselves, may be organized by any of the methods suggested for the whole paper in Chapter V, and the choice of a plan is governed by the same considerations that determine the choice of a plan for the whole work. But in choosing an organization for a paragraph, a writer also considers the preceding and following paragraphs in order to achieve harmony without monotony.

COHERENCE

Regardless of how it is developed, every paragraph must have coherence. Supplying coherence in paragraphs improves style so markedly that when I consult with a discouraged writer I often work on coherence first. Then readers will comment on how much easier and smoother his style is or on how polished it seems, and he will be encouraged to further improvement. Coherence is easy for a writer on science or technology to achieve because his work is likely to be well organized. And the basis of coherence is unity and a plan. When a paragraph is unified and organized, transitions follow easily. Writers use some transitions when they write their first drafts, but coherence is a minor concern at that time. During revision writers can easily provide transitions where they are missing and improve weak ones. This is a better procedure than trying to write all the transitions in a first draft, for when a writer has other things to think about, he may impede the flow of his ideas by worrying about transitions. If a paragraph is unified and well organized, providing transitions is a simple step in revision. A reviser may supply one of the following kinds: (1) pronouns and demonstrative adjectives, (2) conjunctions and other transitional words and phrases, (3) word echo and synonyms, (4) parallel constructions.

[21] J. Robert Oppenheimer, *The Open Mind* (Simon and Schuster, New York, 1955), p. 120.

Pronouns and demonstrative adjectives that refer to antecedents in the preceding sentence connect sentences efficiently if they appear near the beginning of the second sentence. They are common and useful transitions, seldom obtrusive or annoying. Usually most of the necessary pronouns, such as *you, he, she, it, they, I, we, one, each,* and *either,* appear in the first draft. Sometimes demonstratives may be added during revision: coherence between loosely connected sentences may be strengthened by changing *the* to *this, that, these,* or *those.* In the following paragraph *these problems* connects neatly with *the most pressing problems* in the preceding sentence:

> In the epithelial tumors of adult life the most pressing problems in the current study and use of cytotoxic drugs present themselves. These problems fall under the heads of (i) clinical investigation, (ii) host resistance, and (iii) treatment policies in late cancer.

Conjunctions and transitional expressions not only connect elements within a sentence but also connect sentences. A precise use of conjunctions is essential in functional prose. The right conjunction makes reading easier and clearer; the wrong one may stress incorrectly, necessitate rereading, or permanently confuse. Advice on the accurate use of conjunctions to connect parts of sentences appears on pages 180 to 184. Conjunctions that connect the thoughts of two main clauses or sentences vary in meaning and tone; therefore a writer who wishes to choose well should know many of them. Some commonly used conjunctions and transitional words and phrases follow.

ADDITION: *and, again, also, besides, equally important, finally, first (second, third), further, furthermore, last, moreover*

COMPARISON AND CONTRAST: *after all, but, however, in comparison, in like manner, on the other hand, on the contrary, likewise, nevertheless, notwithstanding, still, whereas* (If a sentence contains a comparative or superlative adjective or adverb that compares or contrasts a word or thought with one in the preceding sentence, the adjective or adverb is transitional. For example, in "If x has a greater value," *greater* connects clearly with the value stated in the preceding sentence.)

RESULT: *accordingly, consequently, hence, therefore, thus, wherefore*

EXEMPLIFICATION, REPETITION, SUMMARY, INTENSIFICATION: *as has been stated, as I have said, as well as, for example, for instance, in any event, in brief, indeed, in fact, in other words, in particular, in short, in summary, obviously, of course, that is, to be sure, to sum up*

PURPOSE: *for this purpose, to this end, toward this objective, with this goal*

PLACE: *adjacent to, beyond, here, near, on the other side, opposite to*

TIME: *afterward, at length, after an hour (day, week, year), immediately, in the meantime, meanwhile* (All references to time and place connect by moving readers from one time or place to another or by keeping readers in the same time or place. They are excellent transitions—effective, unobtrusive, organic. And such transitions please readers, because they like to know where they are.)

Long and obvious transitional expressions burden a paper and may irritate readers. A wordy mechanical transition ("Now let us consider the features just mentioned") and sentences that repeat long sections of preceding sentences are usually avoided today because they give a Victorian flavor to prose. Organic transitions, such as word echo, are preferred. Nor do writers of today place heavy transitional words and phrases at the beginnings of sentences unless the connecting thoughts are so difficult that transitions are needed immediately. Transitions are more often placed after the first few words of a sentence, where they are less conspicuous and receive less stress than at the beginning.

Word echo and the use of synonyms, also called *the repetition of key words,* is a common transitional method in functional prose. When main words are repeated, the central idea of a paragraph is stressed, and thus coherence and emphasis reinforce each other. Such repetition is often hardly noticeable because synonyms and synonymous phrases may be used as well as repetitions of a main word. Indeed, even antonyms provide connections, for example, *hot* with *cold, dry* with *wet, economical* with *wasteful, busy* with *idle.*

Parallel constructions also link sentences. Repetitions of sentence patterns connect sentences so closely that other transitions are seldom necessary. Scientists and technologists often use parallel constructions for similar thoughts and thus not only connect the thoughts tightly but make them easier to comprehend because the divisions of thought follow as regularly and clearly as items in a table. The writers of "Sex-Associated Differences in Serum Proteins of Mice" use parallel construction:

> In several animal species certain serum proteins appear to be different in males and females; for example, the relative concentration of albumin in rats, as measured by moving boundary and zone electrophoresis, was found to be higher in females than in males (1). In cattle, males possessed less α-globulin glycoprotein and more β-globulin and γ-globulin glycoproteins than females (2). In toads, the separation of some of the serum components by starch gel electrophoresis has been reported to be different in the two sexes (3). In mice, the concentration of agglutinating antibody to chicken and sheep heteroantigens (4), and to human erythrocytes (5) was found to be higher in females; and, in addition a protein

fraction has recently been described as missing in male mouse serum (Cal A strain) analyzed by starch gel electrophoresis (6).[22]

If a number of sentences are expressed in parallel construction, they are more effective when placed in some logical or emphatic order. A pattern of gradually lengthening parallel sentences is pleasing, parallel sentences in order of climax are interesting, and parallel sentences in logical or chronological plans are easy to understand. But a writer should not be tempted to contort ideas or structure to make sentences parallel, and he should not place unequal ideas in balanced construction.

Example of Effective Coherence

Rachel Carson links closely the sentences in the following paragraph and uses a pleasing variety of transitional methods:

> From the green depths of the offshore Atlantic many paths lead back to the coast. They[a] are paths[b] followed by fish; although unseen and intangible, they are linked with the outflow of waters from the coastal rivers. For thousands upon thousands of years[c] the salmon[d] have known and followed these threads of fresh water that lead them back to the rivers, each returning to the tributary in which it spent the first months or years of life. So,[e] in the summer and fall of 1953,[f] the salmon[g] of the river called Miramichi on the coast of New Brunswick moved in from their feeding grounds in the far Atlantic and ascended their native river. In[h] the upper[i] reaches of the Miramichi, in the streams that gather together a network of shadowed brooks, the salmon[j] deposited their eggs that autumn[k] in beds of gravel over which the stream water flowed swift and cold. Such places,[l] the watersheds of the great coniferous forests of spruce and balsam, of hemlock and pine, provide the kind of spawning grounds that salmon must have in order to survive.[23]

(a) The pronoun *they* in the second sentence refers to *paths* in the first sentence. (b) The word *paths* occurs in the first and second sentences. (c) The time phrase *for thousands upon thousands of years* and the present perfect tense *have known* take the reader over a long span of time from the distant past to the present. (d) The specific word *salmon* echoes the general word *fish* of the preceding sentence. (e) The conjunction *so* prepares the reader for a similar act. (f) The time phrase *in the summer and fall of 1953* moves the reader from the span of time of sentence 3 to specific seasons in a specific year. (g) The word

[22] E. Espinosa, E. Canelo, M. Bravo, and O. González, *Science*, CXLIV (April 24, 1964), 417.
[23] *Silent Spring* (Houghton Mifflin, Boston, 1962), p. 129.

salmon echoes *salmon* in the preceding sentence and *fish* in the second sentence.

Sentences 3 and 4 are subtly parallel. In 3 "the salmon have known and followed these threads of fresh water that lead them back to the rivers, each returning to the tributary in which it spent the first months or years of life." In 4 "the salmon . . . moved in from their feeding grounds in the far Atlantic and ascended their native river." Such parallelism, with each sentence slightly different from the other, is modern. The older writers used more exact parallelism.

(h) The phrase *in the upper reaches of the Miramichi* places the reader. (i) The word *upper* subtly echoes the thought of *ascended* in the preceding sentence. (j) *Salmon* again; it connects with *salmon* in sentences 3 and 4 and *fish* in sentence 2; thus a main word runs through the paragraph. There is no elegant variation here (page 106). (k) The demonstrative *that* and the word *autumn* (echoing *fall* in the preceding sentence) connect the two sentences. But these connectives would come too late in sentence 5 if they were the only connectives between it and sentence 4. (1) *Such places*, the opening words of sentence 6, connect clearly with the closing words of sentence 5, *in beds of gravel over which the stream water flowed swift and cold*. Connecting the end of one sentence with the beginning of the next is a popular technique to achieve coherence.

Tracing the transitions in an editorial, a book, or a well-written article will help a writer who wishes to improve the coherence of his writing. The techniques that he observes in the writing of others will prove useful when he meets problems in revising his own writing to make it coherent. Good writing, like Rachel Carson's, illustrates for him the kinds of transitions and the number of transitions that are to be expected in modern paragraphs. More important to an advanced writer is the fact that good writing demonstrates the close and subtle linking of the sentences of a paragraph and the varied and interesting ways that words and phrases emphasize and strengthen that linking.

The same transitional methods that are used to link sentences within a paragraph are used to connect paragraphs. The best place for connections between paragraphs is early in the first sentence of a new paragraph. Transitions between paragraphs are usually stronger and more numerous than those between sentences because a new paragraph begins a new idea, and the break between ideas is greater than the break between the related sentences of a paragraph. Sometimes paragraphs are part of a larger pattern within an article or chapter, and transitions are easy. One paragraph may be the explanation of a general statement, and the next two paragraphs may be two examples. The connections in such a case are as easy to accomplish as they are in a single paragraph. But occasionally there is a marked break that must be bridged, as for instance in moving from that one paragraph of generalization and the two examples to another idea that is not closely related. And in a few cases part of the thought development of a paper may be a stressing of the break in thought. Then writers often use a sentence of transition or even a short paragraph.

Rachel Carson followed the paragraph just discussed with a brief one that repeats the idea of the preceding paragraph and adds in a sharply contrasting short sentence an important contrast in idea:

> These events repeated a pattern that was age-old, a pattern that had made the Miramichi one of the finest salmon streams in North America. But that year the pattern was to be broken.

How smoothly this paragraph is connected by *these events* to the whole preceding paragraph. How well the *but* and the short sentence of fore-shadowing prepare the reader for a complete change in action. These methods of developing a paragraph and of providing transitions are neither complex nor difficult; therefore the skillful ways in which an artist adapts them to his subject and his purpose are all the more fascinating and, I dare hope, inspiring.

EMPHASIS IN PARAGRAPHS

Excellence of communication depends on conveying clearly to readers not merely ideas and connections between ideas but also the desired emphasis. Correct paragraphing tells readers the divisions of one's subject, and this information helps convey emphasis.

Within a paragraph, emphasis may be secured by attention to paragraph plan, the position of sentences, proportion, repetition, and contrast. Judicious employment of techniques enables a writer to convey subtle emphasis as accurately and precisely as he conveys thoughts by his careful choice of words. Ignorance of techniques may cause a writer to bury ideas that he has worked hard to express clearly and effectively and to emphasize insignificant thoughts so heavily that readers remember nothing else. It may even lead him to persuade readers to the very action that he wants them to avoid. Yet many writers are ignorant of the functioning of the principles of emphasis in paragraphs because their teachers regarded emphasis as advanced work. True, it is advanced work, but it is essential if a writer is to make his points properly. A writer who wishes readers to understand his ideas exactly or to be persuaded or both cannot safely ignore the devices of emphasis.

Contrast in sentences, in their length, grammatical type, and rhetorical type, may be used to make a sentence containing a main thought different, conspicuous, memorable (page 249). A sentence that attracts notice by being agreeably different from surrounding sentences is the best place for a principal thought. Rachel Carson's "But that year the pattern was to be broken" illustrates the use of a short sentence after a number of long ones, a periodic sentence in a passage that has mostly loose sentences, a simple sentence after a number of complex sentences, and the passive voice after many main clauses in the active voice. All these contrasts stress sharply "But that year the pattern was to be broken," which is the major thought not merely of the paragraph but of the chapter. Thus the device of contrast enforces presentation of thought.

Proportion is the principle that bulk is impressive. If a major portion of a paragraph deals with an idea, that idea is stressed. This presents a problem to a writer who must develop at length relatively unimportant material before his readers can grasp a main point. The thoughts in the lengthy development will be stressed at the expense of his main idea unless he prevents this by skillfully using other devices to stress his main point and thus to rectify any incorrect emphasis on the thoughts that bulk so large in his paragraph. But usually the principle of proportion works harmoniously with the development of a paragraph topic. There is a natural tendency to write more about important ideas and to write fleetingly of subordinate thoughts, and in most instances material flows smoothly into this arrangement, fitting it as neatly as a round peg fits a round hole. Thus it is usually not difficult for a writer to be sure that the length of his treatment of ideas is proportionate to their value.

The emphasis that space gives to an idea is a warning against disunity in a paragraph. Any unrelated idea not only spoils the logic of a paragraph but subtracts emphasis from the main subject. An unrelated idea also poses problems of coherence because of the difficulty of connecting it with the other sentences of a paragraph. For these three good reasons digressions in paragraphs should be avoided.

Repetition is a device that requires special skill if it is used to develop a whole paragraph (page 273), but some writers of average ability can repeat main thoughts effectively twice or three times in a paragraph. More advanced writers also find repetition for emphasis a good device on occasion. But used too frequently, it is likely to bore a reader and to make him feel that the reiteration of main points he has already thoroughly grasped insults his intelligence.

Difficult points sometimes benefit from reiteration if the demands of emphasis are met. Each restatement must add something—more vivid language, another facet of the thought, a different point of view. An idea may be expressed positively and then negatively, in a question and then in the answer, in general and then with the addition of detail, impersonally and then personally. The possible variations are countless. So are the writers who do not know this and think that they achieve emphasis by repeating the same thought in the same words. Even a writer's best sentences are not good enough for repetition, but variations may be interesting and effective.

Positioning sentences is an easy way to achieve emphasis. The important positions in a paragraph are the beginning and the ending, and of these two the ending is the more important. Yet many writers carelessly ignore this principle and place a minor thought in the first sentence—even an irrelevant point—and a minor thought in the final sentence—perhaps an afterthought not properly related to the main idea. The stress provided by these positions in paragraphs is too important to throw away.

Clever revisers improve their first drafts spectacularly by moving important thoughts to the first and final positions. Sometimes by this change alone, a cloudy paragraph focuses sharply. This is a technique for a writer in a hurry whose work is clear and fairly correct. How can he gain maximum results from a few minutes of revision? By moving major ideas to positions of prime importance—paragraph beginnings and endings.

INTRODUCTORY AND CONCLUDING PARAGRAPHS

Just as the first and final sentences of a paragraph are the most important, so the first and final paragraphs in a work are the most important. Many writers sense this, worry about these paragraphs unduly, and work over them so fruitlessly that they create fancy paragraphs completely out of keeping with the rest of their work. Whatever else they may be, the first and final paragraphs must be appropriate parts of the whole—on the same subject, in harmonious style and tone. They must enforce the main idea.

Some of the many effective ways to begin a work are discussed in Chapter IV. In general, an opening paragraph should be interesting and informative. If it is easy to read, it encourages readers to continue because they find it satisfying to grasp an idea quickly and easily at the start of a work, especially an idea that opens the subject of the paper for them. Whether a writer starts with prefatory comments on the scope of his work, a definition of his theme, a review of existing knowledge, a survey of his plan of development, an anecdote, an example, a point of view, or a summary of the central idea depends on his subject and his reader. But all readers like a beginning that makes the subject seem interesting and the style clear.

Ironically, the beginning least likely to do that is the one that states baldly that the work is interesting or significant or important (Chapter IV). Readers are not gullible enough to take a writer's word for that at the start; in fact, many of them cynically doubt it. A writer who wants to convince readers that a work is interesting, significant, or important should begin with a paragraph that exemplifies those qualities.

An introduction, like a first meeting, is a promise of what is to come. It sets the tone and style. Its very nature—clear, succinct, thorough, lively—promises what the rest will be like. And a writer should not disappoint his readers. He should not promise a wider coverage, a more scholarly study, a more interesting presentation than he will provide. An introduction is not just a lure to entice a reader; it is also an augury, and it should not be a false one.

A conclusion, too, should be truthful. There are few experiences more annoying, for example, than a speaker who keeps saying that he is ending long before he does end. By the time that he finally reaches his conclusion, his audience has given up; it stopped listening the fourth time he said, "In conclusion."

A good ending is a smooth stop; a reader should know that he has arrived at the conclusion and should not feel inclined to turn the page to find the ending. Nor should a writer present one ending after another, like a guest who stands at the door saying goodby but not leaving. The last paragraph, then, should be strong and final; it should round off the theme effectively.

The content of good endings varies—a restatement of the central idea, an analysis of the significance of the subject, a striking final example, a recommendation, a massing of recommendations or reasons or results, some interesting interpretations or reflections, a forecast flowing naturally from the rest of the paper, an epitome of the important ideas. A last paragraph is not the place to limit the subject—that should have been done near the beginning—or to hedge the conclusions—the conclusions should have been limited when stated—or to offer concessions—these too belong earlier in the paper. And a conclusion is the worst place for an apology. A writer should avoid apologizing for his work. If it is poor, he should rewrite it or scrap it. But if he cannot avoid apologizing for hasty work, he should apologize early in the paper. And if he can, he should apologize so indirectly that readers do not recognize his apology as such but think that he is explaining how the paper was written or what its limitations are.

A conclusion is the place for a good presentation, not a poor one.

It is a reader's last impression of a work, and it should be strong, forceful, convincing, and final. A reader should feel that everything necessary and expected has been covered and that he is ready to have the work draw to its end. The writer may end briskly and forcefully; or he may conclude with wit, a neat restatement of an opening phrase, a clinching repetition of an important idea; or in a stately way he may bring the paper slowly to its final, well-rounded sentence.

In this chapter on paragraphing I have included the basic techniques of good paragraphing. A writer who wishes to improve his paragraphing should examine a sample of at least ten typewritten pages of his writing and ask himself the following questions about his techniques:

1. Have I adapted paragraph length to the format and to my readers?
2. Do my paragraphs vary in length?
3. Have I placed important ideas in the paragraphs that are most different in length?
4. Does each paragraph develop one complete subdivision?
5. Does everything in each paragraph relate to the topic sentence of that paragraph?
6. Have I used a variety of well-chosen methods to develop paragraphs?
7. Are there any other methods I might use?
8. Is each sentence connected with the one before and the one after?
9. Have I supplied strong connections between paragraphs?
10. Have I used a variety of transitional methods or relied on too few?
11. Can I improve my transitions by better choice, better placement, more subtlety?
12. Have I stressed important ideas by contrast? by proportion? by repetition? by position?
13. Do my introductory and concluding paragraphs contain important ideas?
14. Does the introductory paragraph present my topic to readers?
15. Does the concluding paragraph round off my paper?

If a writer will list the errors and weaknesses in his paragraphing and work on them when he revises, he will develop a better paragraph style. Even a writer who has time to apply only one technique will notice an improvement after a few trials, and a writer who perseveres in improving paragraphs will end with a style that efficiently guides his reader to all the facets of his paper and the significance of each.

Chapter XV

Writing Memorandums, Letters, Instructions, and Other Short Forms

"The horror of that moment," the King went on, "I shall never, never, *never* forget!"

"You will, though," the Queen said, "if you don't make a memorandum of it."

Lewis Carroll

MEMORANDUMS

Memorandums convey information and opinions within an organization. Even when sections of a company or government agency are in different parts of the country, memorandums are useful. Letters are generally used for communicating in a more personal way with individuals or for communicating with persons in other organizations and countries. To those who, like field representatives, work independently at a distance from company centers, letters seem more personal than memorandums and therefore link such workers to their companies. Memorandums are suited to the communication of information, suggestions, recommendations, etc., because they do not contain the friendly material of letters and are therefore briefer and because they may be formal or informal.

STANDARD FORMS

Standard forms for memorandums save time and effort; a reader or file clerk finds certain information—name of sender, names of those addressed, subject of the memorandum, etc.—in the same place in each memorandum regardless of its source. The statement of the subject of a memorandum should be meaningful and specific: not, for example,

Change in Bookkeeping Form but *Change in Items 1 to 5 of Bookkeeping Form 104.*

Some writers waste time because they do not develop memorandum forms with blanks for routine information but expend effort writing sentences and even trying to vary the structure and the diction in routine daily reports. To prevent such unnecessary writing, attendance reports and other routine matters, as well as some progress notes like those on construction, should be entered on forms. A supervisor can increase the efficiency of his staff by ensuring through regular checks that material suitable for memorandum forms containing spaces for stated information has not become the subject of memorandums or letters that consume too much of a writer's time.

SELECTION OF READERS

In addressing his memorandums a writer should select his readers carefully. The cost of reading memorandums is great in industry and government, and a writer who carelessly directs a memorandum to readers who do not need it is wasting expensive time. Often the expense is not justified by the value of the memorandum even to the people it should reach. Some lightening of the excessive burden of reading in government and industry today is in the hands of everyone who selects readers for memorandums. Unless readers are fools, they have a poor impression of a writer who wastes their time with pages they should never have received and he should never have written.

LENGTH

The length of memorandums is a controversial subject. Everyone agrees that memorandums should be as short as possible, but not everyone agrees that they should be as long as necessary. Some supervisors and some companies insist that memorandums should never be longer than a page. If such a ruling means that many are incomplete and others are divided into two or more, it accomplishes little good.

A writer should shorten his memorandums by removing superfluous material and superfluous words when he revises (Chapter VIII). And he should organize his memorandums carefully to avoid repetition. But how far beyond that he should go in struggling to shorten his work depends on common sense. If he is addressing one person whose time is more valuable than his own or if he is addressing many people, a writer should revise scrupulously for brevity. But supervisors should not expect writers to produce brief memorandums as fast as they produce long ones. It takes time to be brief.

If a shortened memorandum is not clear, the achievement of brevity has little point. If the brevity makes it difficult to read, the writer has confused saving paper with saving his readers' time. If a memorandum is so incomplete that readers must ask questions to get the information it should have supplied, the omission of information has wasted time. A memorandum should be as brief as is consistent with completeness, clarity, and readability.

STYLE

The principles of clarity that apply to memorandums are the same as those for other writing. Good diction (Chapter XII), sentence structure (Chapter XIII), paragraphing (Chapter XIV), and organization (Chapter V) are the same as for other papers. And meaningful subheads are as useful in memorandums as in reports; they guide the reader, and they aid coherence. The language and subject matter of memorandums should be adapted to the readers, and there should be no ambiguity, due to either sentence structure or diction. The information and the writing should be as specific and concrete as the subject permits. A writer's choice of organization is particularly important in a memorandum; yet many writers fail to consider all possible organizations before selecting one. The first sentence of a memorandum is also important, and writers should be certain that they have chosen an effective way to begin (Chapter IV). Useful as summary beginnings are, they have been employed so often in some companies that they are trite beginnings there. And if a writer does not wish to reveal his main points before he has prepared his reader, other kinds of openings have more appeal.

The style of a memorandum may be formal or informal, depending on the subject and the reader. A memorandum of technical information may be as formal as a technical report. A memorandum of changes in procedure may be formal if it is addressed to a pompous executive and informal if it is addressed to a breezy field representative. Any tendency to make all memorandums routinely formal and cold should be fought. A memorandum to a friendly person with whom one works closely may be as warm and informal, though perhaps not so wordy, as a telephone conversation. Although memorandums do not usually contain the social digressions of a friendly business letter, they may in their own way be friendly too. A supervisor who writes informal friendly memorandums to his staff will get a better response and establish better relationships than one whose writing is stilted and cold. Busy supervisors should not overlook this opportunity to make employees feel like more than robots. Management courses train supervisors so successfully to display warmth and friendliness that they never pass an employee without greeting him. But much of the value of this is lost if they send to these employees memorandums that sound as though they were written by a machine to some cogs.

CARELESSNESS AND INADEQUACY

Carelessness is a common fault in hurried memorandums. Some writers read an inquiry incorrectly and supply the wrong information or only part of the information. Others write memorandums less correctly than reports, and their errors annoy and distract readers. And some few who write hurriedly and neglect revision do not say what they mean. Part of this carelessness is due to a failure to consider memorandums important. A man who writes and receives superfluous memorandums is hardly likely to attach much significance to anything written in that form. Before his memorandums become better, they must become fewer.

Incompleteness, ambiguity, and even complete lack of meaning characterize many memorandums sent to immediate supervisors familiar with a subject.

"Only my boss reads this, and he knows all about it anyway," is the explanation for such writing.

"Then why do you send a memo?"

"Well, for the files, I suppose, or in case someone sends for information when I'm not here."

Pity the reader of those filed confusions! A substitute for the supervisor or the writer, a replacement for one of them, an executive seeking information while they are away, an expert reorganizing systems, an examiner of files trying to decide what to discard—any one of these finds only meaningless or confusing words. Thus the fallacious conviction that "only my boss reads this" is expensive to industry and government. Occasionally justice prevails. Such an incomprehensible memorandum is requested unexpectedly by an executive whom the writer wishes to impress favorably, and then the writer suffers more than his reader. He suffers too if months after filing the memorandum he needs the information in it and cannot understand his own expression.

If a writer does not have sufficient pride to write understandable prose, his supervisor should be responsible for seeing that every paper filed can be understood by a competent reader. And that does not mean the supervisor or the writer, who from their experience can supply missing material and translate meaningless sentences, but a reader who might have to consult the paper in an emergency. Otherwise writing, filing, and storing such papers is wasteful. It would be less expensive and less confusing for the supervisor to state, "I don't believe in files. We don't keep them. If you want to know what we're doing, ask. If we're not here, guess."

LETTERS

Why do men who write good letters of application and good social letters write such poor business letters? is the question about letters that I am asked most often. The answer is that there are three causes of poor business letters.

The instruction in writing given to undergraduates today stresses informal writing like that in freshman themes and formal writing like that in technical reports. Training in letter writing is usually offered only to business majors. When it is given to students specializing in science and the liberal arts and engineering, it concentrates on how to write a letter applying for a job, that being the letter of most immediate concern to students. Some courses do touch briefly on the nuts-and-bolts letters of business—the letter written to order merchandise and the letter correcting an error in an order. But students who are not business majors are seldom trained in the writing of business letters that are more difficult. The handbooks addressed to scientists and engineers except for a few like A. C. Howell's *Handbook of English in Engineering Usage* [1] concentrate on the format of letters and offer little help with writing business letters. And it is clear that many graduate students acquire while writing their theses a style that is particularly unsuitable for letters and not much good for anything else. When a graduate who has had instruction only in essays, theses, and technical reports must write a business letter, he approaches the task without experience and without instruction.

What do government and industry do about this? They usually assign to him the least experienced, least competent secretary or typist available. Together these neophytes write letters for their agency or their company, and they may even write them without any supervision. At the same time the government and industries of the United States spend billions on what their public relations men term "improving the image," the image created at least in part by poor letters.

Some supervisors make it unnecessarily difficult for beginners to write letters; they ask new employees to write letters for supervisors to

[1] 2 ed. (John Wiley and Sons, New York, 1940), pp. 244–282.

sign. Making ghost writers of young scientists and engineers is one way to prevent good performance. To compose a letter in the style of another person requires special skills usually acquired only through long practice. Some few experienced writers can assume now the personality of the president of a company, now of the vice president, and now of the general manager well enough to write speeches, articles, and letters for them all. And some secretaries learn to write letters in the styles of their employers. But to expect young graduates with little training in writing to become ghost writers for supervisors is wasteful of the time of the company, demeaning to any professional worker, and annoying to both writer and supervisor. Under this arrangement each writer of business letters spends time trying to learn not good style but the style of his supervisor; thus a beginner does not develop a letter style suited to him unless he happens to be exactly like his supervisor.

A worker at professional level should sign his own letters. A supervisor's initials or signature of approval may, and for many letters should, be required. But a writer of business letters should be permitted to use and should be encouraged to develop a style of his own that reflects his personality. Such a style will do more credit to his division of the government or of a company than any imitation of the style of another.

A professional man who wishes to learn to write good business letters will learn faster from instruction combined with his own observation than from imitation. The principles of good business correspondence are essentially those of other good writing. The few exceptions to the general rules follow, as does a discussion of some business letters that pose special problems—letters that are contracts; letters that give technical information; and letters of adjustment, apology, gratitude, congratulations, recommendation, and condolence.

THE STYLE OF BUSINESS LETTERS

Style in General

A writer of good letters gives even more consideration to his reader than does a writer of reports and memorandums. They both adapt subject matter and language to their readers' understanding, but a letter writer often drastically modifies his style for his readers. To a stiff and dignified official he writes a formal letter; to a friendly salesman, an informal, even breezy, letter; to a colleague with a good sense of humor, an amusing letter. But all reflect his moods of formality or informality or humor because the styles of all are his, not copies of his correspondents' or his supervisor's or of the styles of letters in books of model letters.

The paragraphs and sentences of good business letters are usually shorter and simpler than those suggested for other writing (Chapters XIII and XIV). Subjects are broken into small units for a letter, and language tends to be informal. Although a letter of information uses the language of a technical report, other business letters may use contractions and informal language if appropriate to the readers.

Letter writers should avoid business clichés, most of which are wordy and pointless (Chapters VIII and XII). And they should not use old-fashioned participial closings or other phrases that are out of date. One undesirable result of the imitation of the letters of others is the copying of antiquated language by generation after generation of letter writers. In some companies the wording of letters has not changed in fifty years.

Courtesy and Friendliness

Courtesy is more important in a business letter than is brevity; therefore letters should never be so brief as to seem curt. A sentence or two of friendly chat are appropriate in correspondence with someone who appreciates a friendly business letter. Social subjects are appropriate in a letter to an acquaintance of long standing or to a friend. A writer should no more restrict himself to business in a business letter than he would on the telephone or in his office. The friendly material may be briefer in a letter, but if he would chat on the telephone to the reader of the letter, he may chat in a letter. If for some subjects, like correcting an error in a routine bill, he would not digress from the subject on the telephone, he does not digress in a letter. But his routine letter must still be courteous.

As a professional man becomes more successful in his career, he writes fewer of these routine letters, and nearly all his letters have personal touches that only he can give them. His letters would seem unfriendly if there were no inquiry about the health of a child who was sick when last the writer saw his correspondent, no recalling of the entertainment offered by his correspondent at their last meeting, no remark about the sport they have been discussing for years. These informal comments are not unimportant or inessential; they are the builders of friendship and good will, which are important to the writer and his employer. Administrators, physicians, and lawyers seem to me to understand the value of encouraging this good will better than most scientists and engineers do. The scientists and engineers who do understand it and have acquired the knack for it are able to establish relationships that contribute to their success. Their associates like them, remember them, enjoy working with them, and want to help them.

Yet many men who are friendly in person are cold and forbidding in their letters. Their business letters read like routine orders for merchandise. Ordering a book, requesting information from an acquaintance, or answering the inquiry of a friend, such men write the same kind of letter. It never occurs to them that an acquaintance may feel rebuffed or that a friend may regret having asked a favor. And they cannot understand why others are chilly or brusque in return.

Such unhappy divergence between the personality of a man and his personality in his writing need not exist. Usually if the personality of his letters is too informal, a writer has little difficulty in making it more formal. But if the tone of his letters is too austere and formal, a writer may have some difficulty changing it. This is due to his failure to see just what needs to be changed. Usually the personality of such letters has been formalized by the absence of pronouns in the first and second persons and by the presence of too many passive verbs (Chapter VII), as well as by the use of old-fashioned business phraseology (Chapter XII). As soon as a writer learns to use *I*, his verbs tend to become active instead of passive. A writer who is stiff and inflexible may fight to retain his business clichés. But replacing trite business phrases with simple conversational English usually completes the metamorphosis from stuffy to informal, from pompous to friendly.

These changes do not occur overnight, nor are they easy for all writers. I have even had to order dictating machines in the shape of telephones to encourage some obstinately stately writers to dictate as though they were friendly with their readers. After a day of such dictating and of reading the results critically, even the most intractably pompous writers loosen up on paper. Only one letter writer complained. He said, "I used to dictate business letters while I was thinking of something else. Now I have to think about the letters." The other transformed writers considered the change well worth the trouble and effort it had required. One spoke the feelings of all of them when he said, "Now I can write like a human being. I used to write like a stuffed shirt; I used to pour out the same old tired phrases like a machine."

The Pronouns I, We, You

A word of caution here about the use of pronouns in the first person is necessary. Most writers worry more than necessary about using *I* too often. They need not strain to avoid beginning letters with *I* if it is appropriate to start that way. And if *I* appears in different positions in the sentences of a letter, it is seldom obtrusive or even noticeable. The people who worry about the number of *I*'s in their writing are seldom those who use too many. A writer who is anxious about his use of *I* should resist the easy but dangerous escape to *we*. For when he uses *I*, he commits only himself; he may commit himself as the shipping manager of his company, but he does not always commit the entire company. A writer who uses *we* commits his company or agency. Another difficulty with *we* is its slipperiness in a writer's mind and the resulting confusion to readers. In one letter of such a writer *we* is the writer alone, his company, his division, he and his wife, and he and those working with him on an experiment. But in one letter *we* is not capable of serving clearly so many meanings (page 198). The confusion that results from *we* signifying first one group and then another is major.

You is not a misleading pronoun in itself, but some misleading advice has been given about *you*, and some good advice has been misunderstood. To dot a letter with frequent *you*'s does not necessarily make it personal or attractive. Too many expressions like "you will agree," "of course, you see," and "you will no doubt find" draw from some readers the well-deserved response, "The hell I will." Most readers do not like to be pushed so hard, and *you* in such expressions is an obvious shove. A writer who has successfully taken his reader's point of view (Chapter VII) can write an effective personal letter without a single *you*. And dozens of *you*'s do not help a letter written by someone who fails to see his reader's point of view; they may in fact make the failure more obtrusive and hence more annoying. "You are hereby notified that your employment in the G. G. Psychology Company will terminate on April fifth," wrote a beginner for his supervisor; and when he was told to soften the blow, he replied, "But I started with *you*." He would not write, "We regret that it is necessary to tell you" or "I regret to tell you" because he considered it self-centered to begin a letter with *I* or *we*. Courteous consideration of the reader is more important than pronouns, and no pronoun can conceal a writer's lack of interest in his reader.

SOME KINDS OF BUSINESS LETTERS

Contractual Letters

Any letter that commits a writer or his organization should be written and revised with care. Such a letter is a legal contract and therefore offers little opportunity for second thoughts after it has been signed and mailed. A writer should be sure that it includes exactly what he wants, that it is complete and accurate, and that it is unambiguous. Too many letters ordering merchandise and equipment lack a necessary specification, such as size, model number, method of shipment, etc.

It is wise to allow twenty-four hours between writing and signing letters of contract, for in the clearer light of another day one may note that he has not said what he intended to say or that his letter is incomplete.

If such a letter must be mailed immediately, the writer should ask a competent fellow worker to check it for him. A hastily written contract should be read by at least two people if it is not read by a lawyer.

Letters of Technical Information

A letter of technical information should contain technical language if it is sent to a technically trained reader; otherwise it should contain such terminology only when it is impossible for a writer to avoid it. Like a technical report, this letter may have headings helpful to readers. If answers to scattered questions are placed under headings, they are more useful to readers; and a writer will find a letter containing unrelated topics easier to write if he uses headings instead of attempting to connect unrelated parts. Lengthy information should be presented in a brief report with a covering letter or in a memorandum. The covering letter introduces the report and may note the occasion for writing or sending it. The report is written like any other. Thus a writer may use one appropriate style in his letter and another in his report. But the writer of a long letter of information should not create a hodgepodge of two or more styles and tones. If there is much information, most readers find a report with a covering letter more useful than a report in letter form.

For internal correspondence some companies use a bastard form that handicaps a writer: they want short reports in letter form. Writers, correctly sensing that letters should be more than pages of information, struggle unsuccessfully to attach opening and closing paragraphs to these "letters." These paragraphs are usually awkward or hackneyed, the opening paragraph acknowledging the request for information and the closing paragraph suggesting that the reader telephone or write if he needs further information, which he will do anyway. Yet without these opening and closing paragraphs, the long section of information constitutes a cold letter.

It would be far better to send the information in a memorandum and thus to avoid these unnecessary difficulties. A memorandum neatly, appropriately, and conveniently conveys information from one person to another in the same company. By supplying in the proper spaces the date of the inquiry, the subject of the inquiry, and other information essential for filing, a writer escapes the awkward task of expressing these details in an opening paragraph. His reader has them in convenient form when he needs them; he does not have to skim through the opening sentences of a letter to locate them. And the memorandum is more convenient for filing than a letter. Moreover, it has unity; there is no occasion for a writer to compose personal sentences to precede and follow the information, for the memorandum does not sound brusque without them. In fact, everyone is happier except, perhaps, the originator of the bastard form.

When letters of information are written by one person and signed by another, they frustrate both. One may not like the opening and closing sentences of the other, and the time the two spend arguing, haggling, writing, and rewriting is a stupid waste of highly trained manpower. I have known a supervisor to argue for nearly two weeks with an assistant, waste the time and patience of others by asking for their opinions, and end by disliking his assistant, who by this time hates him and the letters. When good workable forms like the memorandum of information are available, an administration that requires troublesome letters is seeking and finding difficulties. A company that has many strange requirements of this sort about writing makes poor writers of adequate ones and encourages good writers to hate writing. Only poor writers remain unaffected. New employees suffer even more than others, for they must learn how to meet the strange requirements—if anyone can learn. One of them analyzed it thus: "Everyone at our division writes poorly and hates to write because our division demands poor writing."

Letters of Complaint

The secret of success in letters of complaint is to avoid complaining. Adjustments should be requested politely (and firmly if necessary), claims should be stated clearly and concisely, and arguments should be presented in a way that will move a reader to action. Whining, insults, and pugnacity may occasionally achieve results in conversation or argument, but they are obvious blunders on paper. Without the person's voice, facial expressions, and bodily gestures, they are puerile; and they create a poor impression for the writer and the company or agency he represents. Moreover, angry writers are inclined to present more details than are necessary for a routine adjustment and to cite irrelevant inconveniences but to omit information essential to a claim. An adjuster cannot do what a writer wishes if he cannot understand the letter or does not have the facts he needs.

There would be less vehemence and more clarity in letters of complaint if writers realized what happens to their letters of indignation. The best thing that may happen is that the clerk who receives such a letter will read it; think, "This nut's mad at us"; and make the adjustment in the routine way. But a clerk, impressed by the length and tone of a letter, may send it to the desk of a busy executive, where it will rest until he finds time to answer it and to return it to the clerk who makes adjustments. Sometimes a clerk becomes confused by a long and complicated complaint, misunderstands what is wanted, and gives the writer another occasion for anger. Moreover, letters remain in modern filing systems a long time and may embarrass writers in the future.

Unless a writer thinks that detailing his inconvenience will speed an adjustment, he should omit the details. Of course, if inconvenience is part of a claim, the inconvenience must be described—but preferably in an effective, businesslike way, not heatedly. Clarity, courtesy, and good humor produce desired results in professional correspondence; anger and tears are inappropriate and ineffective.

Letters of Adjustment and Apology

Writing letters of adjustment and apology worries some writers. They can avoid the most common errors of these letters by remembering that adjustments, like contracts, must be unmistakable and that only one apology is necessary for one mistake. The apology should be so complete and sincere the first time that it need not be repeated. When apologizing for a company, a writer should not be excessively humble or condescending. When apologizing for himself, he should apologize in a tone appropriate to the situation and his personality.

A writer of a letter of apology should refrain from promising more than he or his employer can perform; for instance, he may express his hope that an error will not occur again, he may mention the steps taken to prevent its happening again, but he should not promise that it will not happen again. If the promise is broken, his correspondent may consider the writer or the company insincere, or perhaps indifferent. Even though a promise is kept, a correspondent may be dissatisfied, for the excessive apologizing may have led him to think the error or injury more serious than it was.

Usually of greater interest to a reader than an apology is an adjustment. An adjustment favorable to the reader should be placed first in a letter. Pleasing information at the beginning of a letter puts a reader in a good mood. Pleasing information delayed may lead a reader to think that the letter is refusing his request, and his annoyance may not be allayed by the adjustment announced at the end. Letters begin most effectively with something that a reader will be glad to know.

Letters of Gratitude

Like letters of apology, letters of gratitude should not be repetitive. Thanks should be expressed fully and sincerely, and then a writer should end his letter or turn to another subject. There are many ways to develop the expression of thanks. In a letter of personal gratitude a writer may hope that he will be able to return the favor; he may recall with pleasure facets of the hospitality shown to him; he may mention the good results of the help that he received; he may praise the promptness, the graciousness, the generosity of the giver; he may extend an invitation. To be meaningful, such an invitation must be specific as to time and place: "Mary and I hope that you will be our guest at dinner on Thursday, May first, the second night of the ACS meeting in Chicago"; "I will call you when you are in San Francisco next month to arrange lunch or dinner with Bud and George and me"; "I want you to meet the other physicists who benefited from your help. Will you have dinner with us on Monday or Thursday of the week you are in Oak Ridge?" Letters expressing gratitude for a favor to a company are usually shorter and less personal, especially if two companies exchange favors occasionally.

But they should be written. The best advice about thank-you letters is *Don't wonder whether to write them; write them.* No one ever lost a friend for himself or his employer or was refused another favor because he wrote a gracious letter of gratitude. Thank-you notes are easy to postpone and easy to forget. But busy successful men write them promptly. The letters reflect their courteous consideration of others. Such men never underestimate the value of the courtesies which are the foundation of good professional relations, and beginners can profit from their example.

A young corresponding secretary of a chapter of an engineering society may find himself pleasantly remembered by one of the most important engineers in the society because of a prompt and gracious letter of thanks for a speech to the chapter, or he may establish for himself the reputation of a boor by neglecting to write such a letter. A geologist who was surprised to be hired for a position for which some better qualified geologists had applied was even more surprised to learn that his note of thanks for the interview and entertainment had weighed in his favor. A professional man who always writes letters of thanks promptly will have many occasions to be thankful that he does.

Letters to Natives of Other Countries

A writer should be particularly careful to extend courtesies to Asiatics, Europeans, and Latin Americans. They are punctilious about social niceties, and some of them are easily offended by what seems to them the negligence of writers in the United States. The brisk style of a letter that would be considered polite enough in the United States may seem curt in another country. A writer must judge from his correspondence with another country how formal, circumlocutious, and even repetitive his courtesy letters should be. A writer should not jump to the familiarity of first names or an informal style, especially when writing to an older person. It is wiser to wait for him to set such a tone. And a writer should be careful to avoid commands even when he is writing directions. In many countries commands offend a professional man. A command must be disguised as an exceedingly polite request. Brevity is not so important elsewhere as in the United States, and what a writer considers formality befitting only a few occasions may be the rule in other countries. A correspondent must be guided by the letters he receives from other countries and should depart from the principles of good writing in the United States when such a departure seems necessary in order to write politely and effectively to his correspondents.

Letters of Congratulation

A letter of congratulation is another that should not be neglected. This pleasant courtesy is easy to offer colleagues at home or abroad, and the happiness of the recipient far outweighs the small trouble of writing it. Some professional men are meticulous about sending congratulatory notes to those who have competed with them for appointments or promotions and been victorious, but congratulations serve better purposes than demonstrating good sportsmanship. They are particularly pleasing to subordinates, and a good administrator is never too busy to offer them. Distant colleagues are pleased and flattered when their successes, especially their small successes, are noticed with rejoicing. And colleagues close to a writer welcome a letter of congratulation, for it is an indication of personal interest in a world where many people feel that they are only punch cards to their associates.

Letters of congratulation may be sent to those about to retire, to those promoted, to those who receive degrees, to those whose articles or books are published, to anyone, in short, who achieves a success. When a personal relationship exists, congratulations may be offered on honors earned by a child or grandchild, on the birth of a child, on the marriage of a man. (A bride is not congratulated; she is offered warm good wishes.) Greeting cards do not take the place of letters, for letters show that the writer had enough interest to take the trouble to write. On occasions of rejoicing, gracious letters that share the joy increase the joy.

It is not always tactful to be cheery in a letter congratulating a colleague on his retirement. Not everyone is happy about retiring, and a writer should express sentiments appropriate to the feelings of his correspondent. A letter of congratulation on retirement may wish the colleague good health and may hope that he will find satisfaction and pleasure in activities he is known to be contemplating—travel, hobbies, sports, professional activities, or moving to a new home. A specific statement of ways in which the writer or others will miss the person retiring is not amiss, nor are good wishes to the wife or husband of the person who is retiring.

An indication of definite plans to keep in touch by letter or by meetings is welcome. It is not always wise to extend a blanket invitation to a retiring employee to return to visit his friends, for some lonely people haunt the companies where they worked and thus present a difficult problem to whoever invited them, as well as to those who must discourage the visits. However if retired employees are invited to an annual dinner, if the retired colleague is likely to attend meetings of professional societies, if he and the writer are likely to meet at a club, then the letter may express the hope of meeting there.

A writer who is happily anticipating his own retirement may mention that. Younger colleagues may appropriately express gratitude for any help or inspiration that they received. And jingles written for the occasion, company jokes, flattering remarks, another round of teasing about sports or hobbies—all have their place in this letter if they are appropriate to the person addressed. If a man has retired because of illness, it is tactful to omit comments on activities that he no longer may be able to pursue. A letter of congratulation should be designed to make a retiring colleague happy—happy in his prospects, happy in his good friends, happy in his achievements.

Letters of Recommendation

A professional man who never has to write a letter of recommendation is a rarity. But professional men who write useful letters of this type are not legion. A letter of recommendation should not be a panegyric that a reader suspects must be untrue. It should state fairly what the reader should know about the abilities of the person, about his character, and about any deficiencies. A letter mentioning a deficiency may be more helpful than one that omits it. For example, if a competent animal psychologist resents supervision and performs best when he has most independence, a company can try to assign him to an easygoing administrator if it is informed; but if this useful information is concealed, the company may assign him to a martinet with the result that he will soon be requesting another letter of recommendation. A person who has supervised an employee for two years or more should know his strong and weak points well enough to present them fairly and helpfully.

Like many other letters, a letter of recommendation may reveal as much about the writer as about his subject. A professor who does not know one graduate student from another shows his lack of interest when he writes a letter of recommendation for a student. A supervisor who over- or underestimates an employee, who can present no useful comments on an employee, or who does not know one employee from another reveals this in a letter of recommendation. And that letter, displaying his deficiencies as an administrator, may unintentionally disclose the reason that the employee is no longer working for him. The letter of a good supervisor assists an inquirer in understanding and evaluating an applicant, and in the end this is better for the applicant than fulsome praise. As for unloading inefficient and undesirable employees upon other companies by means of letters of false praise, this is a blatant advertisement of a company's or a supervisor's dishonesty. And it is remembered longer than other advertising.

Letters of Condolence

Expressing sympathy tactfully is difficult for so many writers, some of them experienced writers, that I shall treat letters of condolence in more detail than I have treated business letters for other occasions. As in other writing, problems here tend to solve themselves if the writer considers his reader. Letters of condolence are meant to comfort the bereaved persons to whom they are addressed; they are not meant to comfort the writer by affording him an opportunity to unload his feelings. A writer should focus his attention on the recipient and keep it there until the letter is mailed. He should express his sympathy sincerely and simply. To write beyond that, he must consider what will comfort the person whom he is addressing, and that is not necessarily what would comfort him in similar circumstances. Any one of the following subjects or none of them may be appropriate in particular cases, or they may suggest something suitable:

1. Gratitude that the deceased did not suffer long illness and pain
2. A comment that the long suffering and pain of the deceased are ended
3. The writer's appreciation of his association with the deceased and some particulars of the contribution of the deceased to that association
4. A statement that the deceased will be missed by the company or by a division of the company or by a particular group of associates within the company or by the writer
5. A complimentary but not effusive statement of the contribution of the deceased to a field of learning, to a company or division of a company, to a professional society, to his associates, to the writer
6. A complimentary but not effusive statement of the best qualities of the deceased
7. A hope that the family or the persons to whom the letter is addressed will find comfort in the companionship and love they gave the deceased, in the excellent nursing and tender comfort they offered

during an illness, in the children who are carrying on his work or his qualities so well

8. A recollection of the pride in his family or the love for his children expressed by the subject of the letter to his colleagues

9. The excellent reputation of the deceased, the respect accorded him, his many friends

10. A recollection of him in the situation in which the writer will remember him—helping a new employee, modestly receiving acclaim, concentrating all his intellectual powers on a problem, joking during coffee breaks, enjoying a game of golf, etc.

Whatever material he chooses for his letter, a writer should remember that a personal letter of condolence should not be long. More dignified and formal language may be used than for other business letters, but it should be simple. As this is the most personal of business letters, it should not be a copy of someone else's letter or of a model in a book. In this letter sincerity is more important than elegance. A condolence letter represents the writer himself as no other letter can and should never be written by someone else for him. If he is away and cannot be reached, his secretary may write to explain this. And his secretary may also write a condolence letter of his own if he knew the deceased. The family and friends will be more comforted by a separate letter than by a few sentences tagged on to a letter written for an employer in his absence.

A personal letter of condolence should be written by hand on stationery of good quality of a size that suits the handwriting. It should be written promptly, usually the day that one hears of the death. A letter written for a company or a letter written by a secretary for his absent employer may be typewritten on company stationery unless that stationery is not dignified or is otherwise inappropriate.

A letter that an executive writes to express the sympathy of a company or division may have to be formal; but if the executive knew the deceased, it should be personal. If the executive supervised the work of the deceased, his letter will be important to the family. The writer should realize that the family will cherish it and may show it to relatives and friends. Because it will enable them to take pride in the reputation and work of the deceased, in the high regard and affection of his colleagues, in the esteem and respect shown him, it will be a comfort. The writer of such a company letter may include his own sympathy for the bereaved. If his letter is longer than the usual letter of condolence, it does not matter. That an executive took the trouble to write so full a letter may be a comfort in itself.

Besides offering sympathy, a business letter of condolence may offer specific help. Writing for his company, an executive may state that a representative of the company is ready to confer with the widow or her lawyer. A letter about financial arrangements—pension or other benefits, company insurance, salary due, stock transfers, etc.—should be sent promptly if a bereaved family has any financial problems known to the writer. Union officials may also write letters about financial arrangements, and they should take care that these letters are not so coldly businesslike as to be offensive.

If it seems appropriate, a colleague who is also a friend may offer his assistance with specific tasks—funeral arrangements, notifying friends and business associates, helping to receive mourners, etc. If a colleague knows the family, he may find it more helpful to offer such assistance by telephone because he can discuss what needs to be done and how he can be most helpful. General offers of assistance are empty formalities. But specific offers are a comfort and a help: "I'm free all day Thursday to help you"; "Mary would like to do anything she can on Wednesday"; "We will gladly take care of the children until after the services"; "Don't put your dog in a kennel unless you particularly want to; we'll be glad to have him at our house"; "If your boy is interested in a summer job, please ask him to let me know. I am sure that I can find something for him"; "My son will gladly stay with your grandfather if he is not going to the services." A colleague must use his good judgment about the circumstances of the bereaved persons in deciding what help to offer when he writes or telephones.

With obvious modifications the suggestions given here apply also to letters of condolence written to a colleague, an employer, or an employee on the death of a member of his immediate family. A writer knows the recipient of this letter, and therefore he is on firm ground in selecting the type of comfort to offer.

A warning against some common mistakes may be helpful. A letter of condolence should never be maudlin or effusive. A writer should not assume that death is welcome because of long suffering, and he should never in any way imply that the bereaved persons must be relieved or happy. They probably are not, and in any case they do not want to read such comments. A writer may express his own relief that the deceased is no longer in pain, but he should not imply that the family of the deceased shares his sentiments.

A writer should consider carefully before expressing religious sentiments. If the bereaved and the writer share the faith of the deceased, the writer may offer appropriate religious comfort if it seems natural and fitting. But when faiths vary, any religious statements should be carefully examined for acceptability to the bereaved. Christian comfort about an afterlife should not be addressed to a Jewish family unless the writer knows that the family believes in an afterlife. Nor should a Jew express sympathy on a Christian's losing the deceased forever. And a writer should be sure that the bereaved are not atheists before offering to pray for them. The function of a letter of condolence, I repeat, is not to give the writer comfort but to make grief more bearable for the bereaved. Some writers think of a time of death as a time to seek converts. Attempts at religious conversion have no place in a business letter of condolence. As a matter of fact, they should be made, if they are to be made, in person, not by letter. Then at least the man who is trying to convert can see whether he is increasing the emotional problems of the bereaved.

In the writing of a letter of condolence, as of any business letter, common sense is invaluable. If a writer with common sense attempts to allay the grief of bereaved persons, he will not go far wrong in his letter. If, in addition, he writes sincerely and simply, his letter should be a good one.

INSTRUCTIONS AND INSTRUCTION MANUALS

In instructions clarity, completeness, and helpful organization are of main importance. To achieve these a writer must consider his reader constantly. Directions that are clear to an experienced chemist may not be clear to a laboratory assistant, directions that the head of the financial division understands may confuse a new clerk, directions helpful to an editor or printer may puzzle a lawyer, and directions detailed enough for a new clerk will only annoy when addressed to a supervisor. The first consideration, therefore, is always the reader.

KNOWING THE READER

Instructions that are to be used many times, like those for laboratory assistants, clerks, and factory workers, must be clear to all who use them, not just to the present workers. Words alone may not be enough; illustrations may be necessary. If a laboratory worker does not know one flask from another, the required flask should be sketched and a clear caption should appear in the instructions. Moreover, sketches of all flasks, clearly labeled, should be posted near the storage space for flasks. Complicated bookkeeping instructions accompanied by a sample card or page are clearer than words alone can make them. And a lawyer will find printer's galleys easier to correct if he has a sample marked galley as well as a list of printer's symbols. Directions to a factory worker that tell him not to remove the fabric until it is dark blue should include a sample of that color. A writer's first step in preparing directions is, then, to know his readers well enough to estimate what words and illustrations and samples they will need in order to follow the instructions correctly.

KNOWING THE SUBJECT

His second step is to be sure that he knows his subject completely. Complete understanding of an operation usually requires that a writer perform it himself several times. Many mistakes in directions come from a writer's failure to grasp exactly what his reader is supposed to do. A writer who wets his hands in the laboratory sink, soils them with machine oil, or uses them to punch computer cards will understand the operation as somebody who has never tried it cannot possibly understand it. And he will find that if he is friendly, operators and clerks and other workers will supply him with valuable suggestions that he could not get any other way. The best writer of directions that I know says that he never writes instructions; he just records them as workers tell him how to do a job.

ORGANIZING AND OUTLINING

The third step is to outline instructions in the order of performance and to check the outline to be sure that it includes all the steps and lists them in the correct order. I am astonished by the number of printed directions that have caused mistakes for years because they list steps out of order, for example

4. Heat the mixture at 120°F. for 20 minutes. Before heating, test for acidity.
5. To test for acidity. . . .

These directions were rewritten as

4. Test for acidity by. . . .
5. If the mixture is acid, heat it at 120°F. for 20 minutes.
   If it is not acid. . . .

"Can't understand it. We haven't had a spoiled batch all week with the new directions," said the supervisor. "Quite a saving in chemicals and time."

Writers of poorly organized directions are inclined to blame their mistakes on their readers. "The workers don't read the instructions through as they're supposed to," complain the writers. A writer should never rely on a worker's reading all the directions before starting to follow them or on a worker's remembering all the points if he does read the complete directions. For this reason any equipment, supplies, apparatus, machinery, etc., needed for the operation should be listed first. Otherwise workers following the instructions may discover at an awkward moment that they need equipment that someone else is using or material from a distant storeroom.

Any statements about safety should precede the other instructions. If they are not necessary throughout the procedure, safety instructions should be repeated just before the step where precautions are necessary. Safety directions need strong emphasis; some of the visual devices that may be used to stress them are white space surrounding the safety direction, color, capital letters, underlining, asterisks, large type, pictures, and cartoons. A writer should make it impossible for a worker to overlook a safety instruction.

If a worker can follow instructions better by understanding the reason, then explanations may precede a set of directions. They should precede particular steps only if they will not interfere when a worker is performing the task. If sweeping changes are made, explanations are almost essential, for workers tend to approve and defend methods that they understand. They accept change more readily and comfortably if they understand the reasons for it. If they resent changes, they may unconsciously make mistakes. A beginner who has recently managed to master a filing system may be upset out of proportion to the difficulty if he does not understand and accept the reasons for a change. A professor of mathematics can be upset by a new mailbox number if he has not been properly prepared for it. Meetings that offer opportunities for questions are helpful when many workers are much affected by a change, but a meeting is not a substitute for written explanations that a worker can take home to think about. And a writer should never overlook the happy possibility that a worker who reads a rough draft or outline of explanations of changes may suggest a necessary modification of a new system or a way of making the change more efficiently.

CHECKING AND WRITING

Once an outline of necessary explanations and of the instructions has been prepared, a wise writer checks it. The best way is to follow the outline himself, to have an experienced worker follow it, and to have a new worker follow it. Any insertions or other changes may be made easily when the directions are still in outline form. The next step—writing from such a carefully prepared outline—is easy. The best form for directions is the simple command, also called the cookbook imperative: *Enter this sum in columns 4 and 5.*

But directions for a colleague in another country may be an exception. Usually these require more tactful phrasing: *Our bookkeeper suggests that you enter this sum in columns 4 and 5; You can assist us greatly by entering this sum in columns 4 and 5; Please help us to keep our records consistent by entering this sum in columns 4 and 5.* A writer new to foreign correspondence may find these circumlocutions strange, but writers experienced in writing to colleagues in countries where more formal courtesy is usual have found it much easier to employ such punctilious phrases than to write the apologies necessary when they do not. A beginner writing to natives of other countries should consult those who have written to his correspondents, or he should examine the files to learn how formal his instructions should be.

The language of instructions should be simple. Any word that a worker might not understand must be fully defined the first time it is used or it must be replaced. Each step of the instructions should be a new sentence and should be numbered. Illustrations should appear on the page or opposite the page to which they apply, and they should be legible enough so that any lettering or numbering may be read at a glance.

Before instructions are published, a trial of a week or more is advisable. Average workers, experienced and inexperienced, should be selected to test the instructions so that the supervisor and the writer may catch any misunderstandings, omissions, or confusions, which the writer will then correct. Instructions prepared this way are not published until they are foolproof. Although they take time to prepare, they are still a great economy because of the errors, materials, and equipment they save.

And when safety is involved, such care is essential to prevent accidents. An operator's safety may be endangered by a procedure out of order. It is small use to place at the end of job instructions a warning to wear protective clothing. Some worker is almost certain to perform each step in order without reading all the steps and thus to risk injuring himself.

A writer of instructions sent the following directions to be posted above machines in a college language laboratory: "To start this machine, press button B. Before pressing button B, wind all the tape onto the left spool." In the first five minutes of use, thirty of the thirty-three machines were damaged. The other three escaped because one student was absent, one student who was slow was warned by the mistakes of the others, and one student read and followed the instruction to read the directions from beginning to end before performing any operation.

Exact chronological order prevents such accidents. It is the best order for instructions because it leaves nothing to the discretion of the writer or reader. Many accidents might have been prevented by careful checks to be certain that directions were in exact chronology and by supervision of the operator to be sure that he performed the operations in the order listed. These two simple steps promote safety on the job, help an operator to follow directions properly, and train him to observe safety instructions at the right time.

INSTRUCTIONS FOR A SINGLE PERFORMANCE

Instructions to be used once by one person or by a few persons, like an executive's instructions to his secretary or to his assistants, are a somewhat different matter. Although the executive and his secretary or assistant may be so well acquainted that they speak and write a personal shorthand, the directions should be written so as to be clear to anyone substituting for either of them.

A procedure that works well for executives and those they direct follows:

1. The executive discusses the instructions with his secretary or assistant.
2. The secretary or the assistant writes the instructions.
3. The executive corrects or changes the instructions.

An annoying problem is the supervisor who gives oral instructions and then denies them or says that he was misunderstood. Another is the assistant or secretary who seems to understand instructions but then ignores them or changes them to suit his own ideas. The procedure that I have outlined usually solves the problem of the executive who is careless or forgetful and of the assistant or secretary who is a poor listener. Executives who are merely careless or impulsive have an opportunity at step 3 to change their minds before the instructions are followed. And an assistant or secretary who has missed a point should find that out at the same step. But executives who try to weasel out of responsibility for instructions they have given and assistants who wilfully pursue their own way cannot be helped by instruction in writing. Theirs are not problems in writing or reading, and it is wise not to pretend that they are.

Sometimes a writer fails to indicate priorities for a list of tasks. Unless the person following the instructions is so closely attuned to the writer that he automatically performs tasks in the order desired, he is entitled to some indication of the order. This information is urgent when the writer will not be available for consultation about the instructions or when the person performing the tasks is new to the work.

There is never any need to apologize for the explicitness of directions, for the explanations or definitions that accompany them, or for a statement of the order of performance. The directions that require apology are those that are not explicit, clear, and organized.

ABSTRACTS AND SUMMARIES

An abstract, or synopsis, usually accompanies a technical paper. Some technical editors distinguish abstracts and summaries as follows. A descriptive abstract is an expository table of contents expressed in sentences and paragraphs. It outlines the development of the paper, rather than the main ideas. An informative abstract contains the most important points, usually in the order in which they appear in the paper. Although the informative abstract is more useful than the descriptive, many writers prefer to submit descriptive abstracts, perhaps because they are easier to write. The new information storage and retrieval systems may change this predilection.

A summary also presents the most important points but not necessarily in the order of the paper. A summary at the beginning of a paper may epitomize the organization of the paper, the main points, the main points of each section, the results, the conclusions, or the recommendations (Chapter IV). It is often written as a separate document expressed in terms that nontechnical readers can understand. A final summation of main points is useful in some papers to give a comprehensive view of a long or involved exposition (Chapter XIV). And summary sentences may be helpful at the ends of some sections of long reports. But placing a summary at the end of every section or chapter easily leads to monotony and, as every student knows, to skipping all but the summaries.

Whatever kind of summary or abstract is prepared, it should contain only important material selected from the rest of the paper. It is not the place to introduce new material. A summary does, then, involve repetition, but often, because the summary is prepared for nontechnical readers or as a conclusion, this repetition is in other words.

The lengths of abstracts and summaries vary. In a short report or memorandum a few summary sentences may state the problem and either the solution proposed or the progress toward a solution. Anything more than a single page for works of more than fifty pages and a half page for shorter works should be closely examined for unnecessary material and unnecessary words. The extreme brevity of a good summary demands that all details be removed and that only the most significant ideas be stated.

Sometimes these are difficult for a writer to assess while he is close to the final stages of his work. For this reason many researchers write the purposes of a project early and review these and the main topics of the outline of their report to reorient themselves before writing summaries. To summarize effectively a writer must direct his thinking away from the minor points of the final stages of his work that have been absorbing his attention and concentrate on main points, which he may not have considered for some time. Some writers find that discussing the main points of the work with their colleagues helps them to recapture the gist of the material.

In abstracting the work of another, a writer should determine what he will summarize—the various steps of the paper, the main points of each section, the main points of the whole paper, or some combination of these. In reading for his abstract, he should study carefully a descriptive table of contents if one is provided. It will be a useful guide for skimming. As he comes to suitable material, he should note it as briefly as possible. Before he writes, he should reduce these notes by removing subject matter and words wherever he can. When he thinks that he has reduced as much as he can, he should remove a third of what is left. Then he is ready to write an abstract of appropriate brevity.

All writers of technical material strive for brevity; the writer of abstracts must seek the essence of brevity. His style has no room for the unnecessary words listed in Chapter VIII. Whereas other writers should remove most of them when they revise, he must remove all of them. A writer of a summary or abstract must search for appropriate single words to replace phrases, and short words to replace long ones. He must avoid wordy constructions. He does not use a three-word tense like *has been found* when *found* will serve his purpose. He uses the devices of style, like parallelism and subordination, that reduce the number of words. The more miserly he is with words, the better his abstract will be. This does not mean that his style should become telegraphic or cryptic. It means that his style should be completely clear and correct. The summary that concludes a paper should be more than a mere listing of points. It should be an interesting division of the work, polished, brief, and memorable.

Chapter XVI

The Editor and Supervisor
and the Future
Editor and Supervisor

> He taughte, and first he folwed it himselve.
>
> *Chaucer*

SUPERVISING WRITING

Supervising writing is one of the most difficult and least successful kinds of supervision for a number of reasons. Some who are called upon to supervise have no training or experience in supervising or editing, some have training or experience in only one, and some are themselves poor writers. Moreover a man's feelings about his writing are more sensitive and tender than his feelings about his performance in his science or technology. He considers writing, even writing memorandums and reports, more personal work, and he takes criticism as a reflection on his inner self. An engineer will defend at length a dangling modifier or a pronoun without an antecedent, but he will correct an error in engineering the moment it is pointed out to him. Conferences with such a writer may take on all the more unfortunate aspects of attempts to point out personality defects. As though this were not trouble enough, editors and supervisors of writing must cope with the tendency of some writers to confuse other disappointments and annoyances with feelings about the correction of their writing. Such people argue interminably about insignificant details.

The Influence of Other Problems

Many teachers of writing in industry and government are convinced that some writers cannot improve their writing unless their attitudes toward their jobs change. In fact, one editor refused to supervise the writing of engineers because the engineers needed better working conditions in the plant more than they needed editing; therefore he thought that an editor could do little good because the dissatisfaction with management would be transferred to him.

As a woman, I seldom find that anger has been switched from supervisors to me, probably because most of the supervisors are men. Writers may attempt to complain to me about the way a supervisor edits their writing, about the burden of writing, about not being promoted, about lack of appreciation; but even though I change the subject, they seem to consider me sympathetic and believe that if I had time I would listen and take their part. However I do not escape all other problems. When one of the first classes I taught in industry was examining coherence in a book review, a writer interrupted, "Now, I suppose that I'm going to have the same argument with you that I'm always having with my wife. I think that book reviews should sell books, not criticize them." That was one dispute we did not have, but I had to struggle to avoid it and to keep him on the topic of coherence. Thereafter he tried to argue every point in the book with me. It was clear to the rest of the class—most of whom had had medical training—and to me that this writer would never learn from a woman unless he improved his relations with his wife or his understanding of his reactions.

Such extreme cases are, of course, unusual, but they indicate clearly the influence of unrelated troubles and miseries on writing and thus may help editors and supervisors to understand the causes of the otherwise unaccountable truculence of some writers. When advancements are refused, when salary increments are withheld, when working conditions are deteriorating, editing and supervision of writing become more difficult. Even unpopular changes in the cafeteria have affected writers' attitudes. Family arguments, financial worries, and marital failures are also storm signals to supervisors of writing and to editors. A writer may direct at them the impatience and anger that he has not expressed to the person who thwarted or defeated him.

Therefore an inexperienced supervisor of writing or an editor who is a beginner need not feel unsuccessful or incompetent should he meet a contentious writer who is determined that his writing remain as it is. If the editor has not been dictatorial but has tried to be understanding and helpful, he should not blame himself for such a response. Only a psychologist, psychiatrist, or analyst can help some writers; and no one else should waste patience and energy on trying to help them. Unfortunately, such writers always seem to be assigned to inexperienced editors, and inexperienced editors do not realize that they should save their patience and energy for more cooperative writers, who are bound to have difficult days and troublesome writing assignments.

If a usually cooperative writer is in a poor mood for editing and correcting, a supervisor may find it wise to devote their conference to work that is less affected by emotional attitudes, and an editor may judiciously postpone the conference. When postponement is not possible, a supervisor or editor will have to rely on psychology and tact.

Psychology and Tact

It is good psychology, for example, to avoid confronting a writer with a page that seems to have more corrections than original writing. Sometimes this impression results less from the number of corrections than from the untidy, sprawling handwriting of an editor. Changes and corrections made in a small neat handwriting are less obtrusive and less likely to exasperate a writer before he has a chance to read them. But a paper covered with changes puts a writer in an uncooperative mood even on one of his good days.

A complimentary remark never starts a conference badly. There is usually something to admire in a paper—the subject matter, if not some point of style. If his paper is hopeless, the writer may deserve praise for something else, and a competent supervisor tries to have some kind words or admiration ready at the beginning of a conference. It is hard for a writer to dislike a person who thus clearly demonstrates his appreciation. But false compliments are much worse than unsuccessful conferences. They boomerang, for they may be recalled to an editor by a writer who cannot understand how someone who once admired his work is now not even satisfied with it. And the writer who knows a supervisor is lying becomes distrustful and suspicious. I do not suggest that a supervisor sugarcoat the pill of truth, but that he begin a difficult conference with a pleasant comment on the writer or his work. A supervisor who cannot find anything complimentary to say about a writer should not be supervising writers. He is too unperceptive.

To end a conference well, a supervisor has ready a constructive view of the writing. If the present is painful, he turns to a more promising future. Good points in a paper may be used to stress the attractive prospects of a writer, and the value of correcting a few faults or strengthening a few weaknesses may be presented to cheer a disheartened writer. Sometimes it is useful to turn from the paper on which the conference has been concentrated to a writer's next assignment and to help him with that. At other times it may be better to summarize how a writer can improve a poor paper and then to turn the discussion away from writing to some work at which the employee is succeeding or to some work in which he has a special interest.

When a writer resents without apparent reason all criticism given in conference, a supervisor may give him his corrected paper to study, schedule another conference on it, and trust to a session with fellow employees and the passage of time to make the writer more complaisant. A suggestion that a poor writer use a book, take a course, seek tutoring may be a good final note. To be effective, such a suggestion must be specific. What book, what course, what tutor? Will the company pay for the course or part of it? The best way to present such a suggestion is to lend the writer the book to look over, give him a catalogue with the course marked, or be ready with information about a tutor. This help should be most specific for foreign-born writers who have come to the United States recently. They should not be left to flounder in a search for assistance they are poorly equipped to find.

A tactful editor yields a point now and then to a writer. Every educated person knows that some decisions about writing are matters of taste, and writers like to think that their taste will not be ignored. If a supervisor knows that a writer finds it hard to take criticism, the supervisor might occasionally consult him about some debatable point. "Do you think that we might use a pronoun here instead of this synonym? Then we can use the synonym in these other sentences." If the writer stubbornly insists on retaining the synonym, his writing is not much worse, and the relations between supervisor and writer may be better. However an editor or supervisor must use good judgment about yielding because some writers view any concession as a sign of weakness and try to take advantage of the supposed weakness.

Special Problems

One of the most difficult editing problems is the writing of a confused thinker. He uses correct words, appropriate style, and correct constructions, but he does not express the meaning he intends to convey. And the writer apparently does not notice this. Indeed, some supervisors report great difficulty in convincing such a writer that he is not saying what he means. What he intended to state is so firmly fixed in his mind that he cannot see what he has said. Such a writer finds it difficult to see that *a check on the progress of the experiment* is ambiguous; even with the help of a dictionary he will not understand that *check* has two meanings, both possible in the phrase. He is so intent upon one meaning that he refuses to admit another.

Some writers have difficulty whenever exactness is required. They write about "eliminating our present suppliers" and about "incredulous demands" and think readers should understand what they mean. When they plan to send such writing to readers who are not working for their company or government agency, an editor can insist that the reputation of the company or agency demands correct and precise writing. But when they write to their fellow employees, such writers may be difficult to convince. "He knows what I mean" is their defense. Sometimes a reader does know; sometimes he does not; certainly his substitute might not know. A more persuasive reason for care in writing is that a writer who is careless with one kind of writing will make mistakes when he wishes to be correct and accurate.

Time may help such a writer. Although he is unaware of his error at the time that he writes, does not notice it when he revises, and cannot see it when an editor or supervisor points it out, he may struggle with the misstatement, read and reread it, and discuss it with others until he finally sees the error. A course may help a confused or careless writer, particularly if the other members of a course equal or surpass him in rank. Even the stubbornest writer will not defend his clarity against a dozen readers who deny it. The complaints of readers force even the most obdurate writer to reconsider.

But a writer who cannot see what is wrong with "Problems are encountered by changes in the conference hours," may prove difficult to convince of his weaknesses. And when a desire to hedge confuses his thinking further, a writer may be impossible. One doctor who wrote, "There is every reason to expect that side effects will appear," was convinced he was not committing himself in any way. He did not expect any side effects but did not wish to say so. In attempting to evade a commitment, he made himself responsible for exactly the opposite of what he thought.

"If you say, 'There is every reason to believe that it will rain,'" he was told, "you are expressing the opinion that it will rain."

"No, I'm not," he insisted. "I'm saying that it probably won't rain, but I'm not committing myself. I'm hedging."

When a busy director summoned him to ask why the company was investing in a drug that would probably have side effects, he told the director that he had expected the tests to prove the absence of side effects. He was unable to understand how anyone could take any other meaning from his words.

If an editor or supervisor meets such a stupidly stubborn reaction, he must use his authority to change the wording. The writer may fret and fume, but when he is so wrong and so blind, someone must correct his writing.

Explanations of Changes

Most writers are willing to correct writing if an editor can give them a sound reason for the change. Hence a good handbook of writing is useful to an editor or supervisor. After a writer has been shown the rules for a few changes, he will, if he is a reasonable man, accept the editor's word for other rules. If a writer wants to be convinced of every point by reference to authority, a supervisor should explain some reasons and urge the writer to look up the rest himself. But supervisors should not expect writers to be convinced by such silly arguments as, "Well, this is the way I say it"; "I never heard it that way"; or "I like it this way and I'm the boss. When you're the boss, you can write it your way."

Reasonableness and Competence in Editing

There is often more than one acceptable way of phrasing an idea. If a writer's expression is satisfactory, he should not have to change it. And good supervisors remember that editing can be too fussy; there is little point in caviling over unimportant matters, and a sensible person recognizes the occasion on which he should not correct. An editor or supervisor should not be a Professor Twist:

> I give you now Professor Twist
> A conscientious scientist.
> Trustees exclaimed, "He never bungles!"
> And sent him off to distant jungles.
> Camped on a tropic riverside,
> One day he missed his loving bride.
> She had, the guide informed him later,
> Been eaten by an alligator.
> Professor Twist could not but smile.
> "You mean," he said, "a crocodile." [1]

Ogden Nash

A supervisor or editor should be reasonable and sensible. He should not press a writer to produce long papers just to convince readers that the division is working hard or insist that he use elegant diction or unnecessary jargon to convince readers that the subject is difficult. A supervisor who, despite the variety available, insists upon one organization, one beginning, one ending should be training robots not writers. The best supervisors are those who permit their writers to depart from the set methods of a company or division whenever another method is better.

[1] "The Purist," *The Selected Verse of Ogden Nash* (The Modern Library, New York, 1945), p. 229.

To make decisions and to give advice about writing, supervisors must be well informed. But government and industry often neglect the supervisors' training in writing and in supervising writing. Some writing courses are given for everyone but supervisors. The fact that supervisors realize this is foolish is shown by their requests to take or to audit these courses. When they have learned the principles of correct and effective writing, they find editing much easier. Many supervisors and editors need not a course in writing but a course in supervising and editing. Sharing problems, considering various approaches to writing and writers, becoming familiar with the editing of other supervisors, studying the psychology of writing and of writers—all these help supervisors to improve. Some few men may be born supervisors or editors, but most of them have to be trained and educated. Much writing in government and industry and much of the friction associated with editing are due to untrained, unprepared supervisors and editors. That the writing and friction are no worse than they are is due largely to the goodwill and common sense of those supervisors and editors. But common sense is not enough. Knowledge of the techniques of supervising and editing is essential. And by learning to understand some of a writer's difficulties and problems, a supervisor or editor can become more successful.

One difficulty is that a writer needs knowledge of his readers. It helps him to know roughly their education, the extent of their understanding of the subject, and their purpose in reading his paper. To write good instructions, he must know his readers well (Chapter XV). And to compose an effective letter, he should know something of the personality of the man to whom he is writing. These are reasonable requests, and a supervisor should supply what information he has. To insist that a writer need not know anything about his readers is to insist on writing that succeeds only by accident.

Supervisors and editors work better with writers if they realize that good writing takes more time than poor writing and that to write something in a hundred words takes longer than to write it in a thousand. A man who is learning to write better needs time; corrections and changes require careful thought, especially at first.

A writer frequently interrupted or otherwise distracted is a slower, poorer writer than he need be. At least while he is writing a first draft, a writer should be free of interruptions and able to work in quiet surroundings that are not distracting (Chapter III). If he cannot close his office door or if there is no place for him to write except a noisy laboratory, it is an economy to send him to a library or the office of an absent executive. Many errors are avoided and time and effort are saved when a writer has a quiet place to work.

A writer also needs time to plan his writing. A period of mulling over a paper helps him find better ways to write it. He needs time to outline, time to write, time to put the paper aside after writing it, and time to revise (Chapter II). Frequently the back of his mind will be concerned with his writing while he is off the job. During dinner a phrase he wants may pop into his head; while reading his evening paper, he may spot a type of ending that he can use; during a bowling game a better way of beginning a report may suddenly come to him. And this costs his company or the government nothing but a little care in scheduling writing. If he can spread writing and revising, a writer has time to work on the paper in his mind. Therefore a supervisor's scheduling of writing is of major importance. It is not something for a supervisor to neglect or to take care of when he has nothing else to do; scheduling writing is an urgent task.

A good supervisor or editor is ready to help a writer from the first plan to the last word of the final draft. If a writer organizes poorly or if he has a long, difficult report to organize, a conference on the outline may save many alterations later. Conferring on outlines is also useful for supervisors and writers who tend to disagree on the purpose or scope or organization of papers. And a supervisor can tell from a detailed outline whether a writer has understood the assignment (Chapter VI). Inexperienced workers and new workers benefit much from discussion of their outlines, for they gain a clearer idea of what is required. The old method of training a professional man by letting him learn to write reports by reading those in the files is far inferior to guidance from a supervisor or editor. Imitating old reports may introduce a writer to new mistakes, confirm him in bad habits, and dam his originality.

A writer needs sensible answers to sensible questions. In some divisions of industry and government these are available. Patient, competent supervisors teach young administrators, scientists, and engineers the principles of good writing. But in the many divisions where supervisors know no more about writing than new employees do, some of the supervisors are sensitive and try to cover their deficiency by pedantic insistence on their own expressions. The young people soon learn that the only way to get a supervisor's approval on a document is to write it in his style. And his style may be antiquated, pompous, and verbose. Imitating such writing is not a salutary experience for a beginner. Some engineers and scientists have imitated the writing of supervisor after supervisor, and their own styles—though it may not be fair to call them that—are patchworks of the worst features of the writing of five or six supervisors. Imitators learn quickly that it is the poor characteristics of his style that a supervisor likes to have reproduced.

An editor or supervisor should keep informed of changes in English. To recommend style that was out of date twenty years ago, to punctuate according to rules current when the supervisor was in college, and to insist on old-fashioned business jargon is to court trouble. Writers lose respect for a supervisor who is out of date.

A supervisor or editor who is informed, who will look up a rule, who will listen to an intelligent point of view is a comfort to a writer. Professional men remember gratefully those executives who trained them to be better writers. Supervisors would be surprised at how often when I comment on a good point in a paper, a middle-aged or elderly writer will say, "Oh, I was trained by an excellent man," or "My first supervisor was a great help to me. I was a terrible writer before I worked for him," or even, "I guess my boss finally taught me something about writing. You know, he's been pretty patient with me. I never learned anything about writing until I worked for him." Contentious, troublesome, irritating though writers may be, they are grateful ever after to the person who helps them to write better. That is a thought for the day when a supervisor feels that he does not want to see another writer— ever or when an editor is certain he chose the wrong profession.

Company Motivation

Many of the tribulations of supervisors and of editors disappear in a company that has an atmosphere conducive to the improvement of writing. When good writing is important in a company, employees are eager for help. But writing is not important because management says it is. Good writing is important when it is recognized as a part of an employee's work that counts toward advancement. As soon as advancement is based partly on writing skills and performance and as soon as this is known in a company, the supervision of writing becomes less of a problem and writers appreciate good editing.

Consultants on writing and teachers of writing immediately notice an atmosphere favorable to writers, because these consultants are welcomed with the same enthusiasm that a specialist who can solve a difficult engineering problem receives. When they return a second time, employees seek them out to ask questions and to discuss progress. The motivation for courses that is required elsewhere is superfluous in such an atmosphere. Writers are eager to improve, and unless a consultant or instructor is hopeless, his writers remain eager, interested, and alert. A consultant finds that employees could not be more intense about improving their writing if the company were expecting to make a monthly profit of several million dollars through writing. And good writing does profit such companies by saving expensive reading time, by keeping scientists informed, and by giving executives clear and complete information for decisions.

BENEFITING FROM SUPERVISION OF WRITING AND FROM EDITING

Even excellent supervisors and editors cannot summon forth good writing by themselves. A poor supervisor and a cooperative writer can accomplish more than an excellent supervisor and an uncooperative writer. Some workers do not benefit from supervision and editing because they do not know how to benefit.

To improve, a writer should pay attention, ask intelligent questions, and try to apply whatever seems to him useful. Obviously if, instead of trying to learn, he spends his time planning his next argument, he will not improve. A conference on writing is not an opportunity for a writer to display his debating skills, to demonstrate that he knows more than his supervisor, or to release his irritations. It is an opportunity to learn to improve writing.

A little reasonableness on a writer's part helps his editor or supervisor to instruct him more efficiently in the allotted time. A writer should try to think of his writing as impersonally as he thinks of his mathematics or science because a touchy, resentful writer is difficult to help and therefore injures himself more than any adverse criticism from an editor or supervisor can injure him.

A writer can also learn much from the corrections and changes made by an editor working for a publisher. Yet few writers realize this. Many approach an editor's changes antagonistically and fight bitterly although they can accomplish nothing by displaying bad temper and ignorance. But a writer who examines changes, studies the reasons for them, and tries to improve his next paper can learn much about writing.

Some years ago I instructed a new magazine editor by demonstrating on the two most poorly written papers awaiting publication. To save time I performed all the editing that would be desirable under the best circumstances, which are certainly not those that generally prevail in the editorial offices of professional journals, and I indicated the editing that might be omitted in more normal circumstances. Then the editor and I discussed points that he had noticed, and we marked one manuscript a little more. At the end of the day that paper had been edited more thoroughly than any ever published in the magazine. To spare the feelings of the writer I suggested that the editor erase some of the optional changes.

A few weeks later the editor told me that the edited manuscript with all our changes had been sent to the printer by mistake, and galleys had been mailed to the author. The editor was awaiting the writer's response with trepidation because the editor had not removed those optional corrections. The writer's galleys, however, were returned without comment, and the editor and I never thought about our zealous editing until more than a year later. We were reminded of it when the writer's next paper received an award as the best paper of the year.

We rushed to examine the manuscript of the prize paper and found that it contained not one of the errors or weaknesses, not even one of the wordy expressions, of the paper we had dissected. Instead of damning the editor who had made so many changes, this writer had learned everything that he could learn from the meticulous editing. And that, as shown by the subsequent award, was more than many writers learn during a whole course.

Most of the editors and supervisors I meet are seriously concerned about improving writing and about learning how to help writers. A writer should not spurn this goodwill. If he realizes that a supervisor or editor is trying to help him improve a skill important to his career, he may be more tolerant of adverse criticism.

Nobody suffers from his failure to improve as much as a writer himself. If he consciously or unconsciously attempts to revenge himself upon a supervisor or a company by refusing to learn to write better, he damages his own career. His supervisor and his company will succeed in spite of his lack of improvement. He should ask himself, "Will I?"

A writer sometimes forgets that he is likely to be a supervisor of writers himself soon. In industry and government, the man whose work is edited today may be editing tomorrow. He can prepare himself by taking advantage of advice, suggestions, information, and training. As a supervisor, he will have to do more than express his own thoughts: he will have to know whether another writer's expression is correct and effective; he will have to explain, not just change; he will have to assume the writer's point of view and adapt his instruction and advice to it; and he will need patience and understanding.

Since none of this will come to him with the title of editor or supervisor, a writer should seize every opportunity to learn. In every conference about his writing, he should acquire as much as he can of the principles of writing and the techniques of editing and supervising.

An intelligent professional man can learn from poor as well as from good examples: one clever chemist who is now the best supervisor of writers in his company told me that he had prepared for supervision by noting carefully the supervisory mistakes that he intended to avoid.

That chemist is the antithesis of the complainer who spends his time fussing over every change in his writing, criticizing others sharply, and feeling unappreciated. Such a complainer becomes the poorest of editors or supervisors not only because he has learned little about writing and supervising but also because he is likely to switch from destructive criticism of his supervisor to destructive criticism of his writers. Only by using his energies for learning rather than lamenting can he hope to become a better writer and a better prospect for promotion to a supervisory or editorial position. By examining carefully an editor's changes, a writer can discover whether they are good or bad, whether he should make them when he supervises or avoid them. By learning good administrative techniques and by rejecting poor ones, particularly those to which he is prone, a writer can prepare himself to help others. And by taking a more broadminded view of others, even of his supervisor, and a more critical view of himself and his writing, he will become better prepared and better suited to help and develop others. Then when opportunities arise, when promotions come, he will be ready.

Index